Jimmie Foxx

Jimmie Foxx

The Life and Times
of a Baseball Hall of Famer,
1907–1967

W. HARRISON DANIEL

McFarland & Company, Inc., Publishers
Jefferson, North Carolina, and London

For that Magnificent Red Head,
who is as great a baseball fan
as her father used to be

Frontispiece: Foxx in uniform, ca. 1927-28 (courtesy Easton, Md., *Star Democrat*).

The present work is a reprint of the library bound edition of Jimmie Foxx: The Life and Times of a Baseball Hall of Famer, *1907–1967, first published in 1996 by McFarland.*

LIBRARY OF CONGRESS CATALOGUING-IN-PUBLICATION DATA

Daniel, W. Harrison.
    Jimmie Foxx : the life and times of a baseball Hall of Famer,
1907–1967 / W. Harrison Daniel.
        p.   cm.
    Includes bibliographical references and index.

    ISBN-13: 978-0-7864-1867-1
    (softcover : 50# alk. paper) ∞

    1. Foxx, Jimmie.   2. Baseball players—United States—
Biography.   I. Title.
GV865.F64D36   2004
796.357'092—dc20
[B]   96-34665
                                                 CIP

British Library cataloguing data are available

On the cover: "Jimmie Foxx," original painting by Arthur K. Miller/
The Art of the Game ©2003

Manufactured in the United States of America

McFarland & Company, Inc., Publishers
   Box 611, Jefferson, North Carolina 28640
   www.mcfarlandpub.com

Contents

Acknowledgments

A number of persons have kindly and patiently assisted me in the years that I have been researching this project. I am grateful to each for their help, and I reiterate what every scholar knows: it is the competent, cooperative, and friendly persons one encounters in research that make it such a rewarding experience. Among those who have graciously assisted me in researching this project are the following:

Nina Biddle, Minneapolis Public Library; Bill Boles, library of the *Boston Globe*; Charles F. Bryan, Jr., Virginia Historical Society; Nanci Canaday, Sumterville, Florida, for photographs and a number of xerox items pertaining to her stepfather; Tom Clark, library of the *Boston Herald*; Richard Dalrymple, University of Miami, Florida, Sports Information Department; Barbara Everett, librarian, Sudlersville Memorial Library; James Emory Foxx, Jr., II, Lakewood, Ohio; W. Kenneth Foxx, Decatur, Alabama; S. Dell Foxx, III, for the loan of two scrapbooks of data concerning his Uncle Jim; Steven Geitschier, director of historical records, *The Sporting News*; Anne Margaret Daniel-Grobler, Washington, D.C.; Dr. Van Eyk Grobler, Easton, Maryland, for photographs; Tom Heitz, librarian, Baseball Library, Cooperstown, New York; William J. Jenkinson, Willow Grove, Pennsylvania; Littleton Maxwell, library staff, University of Richmond; Scotti Oliver, curator, Maryland Room, Talbot County Free Library, Easton, Maryland; Carol Pickerl, archivist, Northern Indiana Historical Society, South Bend, Indiana; Sue Ratchford, interlibrary loan librarian, University of Richmond; Denise Riley, editor, Eastern Maryland *Star Democrat*; Greg Schwalenberg, curator, Babe Ruth Museum, Baltimore; Irene Shubert, Library of Congress, for *Real Life Comics* #41; Bill Stout, library staff, Temple University; John Treadway, University of Richmond; Nancy Vick, interlibrary loan librarian, University of Richmond; Loretta C. Walls, Sudlersville, Maryland, for photographs; Mary Anne Wilbourne, University of Richmond; Chet Williamson, Elizabethtown, Pennsylvania, for xerox copy of *How I Bat*; librarian, office of the *Philadelphia*

Inquirer; librarian, office of *The Queen Anne's County Record-Observer*, Centreville, Maryland; colleagues in the Department of History, University of Richmond, for released time; and the Faculty Research Committee, University of Richmond, for financial assistance.

Preface

From the time I began to read newspapers until I was a student in college I was a consummate baseball fan. I made scrapbooks from box scores and pictures of players which I clipped from newspapers. I memorized batting averages, pitchers' records and numerous baseball statistics and data. I collected pictures of baseball players which came with chewing gum and those featured on various cereal packages. I requested and obtained autographs, via postal card, from such players as Lou Gehrig and Bob Feller, and on one occasion when the Yankees and Dodgers played a spring exhibition game in my small home town in central Virginia I obtained autographs of practically the entire team of both contestants.

I have been asked many times in recent years, as I was engaged in research for this book, "How did you get interested in Foxx?" The truth is I don't know. My interest in Foxx dates from my earliest memories of newspaper reading. Maybe I was attracted to him because it was the first time that I had ever seen Foxx spelled with two x's. Maybe I was interested in him because he was a right-handed batter, and at a time when the press gave most attention to such left-handed sluggers as Babe Ruth and Lou Gehrig, he was something of an example for right-handed kids; he was proof positive that right-handed players could also be sluggers. Perhaps I was attracted to Foxx because he played first base, and as a kid I tried to play first base and I was right-handed.

I followed Foxx's major league career until it ended in 1945 and I have followed major league baseball, though at a distance, for the past fifty years. However, throughout a teaching career, when my research and publications focused on other subjects, interest in Foxx persisted. I have always kept, in the recesses of my mind, the aim of doing a life-and-times study of my childhood hero. Five years ago, after completing a local history project which focused on the University of Richmond, I began serious research on Foxx and his times.

In this study I have focused attention on the life and career of Jimmie Foxx; however, I have attempted to relate his career to two overall concerns: (1) the developments or changes in major league baseball from the 1920s to

1945, and (2) those events in American society during these same years which had a significant impact on baseball—specifically the Great Depression and World War II. I have also tried to present as completely as possible an account of Foxx's post-baseball years, from his retirement in 1945 to his tragic death at age 59 in 1967.

One decision that I had to make in preparing this study was how to spell his given name. Would it be "Jimmy" or "Jimmie"? Sportswriters throughout his career spelled it both ways and used the names interchangeably. The memorial erected to his memory by his home town spells his name "Jimmy." One account, which I heard at Sudlersville, was that as a boy he was called "Jim" or "Jimmy" and that he spelled his name "Jimmy" when he was in high school. But, after he went to Philadelphia to play for the Athletics, he changed the spelling of his name and began using "Jimmie." At the Baseball Hall of Fame Museum and Library in Cooperstown, New York, the baseball and bat which he autographed are signed "Jimmie." However, his memorial plaque in the Hall of Fame reads "Jimmy." I concluded that the Hall of Fame officials avoided making a decision by using both appellations or ignoring the inconsistency. However, Foxx's official autograph or signature in the Baseball Library reads "Jimmie." Officials at Cooperstown only shrugged their shoulders when I inquired about the inconsistency in the spelling of Foxx's given name. I was probably as ambivalent or uncertain as others about which spelling to use until I talked with Foxx's stepdaughter, Ms. Nanci Canaday. She informed me that "Dad always spelled his name J-i-m-m-i-e." That was good enough for me; I have also spelled his name "Jimmie."

One

Schoolboy Athlete

At the conclusion of the World Series on October 12, 1907, the *New York Times* declared that "the greatest baseball season ever known has just closed." The combined attendance for the American and National leagues exceeded 6.1 million; this was over a quarter-million more than attendance at major league baseball games in any previous season. Despite the fact that Ty Cobb won his third batting title in 1907, he and his Detroit Tiger teammates lost the World Series to the Chicago Cubs in four straight games.[1]

Ten days after the close of the baseball season, on October 22, in a two-story frame farm house in Queen Anne's County, Maryland, a healthy and physically gifted baby boy was born. His parents were Samuel Dell Foxx and Martha (Mattie) Smith Foxx. Foxx was a tenant farmer, and the family resided about three miles from the crossroads village of Sudlersville. The Foxx and Smith families had lived in the area for several generations. Mattie descended from English forebears and Foxx was of Irish ancestry. The Foxx family were members of Calvary Methodist Episcopal Church in Sudlersville.[2] Dell and Mattie named their first-born child James Emory, giving him one name from each of his grandfathers: Joseph Emory Smith and James Benton Foxx.[3]

Grandfather Foxx was a Civil War veteran, and although he and the Foxx family were residents of Maryland, he had volunteered and fought for the Confederacy. A close relationship would develop between Foxx and his grandson, and he would often entertain the youngster with stories relating to the war and his experiences as a drummer boy in that conflict. It is claimed that Jimmie was so impressed by the stories of his grandfather that during World War I, when he was ten years old, he sought, unsuccessfully, to emulate his grandfather by joining the army as a drummer boy.

Jimmie grew up on the farm, and he performed an increasing number of chores as he grew into adolescence. These included milking cows, chopping and harvesting corn, plowing the soil for planting, cleaning stables, driving the milk wagon to the railroad station in Sudlersville, and often loading and unloading supplies such as sacks of fertilizer, grain, and other items. Farm work, Jimmie would later claim, helped him to develop strong wrist, arm, leg,

1

Jimmie and his mother, Martha Smith Foxx (courtesy Sudlersville Memorial Library).

and back muscles.[4] When he was eight years old Dell and Mattie Foxx's second and last child was born. He was named after his father, Samuel Dell Foxx, Jr. Despite the age difference between the two boys, a warm, supportive, and enduring relationship would develop between Jimmie and his young brother Sammy Dell.

The social and economic center of activities for many in the area where the Foxx family lived was Sudlersville. In the early twentieth century Sudlersville was a village of approximately 420 inhabitants. It derived its name from one of the earliest families to settle in the region— the Sudler family.[5] This village was "town" for many of the farm families in Queen Anne's County and adjoining areas. Here were located the post office, the bank, the railroad depot where farmers came to ship milk cans to the Harbison Dairy in Philadelphia; there were also several hardware stores, insurance offices, restaurants, dry goods and grocery stores, a cannery, several barber shops, a drug store, physicians' offices, and the school the Foxx boys would attend.[6]

By the time Jimmie Foxx was twelve years old his talents as an athlete were beginning to attract attention in his home county and beyond. This versatile youngster's first hero and role model was track star Charles W. "Charlie" Paddock. For fifteen years, beginning in 1913, Paddock set or equalled a number of world records in track events, and he represented the United States in the Olympic Games in 1920. Among the records held by this "fastest human being" were in the 100-yard and 100-meter dashes, and the 220- and 300-yard sprints.[7]

Jimmie read about the track exploits of Paddock and envisioned himself as one day being a great sprinter. When he was a preteen he began competing in county school track meets, and by the time he was thirteen he was attracting attention beyond his local school. In May, 1921, at a track meet which included school participants from three of Maryland's Eastern Shore counties, Foxx won first place in two events in the junior unlimited class: one was the 80-yard dash, the other the running high jump.[8] The following year at the Queen Anne's County Olympiad, a track meet featuring the best performers from twenty high schools, Jimmie again won the 80-yard dash and was first in the high jump competition with a jump of five feet, one inch.⁹

Each spring the Maryland State High School track meet was held in Baltimore. This involved competition among the best high school athletes from all areas of the state. The event, often referred to by the press as the Maryland Olympiad, attracted attention throughout the state. Foxx first appeared in this event in the spring of 1922, when he was fourteen years old. Athletes from Queen Anne's County won fifth place in the state competition, but Jimmie won first place in the 80-yard dash; he also broke the state record of eight and four-fifth seconds and established a new record of eight and three-fifth seconds for this event.¹⁰ At the Maryland State High School track meet in 1923, Jimmie won the 220-yard dash with a time of twenty-three seconds and the high jump event with a leap of five feet, eight inches.¹¹

Each year at the conclusion of the state olympiad in Baltimore, sportswriters covering the event selected a star state athlete for the year. In 1923 they chose fifteen-year-old Jimmie Foxx, the muscular, 165-pound youngster from Sudlersville High School. In making their selection the writers were not limited to consideration of an athlete's track performances. They noted that Jimmie was a member of his high school basketball team, that he was Sudlersville High's champion in weight events, and that he participated in numerous track events, although in the state olympiad he was limited to competing in only two.¹² The sportswriters were of the opinion that young Foxx was one of the most promising athletes they had ever seen and envisioned "a great future for him."¹³ Some years later Foxx declared that winning the 220-yard dash and high jump and being named the outstanding high school athlete in Maryland was the greatest thrill of his boyhood.¹⁴

Jimmie's last appearance as a high school track star was at a local county meet early in May, 1924, when he was a junior in high school. In this event he broke the county record for the running high jump and for the 100-yard dash.¹⁵ Jimmie did not participate in the 1924 state olympiad at Baltimore later that spring. By the time that event was held, Jimmie had embarked on his professional career in another sport.

During the same years that Jimmie was gaining attention as a high school track star, he was also an active member of the Sudlersville High soccer team. Since the local county schools in the area did not participate in football, soccer season was in the autumn, during October and November. Jimmie was a member of his high school soccer team during his sophomore and junior years.¹⁶ He was a forward on the Sudlersville soccer team and competed against schools at Centreville, Stevensville, Queen Anne and other local areas. In 1923 Foxx was chosen captain of the Sudlersville soccer team. This year they won the tri-county championship with a record of four wins and one loss. In a crucial game with Centreville High School it was reported that the skillful playing of Jimmie Foxx was a key factor in Sudlersville's 1-0 victory.¹⁷

Sudlersville High School soccer team; Foxx is seated in front with ball (courtesy Sudlersville Memorial Library).

The winter sport at Sudlersville High and other schools in the region was basketball. Sandwiched between the soccer and baseball seasons, basketball games were scheduled from early January to mid–March. Jimmie, who was 5' 11" at age thirteen, was a member of the Sudlersville High basketball team during the years he was a member of the soccer team. Foxx played center and was elected team captain his junior year (1923–24). In the opening game of this season Sudlersville defeated Centreville by a score of 15-8 and it was noted that Foxx starred throughout the contest.[18] Two weeks later, in a game played at the Washington College gymnasium in Chestertown as a preliminary game to one between Washington College and Western Maryland, Sudlersville defeated George Biddle High School of Cecilton 31-9. In this game Jimmie had three field goals.[19] In March, at the county basketball tournament, held in the Washington College gymnasium, Sudlersville won the Queen Anne's County basketball championship by defeating Centreville 33-18. Team captain and center Jimmie Foxx led the Sudlersville champions in season scoring with eighty-eight points; the teammate with the second highest score had fifty.[20] When Jimmie was a high school senior (1924–25) he was not permitted to play soccer or basketball. Connie Mack, the owner of the baseball team which had signed Jimmie to a contract in the summer of 1924, prohibited his participating in these sports. Mack feared that Jimmie might suffer an injury which would "jeopardize his baseball future."[21]

Although Jimmie Foxx was an outstanding high school track star and his performances in soccer and basketball were at a level considerably above average, it was in baseball that he early exhibited a rare and exceptional talent. Other sports Jimmie learned at school, but baseball was something which he was introduced to before he learned to walk. His father, Dell Foxx, had been for a number of years one of the most popular baseball players on the Eastern Shore. He was a catcher and played with various teams in the county. Some maintain that Dell Foxx could have had a professional baseball career of his own but that he elected to stay home and fulfill family responsibilities which fell to him when his father died. When Jimmie was a child his father taught him to throw and catch a baseball. He also instructed him in hitting and served as batting practice pitcher for his son.[22]

From the time he was twelve years old Jimmie was playing baseball during the summer with county league teams comprised of adults, one of whom was his father. Before Jimmie became a high school baseball star he was attracting attention by his summer play for county league teams. It appears that the first mention of his baseball playing at this level was in the summer of 1921, when Foxx was just thirteen. The *Centreville Observer* for August 27, 1921, notes that in a county league game Sudlersville defeated Bridgetown 9-4. In this game Foxx was the catcher, and he scored two runs. Later that week Sudlersville lost to Denton 2-1; Jimmie also caught this game and had two hits. The umpires for these games were Dell Foxx and a man named Emerson. On other occasions in these county games Jimmie would pitch and his father would be the catcher.[23] Jimmie later recalled an experience from the 1921 season. He noted that all of the other players in the league were older than he was and that the pitcher he faced in his first game was a man about thirty years of age. The first time Foxx was at bat he stroked a fast ball for a base hit. After that hit, he recalled, "I felt as if I could hit any pitcher in the business. That hit gave me confidence."[24] Confidence on the playing field would be an abiding feature of Jimmie's career.

The following summer, 1922, Jimmie received his first money for playing baseball. A representative of the Goldsborough team in the Caroline County League asked him to play for his team. The representative agreed to pay Jimmie one dollar for an "experimental game." In this game Jimmie played second base and hit two long home runs into the woods beyond the playing area. Goldsborough officials were so impressed with the play of Foxx that they offered to make him a regular and pay him three dollars a game.[25]

In the summer of 1923, the interval between his sophomore and junior year in high school, Jimmie played for the Ridgely team of the Caroline County League. He was paid twenty dollars a week for playing three games — on Saturday, Sunday and Wednesday. He demonstrated his versatility by playing several positions for the Ridgely team — among them catching, third base, pitching, and the outfield. However, the feature of Foxx's play which attracted the most attention was his hitting, especially the long home runs. It was during the 1923 season that a scout from the Dover, Delaware, club of the Eastern Shore League witnessed one of Jimmie's long distance home runs. He was so impressed that he offered Jimmie a contract for thirty-five dollars a week and expenses. Jimmie would have accepted this offer, but his mother intervened, explaining that he was too young to leave home.[26]

In addition to playing baseball for county league teams, Jimmie was also playing baseball for Sudlersville High School, where he played a variety of positions, including pitching, catching, the outfield, and various infield positions. In his junior year, the last one during which he played high school baseball, Jimmie had a batting average of .552. In one game he struck out eighteen batters. In addition to his hitting and pitching, Foxx was always a base-stealing threat and was a high school leader in this category with eight in 1924.[27]

It was customary on the Eastern Shore that after the close of the high school baseball season All-Star teams, representing the best players from various county high schools, were formed to compete against each other and also against visiting teams. These games were usually played in June and did not interfere with county league play. In 1923, when Foxx was fifteen years old and before the beginning of his junior year at Sudlersville High, he was chosen a member of the Queen Anne's All-Star baseball team. During the month of June the All-Stars played a number of games. In one against a Washington College reserve squad, the All-Stars won 10-1. Jimmie caught this game and he had one hit in five times at bat. In a later game against Beacon Business College, he was four for five with two singles, a triple, and a home run. Although a team from Gettysburg, Pennsylvania, defeated the Queen Anne's All-Stars 6-5, Foxx was four for five in this game and two of his hits were triples. At the conclusion of the All-Star games, Foxx emerged as the team's leading hitter with an average of .454.[28]

As Jimmie became more active in baseball, his heroes and role models began to shift from Olympic track star Charles Paddock to major league baseball stars. Some years later, while reminiscing with a Philadelphia sportswriter, Foxx stated that by the time he was fifteen years old his "heroes" were Rogers Hornsby and Harry Heilmann, both, like Jimmie, right-handed hitters.[29]

In the spring of 1924 Jimmie was a sixteen-year-old high school junior, and this would be his last year as a high school baseball player. The high school baseball season extended from early April to late May. Foxx participated in all of Sudlersville's games—playing in the outfield, catching, and pitching. Whatever position he played it did not affect his hitting; he hit well in all games. For example, in an early game against Stevensville he was three for four, with a double, triple, and home run; in another contest he was three for five; in a game against Centreville he was three for four. In a game near the close of the season Sudlersville lost to Centreville but in this contest Jimmie struck out eighteen of the opposing hitters, walked one batter, was two for four at bat, and stole a base. When the high school baseball season ended, Foxx was the leading hitter among high school players in the region. His batting average was .552.[30]

Although Jimmie was an outstanding high school star in track, soccer, basketball, and baseball he was not simply a high school jock. Foxx was also interested in the theater, and he performed as a high school thespian. In the spring of his junior year he had a role in the class play. This production, entitled "Miss Cherry Blossom," was presented at Memorial Hall in Sudlersville during the last week of April. The setting of the play was in Japan, and it was reported that Jimmie gave "a fine performance," playing the part of a "Japanese politician of high rank."[31] Jimmie also compiled an average or better academic record in high school. Although his academic record was modest when compared with his athletic achievements, his performance in such subjects as English, geometry, history, and chemistry was satisfactory or better. For example, in his sophomore year his grades in plane geometry, European history, and Latin were in the C category; his English grade was B. His grades for the junior year included a B in English and agriculture and Cs in algebra and chemistry.[32]

In the spring of 1924 one of the most remarkable careers in professional baseball began when sixteen-year-old Jimmie Foxx signed to play for the Easton, Maryland, club in the class D Eastern Shore League. This league was only two years old and it was Easton's first year in the league. The sponsors of Easton's entry had acquired the services of the former major league notable and now resident of Trappe, Maryland, John Franklin "Home Run" Baker to manage the team. Baker a native of Maryland, had retired from baseball and had been living on the Eastern Shore for several years. Baker and Ty Cobb were two of the best-known major league baseball players in the opening decades of the twentieth century. Baker played third base for the Philadelphia Athletics from 1908 to 1915 and led the American League in home runs four times. From 1915 to 1921 he was a member of the New York Yankees. In the 1911 World Series against the New York Giants, which the Athletics won four games to two, Baker was the hero. His home runs off Christy Mathewson and Rube Marquard, which propelled the Athletics to the championship, prompted sportswriters to give him the nickname "Home Run," a moniker which clung to him until his death sixty-five years later. Baker's lifetime batting average was .308 and his home run total was ninety-three; he was elected to the Baseball Hall of Fame in 1955.[33]

The Eastern Shore League, which began operating in 1922, consisted of six teams from Maryland, Delaware, and Virginia. Easton was not one of the founding members of the league but joined it two years later. During the winter of 1923–24 the sponsors of the Easton franchise employed Frank Baker to manage their entry. Baker's first task was to assemble a team and have it ready

Easton Farmers of the Eastern Shore League, 1924. Jimmie Foxx is the middle man in the back row, with right hand on hip (courtesy Easton, Md., *Star Democrat*).

for the opening date, May 30, 1924. One position he would not have to worry about filling was third base—Baker would play this position himself.[34]

One possible recruit who interested Baker was the high school youngster in Sudlersville. Baker had first noticed the play and especially the hitting of Foxx in 1922, when Jimmie was playing in the local county league. In the winter of 1923–24, Baker wrote Foxx a letter informing him about Easton's entry in the Eastern Shore League, briefing him on some of the other teams and noting that the season would open on May 30. Baker also stated that he had heard about Foxx's play and that it had been suggested to him Foxx might like to try out for the Easton club. Baker concluded by inviting Jimmie to come to Easton and talk with him about the upcoming season. This invitation received the approval of his parents, and Jimmie went to Easton in early April, about the time Baker's other recruits began pre-season training. Baker talked with the youngster and was impressed with his hitting. He noted that Foxx had played at various positions and he informed Jimmie that he would like for him to be one of Easton's catchers. Before the visit was concluded Foxx was offered a contract to play for Easton at a salary of $100.00 a month. Although this was less than one-half of Easton's top salary of $250.00 a month, it was considerably more than Jimmie had received from county teams in previous summers.[35] Jimmie returned home, completed the second semester of his junior year in high school, played high school baseball, and signed the contract with

Easton. He joined the Easton Farmers for their opening game against Dover on May 30.[36]

In 1924 the Eastern Shore League consisted of six teams, four of which were located in Maryland: Cambridge, Salisbury, Crisfield, and Easton. The other two were Parksley, Virginia, and Dover, Delaware. A sporting news feature in the May 10 issue of the *Easton Star-Democrat* announced that the upcoming baseball season would open on May 30 and close on September 1. Each team would play an eighty-game schedule; forty at home and forty away. Easton's home field was Federal Park.[37]

The first mention of Jimmie Foxx in the Easton newspaper was on May 24, a week before the season's opener. Although the writer misspelled his name by referring to him as Fox, all else in the article was correct. It stated that Jimmie was

> a young man, in his teens, but he is good behind the bat. His arm is strong, he is fast, and besides can play the infield. Many predict that he will be in the big leagues in two or three years time. He is said to be a hard hitter.[38]

This youngster was behind the bat for Easton's opening game against Dover. There were 2,269 fans in Federal Park for the contest, and although Easton lost 7-2 the crowd was impressed by the young catcher. In the sixth inning and with a runner on base, the count three and two on Foxx, the youngster "did the Babe Ruth stunt and put the ball over the left field fence."[39]

The opening day loss by the Easton Farmers was the forerunner of what was to be a miserable season for them. They would conclude the season with a record of twenty-three wins and fifty-seven losses for a winning percentage of only .281; each of the other five teams in the league would play .500 or better ball.[40] Despite the fact that the team floundered, Easton and supporters of the Farmers led the league in attendance: 33,293 fans witnessed their home games. This was 10,000 more than any other town in the league.[41]

Perhaps the principal attraction of the Farmers was their sixteen-year-old schoolboy catcher. Jimmie was acutely aware that he was a boy playing a man's game, and in an attempt to appear more "grown up" he began to chew tobacco, as many of the older players did. He continued this practice after he joined the Athletics and soon added another type of activity which he associated with manhood—he began smoking cigars, a practice he would continue for the rest of his life.[42] Jimmie participated in seventy-six of Easton's eighty games, and although he caught most of these contests, Baker utilized his versatility by occasionally playing him in the outfield and at other times having him relieve the manager at third base. During the first half of the season Foxx was hitting slightly over .300 or .309 after forty-six games. His average was second to the club leader, manager Baker's .319. At this time Foxx's hits included five doubles, three triples, and five home runs.[43] Early in the season the press noted that Foxx was "stinging the ball" and that his hits "travel fast." In one game his ninth inning home run was "over the deep left field fence," and in another it was exclaimed that he hit one of the "longest balls ever seen in Easton." This was a home run to deep center field.[44] Throughout the summer the *Centreville Observer* (which spelled his name correctly) reported that Foxx was playing brilliantly for Easton, that he was "a pillar of strength" for the team, that he was a "hard-working player" who was "playing gilt-edge ball for Baker."[45]

Baker established a close rapport with his young protégé. He was impressed by the youngster's natural talent, by his enthusiasm for the game, and by his friendly and cooperative attitude. Jimmie would play wherever Baker suggested, and he performed well at any position. Jimmie, in turn, idolized "Home Run" Baker, his manager, former major league star, and World Series hero. He listened to Baker's advice and instructions. Baker was satisfied with every aspect of Foxx's play, with one exception. Throughout his high school and county league play Jimmie had been mainly a right-handed batter, but occasionally he would hit from the left side of the plate. Jimmie was a switch-hitter before switch-hitting became acceptable in professional baseball. Baker told him that "no good hitter has to turn around," and he instructed Jimmie to hit right-handed. This was advice or instruction which Jimmie accepted, and he gave up switch-hitting.[46]

Among the 33,000-plus who attended Easton's home games in 1924, two were rather special guests. One was Judge Kenesaw Mountain Landis, commissioner of baseball since 1920. The office of commissioner was created by major league baseball owners following the Black Sox scandal in 1919. This scandal involved gamblers who bribed Chicago White Sox players to throw the World Series to the Cincinnati Reds. This scandal tarnished the reputation of the all-American game, led to the banishment of the White Sox players from baseball, and the appointment of a commissioner with authority to oversee the activities of baseball, to restore the integrity of the game, and to supervise the practices and activities of all associated with the game. Landis, who was a federal judge at the time of his appointment, would serve as the unquestioned "czar" of baseball until his death in 1944.[47]

Prior to the opening of the season, officials of the Easton club had invited Landis to visit the town and to be a guest at one of the home games. Landis accepted this invitation and also relayed some complimentary comments about Easton's manager Frank Baker.[48] The commissioner's visit to Easton was delayed until the last month of the season. On August 9, there was a notice in the *Star-Democrat* announcing that Judge Landis would be in Easton on August 15, that he would be a guest at the Rotary Club luncheon and later that afternoon attend the game between Easton and Crisfield. After welcoming remarks at the luncheon, Landis made a brief speech to the Rotary gathering and their guests. He commended the Easton sponsors and fans for their support of the baseball club, spoke kindly of Frank Baker, and "declared his love for the hospitality of the Eastern Shore." That afternoon it was reported that a "holiday festival atmosphere" prevailed at the game. More than 3,000 fans filed into Federal Park to see the Farmers play the Crisfield Crabbers. Easton was victorious in this contest 4-1; Foxx was two for four that afternoon, getting a single and a home run—a massive drive over the left field fence which the judge described as "a dandy."[49]

Before the season was half over Baker was so convinced of the immense potential of his versatile young hitter that he sought to make a major league connection for him. On one occasion when there was an off day and when the Yankees were in Philadelphia for a series with the Athletics, Baker went to Philadelphia. He visited the Yankees, talked with some of his former teammates, and tried to interest Manager Miller Huggins in his sixteen-year-old power hitter. Huggins, whose contingent featured a number of power hitters, including George Herman "Babe" Ruth, who had hit fifty-four home runs in 1920 and fifty-nine in 1921, was hardly interested in high school phenomenons. Some years later Colonel Jacob Rupert of the Yankees would bemoan the fact that the Yankees had passed up the opportunity to acquire Foxx in 1924. His "Murderers' Row" would have been even more deadly with Foxx in the lineup along with Ruth, Gehrig, Meusel, and Combs.[50] After his visit with Huggins, Baker went to see his old manager and one of the owners of the Athletics, Connie Mack. Although Mack had sold Baker to the Yankees in 1915, the two men had maintained a cordial relationship. Baker had been a premier third baseman for the Athletics, a leading home run hitter, and one who consistently hit better than .300. Mack respected Baker's judgment and his knowledge of the game. When Baker told Mack about Foxx he received a more positive response than he had from Huggins. Reportedly Mack told him that if Foxx was as good as Baker said he was, the boy "was worth looking at."

Baker's visit with Mack prompted the appearance in Easton of the second special visitor in the summer of 1924. In July, Mack sent Mike Brennan, a scout for the Athletics, to Easton to observe the play and hitting of young Foxx, to evaluate his potential as a major league player, and to report to Mack his assessment of the youngster. Brennan followed the Easton club for more than two weeks. He carefully observed and evaluated every aspect of the play of this talented youngster. He noted that although he was only sixteen, he had the build and strength of a man of twenty-five. Foxx, he noted, was nearly six feet tall, weighed 170 to 175 pounds and was "all muscle." He observed that Foxx was a skilled catcher and could handle all pitchers whether young or old. Brennan also stated that Jimmie could snap the ball to second base from a squatting position. Whenever he was on base he was a constant threat to steal; Brennan said that Foxx was perhaps the fastest man in the league. But what impressed Brennan more than anything else was the hitting power of Foxx. During the time he was observing him Jimmie had a number of extra base hits, including several long home runs. Brennan reported that it was "common knowledge around the league" that young Foxx hit the ball harder and farther than anyone else in the league, that he was a "terror to any pitcher" in the league.[51]

The report of Brennan and the recommendation of Baker convinced Mack that the young man was worth taking a chance on, and by the end of July it was announced that the Athletics had purchased Foxx from Easton for $2000.00. However, Jimmie would not report to the Philadelphia club until after the close of the Eastern Shore League's season.[52] Foxx later recalled that he was "stunned" when he learned that Baker had recommended him to Connie Mack, and Mack would later recall that Jimmie Foxx was a "gift" from Baker. Probably he did consider Jimmie a gift when one recalls that a couple of years earlier he paid the Baltimore Orioles $100,000.00 for Robert "Lefty" Grove, purchased Al Simmons from the Milwaukee Brewers for $35,000.00, and that he bought the Portland franchise in the Pacific Coast League in order to acquire Gordon S. "Mickey" Cochrane.[53]

Connie Mack joked that he would probably be accused of "robbing the cradle" by purchasing the sixteen-year-old Foxx. Foxx, however, was not the first high school teenager Mack had signed. Fifteen years earlier, in 1909, he had signed another high school youngster, eighteen-year-old John Phalen "Stuffy" McInnis. McInnis was with the Athletics from 1909 to 1917, was a teammate of Baker, and was the first baseman on Mack's $100,000.00 infield and pennant winning teams of 1911–14. After his major league career, McInnis was the baseball coach at Harvard University.[54]

Foxx finished the season with Easton; his final batting average was .296, three percentage points above his manager, Frank Baker. His fielding average was .966. Foxx's complete statistical record for the 1924 season was as follows: he played in 76 games, was at bat 260 times, collected seventy-seven hits and scored thirty-three runs. Among his seventy-seven hits were eleven doubles, two triples, and ten home runs. He received twenty-two walks, struck out forty-one times, stole eight bases, and was hit by pitchers four times.[55] Throughout the season the Easton *Star-Democrat* invariably spelled his name with one x. This, however, never seemed to bother Jimmie; he never had an identity problem, for his energies and attention were focused on the game he loved—baseball.

After the close of the Eastern Shore League's season, the directors of the Easton club arranged a couple of exhibition games, with the proceeds going to "benefit the players." It was a way of providing a sort of bonus for the players and of showing the management's appreciation for their services during the past season. One of these contests was with the Talbot County All-Stars, and the other was with the Wilkins Club of Baltimore. In the game with the All-Stars Foxx played third base and was three for five at bat, having a double and two singles in a game Easton won 11-3. Foxx was the catcher in the game with the Baltimore club. Easton won this contest 9-1, and Foxx was one for three; his hit was a home run.[56]

Following the exhibition games, Foxx also participated in what was locally referred to as the "little World Series." This was a six-game play-off between the champions of the Eastern Shore League and the Blue Ridge League. Parksley, Virginia, located on the Eastern Shore in Accomac County, was the pennant winner in the Eastern Shore League. The Blue Ridge League, also a class D organization, consisted of Martinsburg, West Virginia, Frederick and Hagerstown, Maryland, and three Pennsylvania towns: Hanover, Chambersburg, and Waynesboro. The pennant winner in the Blue Ridge League was Martinsburg.[57] The play-off games included members of the winning teams plus several of the best players from other teams in the circuit. The *Centreville Observer* reported that Foxx was "drafted" to play for Parksley. In the first game Foxx was the catcher for Parksley and the hero of a game which Parksley won 17-0. A Baltimore sports writer covering the game stated that Foxx performed behind the bat like a veteran and that he made the fans "mildly insane" with his spectacular hitting. He had two home runs and a double. Parksley won the series four games to two and the *Centreville Observer* declared Foxx the star of the series. He had four home runs, one of which was described as the longest ever hit on the Eastern Shore, and posted a batting average for the series of .391.[58]

It was during one of the series games at Martinsburg that Foxx received a telephone call from Philadelphia. It was from Connie Mack, requesting that Jimmie come to see him as soon as the games were over. Foxx took the train the next day for Philadelphia and saw the city and Shibe Park for the first time. He was thrilled with the thought of going to the major leagues, but he was also a bit apprehensive. He was only sixteen years old, and he had never been to Philadelphia or so far away from home. However, Mack met him when he arrived in the city, and his fatherly demeanor and treatment put the youngster at ease. Years later Foxx recalled in an interview with a sportswriter, that "the best break" he ever had in baseball was "breaking in under the direction of Connie Mack." He said Mack was "always great with kids." "He gives you hell," said Jimmie, "at the right time and he babies you at the right time. But most of the time he lets you alone to play the game your way."[59] Shibe Park, which would be Jimmie's baseball home for the next eleven years, was undergoing some renovations. However, Jimmie noted the spaciousness of the park, with its dimensions of approximately 330' down the line to the left and right field fences and 468' to the center field wall. In a short while Jimmie would be as comfortable in Shibe Park as he was on the sand lots of Queen Anne's County.[60]

Jimmie did not return home until after the close of the American League season. Mack gave him a uniform and locker, and he remained with the Athletics throughout the month of September. His youth attracted the attention of sportswriters who claimed that Foxx was the youngest player ever sold by one ball club to another.[61] Foxx did not appear in any of the Athletics' games during the last month of the 1924 season. He sat on the bench and listened to Mack and other players discuss various aspects of the game. As one observer remarked, he sat quietly on the bench but was constantly alert, observing, listening, and learning from his manager and teammates. During these weeks Foxx often caught batting practice: he also worked out at third base and was allowed a turn at hitting in batting practice. The more Mack and his executive son, Earl, saw of Jimmie, the more pleased they were with the youngster. Mack referred to him as "a diamond in the rough" and as "a jewel." That fall, at a meeting of baseball executives, he declared that he had "never seen a youngster with as much potential as Foxx."[62]

In late September the Athletics made their last western road trip of the season, and Foxx accompanied the team. On this trip they played several exhibition games and Jimmie saw action in some of these contests; in each one that he played he hit well. In one exhibition game against the Cincinnati Reds, played at Erie, Pennsylvania, Foxx hit a game-winning triple off the southpaw ace, Eppa Rixey. The previous season Rixey had been a twenty-game winner for the Reds.[63]

After the close of the baseball season Foxx returned to Sudlersville and began his senior year in high school. On October 22 he observed his seventeenth birthday. This autumn was similar to past ones in most respects; he was kept busy with farm work and occupied with his studies. However, one startling difference this semester was that he did not compete in soccer and basketball. He sometimes served as a referee for soccer matches, but Connie Mack forbade him to participate in soccer and basketball. The Athletics owner took every precaution against possible injury to his recently acquired baseball "jewel."[64]

Foxx remained in school until February, 1925, when the major leagues began spring training. At this time he left school and went to Fort Myers, Florida, where the Athletics' spring training facilities were located. Jimmie had signed a one-year contract with the Philadelphia club which would pay him $2,000.00 for the 1925 season.[65] Jimmie's mother, who had opposed his signing with Dover in 1923 because he was too young, was not enthusiastic about her son leaving high school and going away from home. She had wanted him to complete high school and go to college so that he would have the possibility of a better life than she and his father had experienced as tenant farmers. However, she knew that Jimmie's main desire in life was to play baseball and that the opportunity to play with the Athletics was one that should not be dismissed. In the end she supported her son's wish to leave school and go to spring training with the Athletics.[66] Jimmie's formal education ended when he left Sudlersville for spring training in 1925. Later that year, on June 19, his class graduated; seventeen young men and women were given diplomas. Foxx did not graduate but the school and his classmates honored him by presenting him a certificate, designating him as honorary member of the class.[67]

When Jimmie left home to join the Athletics, his county newspaper, the *Centreville Observer*, expressed sentiments of pride in the young man and asserted that although Jimmie was young, his home training had instilled in him a sense of values which would guide him in his new environment. His mother, the editor declared, was a "kind, gentle, affectionate" woman who had started Jimmie right. She had brought him up in the Methodist Sunday School and church and had informed him "of the pitfalls and temptations" that beset young men as they "brush shoulders with the world." The editor assured his readers that Jimmie's home training would serve as a guide for living and that he along with "everybody" else in the county hoped that Jimmie would "prove a real success in the majors."

Notes

1. *New York Times* (New York), October 13, 1907.
2. Most accounts maintain that the Foxx family migrated to America from Ireland; however, some claim that the family was of French origin. Those who claim that the ancestry was French speculate that the family name was originally De Foix or perhaps Faux, and that it was later changed to Foxx. Jimmie always maintained that his parents and grandparents were born in America and that his grandfather spelled the family name Foxx. For example see: the *Philadelphia Inquirer* (Philadelphia, Pennsylvania), June 2, 1932; Charles H.L. Johnston, *Famous American Athletes of Today*, Fourth Series (Boston: L.C. Page and Company, 1934), p. 57; F.C. Lane, "The Strong Slugger of the Fighting A's," *Baseball Magazine* (September, 1929). Calvary Methodist Episcopal Church was affiliated with the northern branch of this denomination. Also located in Sudlersville was Asbury Methodist Episcopal Church, South. In 1939 the northern and southern divisions of the Methodist Episcopal Church merged, thereby healing a split of ninety-five years. At this time the separate Methodist congregations in Sudlersville united to form one Methodist church.
3. See Foxx genealogical chart in Sudlersville Memorial Library, Sudlersville, Maryland.
4. *Time*, July 29, 1929.
5. *Centreville Observer* (Centreville, Maryland), April 22, 1922.
6. Paul W. Phillips, *Sudlersville, Queen Anne's County on Maryland's Eastern Shore* (n.p.: n.p., n.d.), pp. 24–30.
7. David L. Porter, editor, *Biographical Dictionary of American Sports* (Westport, Connecticut: Greenwood Press, 1988), pp. 616–517.
8. *Centreville Observer*, May 21, 1921; Bob Broeg, *Super Stars of Baseball* (St. Louis: The Sporting News, 1971), p. 83.
9. *Centreville Observer*, May 20, 1922.
10. *Ibid.*, June 17, 1922
11. *Ibid.*, June 16, 1923.
12. *Ibid.*, June 16, 19, 1923.

13. Undated item from the *Baltimore Sun*, in Foxx files, Talbot County Free Library, Easton, Maryland.

14. Jimmie Foxx, "When I Was a Boy," in *St. Nicholas Magazine* (November, 1925), p. 20.

15. *Centreville Observer*, May 17, 1924.

16. *Ibid.*, October 21, 1922.

17. *Ibid.*, November 3, 1923; *Queen Anne's Record-Observer* (Centreville, Maryland), July 27, 1939.

18. *Centreville Observer*, January 19, November 15, 1924.

19. *Ibid.*, February 2, 1924.

20. *Ibid.*, March 8, 15, 1924.

21. *Philadelphia Evening Bulletin*, January 27, 1925.

22. *Centreville Observer*, September 27, 1924; *Philadelphia Evening Bulletin*, August 13, 1928, November 14, 1929.

23. *Centreville Observer*, August 27, 1921; *Philadelphia Inquirer*, September 4, 1932.

24. *Philadelphia Evening Bulletin*, August 13, 1928.

25. Jimmie Foxx, "I'm Glad I Was a Ballplayer," in *Sport* (March, 1952), p. 49.

26. *Ibid.*, undated item in Foxx files, *Boston Herald*.

27. *Centreville Observer*, April 26, May 2, 10, 17, 1924.

28. *Ibid.*, June 2, 9, 16, 1923.

29. *Philadelphia Evening Bulletin*, November 23, 1954.

30. *Centreville Observer*, May 2, 10, 17, 1924.

31. *The Sudlersville High School Forum*, May, 1924. Copy in Sudlersville Memorial Library.

32. See copies of report cards in Foxx files, Sudlersville Memorial Library.

33. Harry Grayson, *They Played the Game, The Story of Baseball Greats* (Freeport, New York: Books for Libraries Press, 1944), pp. 42–43; George Sullivan, *Sluggers: Twenty-Seven of Baseball's Greatest* (New York: Atheneum, 1991), pp. 64–65.

34. *The Sporting News* (St. Louis, Missouri), April 3, 1924.

35. *Queen Anne's Record-Observer*, undated item in Foxx files, Sudlersville Memorial Library.

36. There are several accounts concerning Foxx's invitation to Easton. One is that one day in the spring Jimmie received a penny post card from Baker, asking him to come to Easton and talk with him about playing for the team. The other is that Jimmie's father, Sam Dell, who knew Baker, had visited with him and told him about his son's playing and suggested that Baker talk with him. A third account is that Jimmie received a letter from Baker, during the winter of 1923–24, inviting him to come to Easton to talk about trying out for the team. Baker noted in this letter that several people had recommended Jimmie to him. The facts are: by 1924 anyone on the Eastern Shore who was interested in sports knew of Jimmie Foxx and his talents as a baseball player. And as early as 1922 Baker had seen and been impressed with the playing of the youngster. See *Philadelphia Evening Bulletin*, February 21, 1930; undated newspaper item in Foxx files, Baseball Library, Cooperstown, New York; *Star Democrat* (Easton, Maryland), undated clipping, Samuel Dell Foxx, III, scrapbook number one.

37. William W. Mowbray, *The Eastern Shore Baseball League* (Centreville: Tidewater Publishers, 1989), p. 30; *Star Democrat*, May 10, 1924.
38. *Star Democrat*, May 24, 1924.
39. *Ibid.*, June 7, 1924.
40. Mowbray, *The Eastern Shore League*, p. 30.
41. *Star-Democrat*, September 13, 1924.
42. *Philadelphia Evening Bulletin*, April 18, 1933; Norman Macht, manuscript sketch of Jimmie Foxx in Sudlersville Memorial Library.
43. *Star-Democrat*, August 2, 1924.
44. *Ibid.*, July 5, August 2, 1924.
45. *Centreville Observer*, July 5, 7, 14, 21, August 16, 1924.
46. Assorted clippings, 1929, in Foxx files, Baseball Library, Cooperstown, New York.
47. Charles C. Alexander, *Our Game, An American Baseball History* (New York: Henry Holt and Company, 1991), pp. 134-35.
48. *Star-Democrat*, May 17, 1924.
49. *Ibid.*, August 9, 16, 23, 1924; *Centreville Observer*, August 23, 1924.
50. *Philadelphia Evening Bulletin*, July 18, 1932. An earlier "twist of fate" also prevented Foxx and Ruth from being teammates. In 1914 Jack Dunn of the Baltimore Orioles had offered Ruth to Connie Mack, giving Mack his first chance on another remarkable youngster. Mack, however, passed on Ruth, and Dunn later sold him to the Red Sox. See *Philadelphia Inquirer*, August 6, 1988.
51. *Star-Democrat*, August 2, 1924; *Philadelphia Evening Bulletin*, July 30, 31, 1924, November 14, 1929.
52. *Philadelphia Evening Bulletin*, July 31, 1924; *Star-Democrat*, August 2, 1924.
53. *The Sporting News*, October 16, December 4, 1924, January 12, 1955; *Philadelphia Evening Bulletin*, August 13, 1928.
54. Jerome C. Romanowski, *The Mackmen* (Camden, N. J.: Graphic Press, 1979), p. 32.
55. *The Sporting News*, January 1, 1925.
56. *Star-Democrat*, September 6, 1924.
57. Robert Obojski, *Bush League, A History of Minor League Baseball* (New York: Macmillan Company, 1975), p. 330.
58. *Star-Democrat*, September 6, 1924; *Centreville Observer*, September 13, 1924.
59. *Philadelphia Evening Bulletin*, August 13, 1928; Ed Rumill, "Looking Backward With Jimmie Foxx," in *Baseball Magazine* (November, 1944), p. 421.
60. Bruce Kuklick, *To Every Thing a Season: Shibe Park and Urban Philadelphia, 1909-1976* (Princeton, N. J.: Princeton University Press, 1991), p. 53.
61. Foxx, "I'm Glad I Was a Ballplayer," p. 78; *Centreville Observer*, September 13, 1924; *Philadelphia Evening Bulletin*, December 28, 1928.
62. Broeg, *Super Stars of Baseball*, p. 84; *Philadelphia Evening Bulletin*, December 22, 28, 1924; *Boston Daily Record* (Boston, Massachusetts), August 15, 1932.
63. *Centreville Observer*, September 20, 1924; *Philadelphia Evening Bulletin*, December 22, 1924.
64. *Centreville Observer*, October 18, 25, November 1, 1924.

65. Foxx, "I'm Glad I Was a Ballplayer," p. 78.

66. *Queen Anne's Record-Observer*, July 27, 1939; *Delaware State News* (Dover), March 18, 1979.

67. Assorted, undated clippings, *Delaware State News*, in Foxx files, Sudlersville Memorial Library.

68. *Centreville Observer*, September 27, 1924.

Two
Years of Apprenticeship, 1925–1928

In February, 1925, Jimmie Foxx left home and his Sudlersville High School classmates to accompany the Philadelphia Athletics to spring training at Fort Myers, Florida. It had been arranged for Jimmie to meet the team train at Baltimore for the journey to Florida. However, Connie Mack was taking no chances on the possibility that his seventeen-year-old farm-boy prospect would become confused and not make the proper railway connections. He assigned Eddie Rommel to meet Jimmie in Baltimore, accompany him to the railroad depot, and board the train with him. Rommel was ten years older than Jimmie and had been a prominent member of the Athletics pitching staff since 1920.[1]

The Athletics were the first major league team to begin spring training in 1925, and sportswriters from the Philadelphia papers as well as *The Sporting News* were interested in the young men Connie Mack was assembling: among them were Gordon S. "Mickey" Cochrane, Aloysius "Al" Simmons, Robert M. "Lefty" Grove, and Foxx. *The Sporting News*, which had first mentioned Foxx in its December 13, 1924 issue, would continue to misspell his last name until its March 4, 1926 issue. From that date on *The Sporting News* was aware that his name was Foxx. However, there is no indication that the misspelling of his name ever bothered Jimmie.

Before the exhibition or Grapefruit League season began, sportswriters covered the Athletics inter-squad games. For three successive weeks in March there were feature stories about the Athletics and Foxx figured prominently in each. In one he was referred to as a seventeen-year-old catcher, perhaps the youngest player in the major leagues. Although he was young, he showed "real class," could hit with power, was "surprisingly smooth in handling pitchers," and he was fast—could circle the bases in thirteen and four-fifths seconds.[2] Jimmie's hitting began to attract attention when, in one of the early inter-squad games, he hit two home runs. It was the home run he hit in a practice game during the first week of March that created the most interest. It was

19

reported that Foxx "hit the longest home run ever seen here [in Fort Myers]" and his teammates declared it would have cleared the center field wall at Shibe Park, which was 468' from home plate. Shortly after this tremendous blast, *The Sporting News* ran a feature on Jimmie and printed an eight-by-six-inch photograph of him on the first page of its March 19 issue.[3]

Power hitting, and especially the home run, was a distinguishing feature of major league baseball as it was developing in the 1920s. Prior to 1920 baseball was primarily a game of low scores, featuring the hit and run, stolen base, squeeze play, and bunt. The player who typified best the type of play prior to 1920 was perhaps Ty Cobb. But the game of baseball began to change in 1920. In this year a new ball was adopted by the major leagues; it was the same size as formerly, but the center contained more rubber, the yarn was of a different grade and was more tightly woven. It came to be called the "lively ball" since it had greater resiliency than the pre–1920 "dead ball." Another change in the game also concerned the ball. In 1920 baseball owners and officials banned certain pitches and forbade pitchers from tampering with the ball. Pitchers were no longer allowed to scuff up the ball or use any abrasive substance on it. The spitball was also outlawed, except for those seventeen veterans who currently used it as their principal delivery.[4] At the time of the spitball rule (1920), the pitch was also banned from the minors. The rule concerning this pitch was that, when the current crop of spitball pitchers passed from the scene, there would be no more spitball pitchers allowed in organized baseball. The lively ball, the outlawing of "trick" pitches, and the use of bats with more finely tapered handles which would allow hitters more snap in their swing all resulted in higher scoring games and an increase in home runs. The player who best typified the game of baseball as it developed in the 1920s was Babe Ruth. Prior to 1920, major league home run leaders usually hit ten, twelve, or thirteen home runs a season. In 1920 Ruth hit fifty-four and a year later fifty-nine. The home run became a favorite with the fans and helped to make Ruth the game's most recognized player. The emphasis on the home run and high scoring games were popular, and attendance in major league parks increased. To insure that the long ball became a staple of the game, some owners moved outfield fences in, giving the hitters a more attractive target. The lively ball, outlawing certain pitches, bringing in the fence and the emphasis on the home run resulted in a game that was popular with the fans but took its toll on pitchers. For example, since the 1920s only three major league pitchers—Lefty Grove, Dizzy Dean, and Dennis McLain—have experienced thirty wins a season.[5]

One practice that baseball owners had discussed from time to time since the 1880s was finally adopted as a regular policy in the 1920s. This was the adoption or establishment of Ladies Day at the ball park. The practice of admitting female fans to games without admission charge on certain days of the week was begun on a regular basis in 1924 by the Cincinnati Reds. The Cincinnati club designated various Mondays during the season Ladies Day.

Within a few years other clubs followed Cincinnati's example; they would announce that on various days, usually a Monday or Friday, Ladies Day would be observed and all female fans admitted free of charge. Before the end of the thirties Ladies Day was an established custom at major league parks. It was maintained that some women were interested in baseball and that others would become fans if given the opportunity to become acquainted with the game and its players. Ladies Day was designed to create fans who would become cash customers, paying their admission to the park during the other days of the week.[6]

Throughout the spring exhibition games of 1925, Jimmie alternated with Cochrane and the veteran Cy Perkins at catching. However, when the season began, Foxx was the third-string catcher. Until well into June Jimmie generally sat on the bench, caught batting practice, and was used occasionally to pinch hit. It was in a game with the Senators on May 27, when Foxx was inserted to pinch hit for Lefty Grove in the eighth inning, that he recorded his first major league hit. It was a line drive double off the southpaw veteran, Sylveanus "Vean" Gregg.[7]

In late June Connie Mack decided to option Jimmie to the Providence, Rhode Island, Grays of the International League; this would permit Foxx to accumulate playing time, would lessen the risk of Jimmie gaining too much weight by sitting on the Athletics' bench, and more important to Mack, it would place Jimmie under the tutelage and guidance of a highly respected and knowledgeable baseball man, Frank Shaughnessy, manager of the Providence club. Shaughnessy had been in baseball for many years; he devised a play-off system, which was adopted by the minor leagues, to determine a league's championship club. Later he would serve for a number of years as president of the International League.[8]

Providence was not a farm club of the Athletics. The farm system, however, was being developed in the 1920s and was a major innovation in baseball. Branch Rickey, the general manager of the St. Louis Cardinals, is credited with creating the first farm system for the development of major league prospects. Under this procedure the major league club would own and operate a number of minor league clubs for the development of young players. Begun by Rickey in 1921, most major league clubs followed his example within the next ten to twelve years. Under this system a club would sign a player for a nominal sum and allow him to develop his skills in the minors until ready for the majors; then he would be brought up. Previously minor league clubs were independently owned and operated. They would develop players and then sell them for the highest price possible to some major league club. For example, Connie Mack paid the Baltimore club $100,000.00 in 1924 for Grove.[9]

In 1925 and after a seven year hiatus, Providence was once again a member of the International League, which at this time was a double A organization.

Other members of the eight-team league were Baltimore, Reading, Jersey City, Rochester, Syracuse, Toronto, and Montreal. The inhabitants of Providence were enthusiastic about the return of baseball to the city. They had renovated and enlarged the seating capacity of Kinsley Park, the stadium, to 8,000 and they were optimistic about the Grays. The team, however, was off to a slow start and by mid–June the Grays were floundering and were in seventh place in league standings. Shaughnessy needed help and in desperation he contacted personnel and sought help from various major league clubs including the Yankees, Senators, and Athletics.[10]

On June 23, Shaughnessy was informed by Connie Mack that he was optioning Jimmie Foxx to the Grays, subject to recall at any time, and that the young catcher would report to the team when it was in Jersey City for a series with the Skeeters.[11] Two days later the *Providence Journal* reported that the young catcher, "Fox" (the Providence press spelled his name with one x the entire nine weeks Jimmie was with the Grays), had joined the Grays and that "he looks good in practice." Readers were informed that on the basis of a fine record he compiled the previous season in the Eastern Shore League, Connie Mack had purchased the youngster from Easton. Although the Providence reporter questioned how well Foxx might "do against class AA company," he concluded that Connie Mack "must have seen something worthwhile in him."[12]

Shortly after Jimmie joined the Grays their regular catcher, Byrd Lynn, was sidelined with a minor spike wound. Lynn had been the backup catcher for Ray Schalk of the White Sox from 1916 to 1920, and he was considered one of the best catchers in the minor leagues. On June 28 his injury caused him to sit out a doubleheader in Baltimore. Foxx caught both of these games, which marked his first appearance in the International League. Although the Grays lost both games to the league-leading Orioles, Jimmie had a hit in each game and was two for five for the day; both hits were singles. The reporter covering the team for the *Providence Journal* wrote that Foxx "looked like a sweet catcher," he "handled his pitchers firmly," and "showed a lot of pep." When an Oriole base runner tested the youngster and attempted to steal, Jimmie "threw the man out." In addition to his "sweet" catching it was noted that Foxx displayed "great speed" on the base paths.[13]

For the next week, until July 6, Jimmie caught while Lynn was recovering. During this time he hit eighth in the lineup, just ahead of the pitcher. On June 30, in a game at Baltimore, Jimmie was three for four. This prompted the writer covering the contest to exclaim, "Foxx gave a snappy exhibition behind the plate and he led the team in hitting, collecting a double and two singles."[14] With Lynn's recovery, Shaughnessy began to vary his use of Jimmie's talents: sometimes in doubleheaders or late in a game he would insert Foxx into the lineup to relieve Lynn; at other times he used Foxx as a pinch hitter or as a pinch runner. By mid–July Shaughnessy was also having Jimmie play right field, and occasionally he shifted him to first base.[15]

It seems to have made no difference to Jimmie what position Shaughnessy asked him to play. He performed well at each and consistently hit .300 or better. A story in the Providence press on July 24 declared, "Foxx is showing up remarkably well and has proven of great value to the team. His hitting has been fine and he has worked splendidly behind the bat, at first base, and in right field."[16] The following day, in a doubleheader against Reading, Jimmie shared time at first base and in right field; he also hit five for seven, getting a triple, double, and three singles. Also on this day he slightly injured a knee, which would sideline him for a couple of days. Three days later Jimmie was in right field for the Grays in a game at Jersey City. In this contest he was four for six with a triple, two doubles, and a single; he also stole a base and scored three runs.[17] Although Foxx was performing well, the Grays remained firmly entrenched in seventh place, one step from the cellar of the International League.

The end of July the Grays returned to their home ground, Kinsley Park, after a long road trip on which they won twelve and lost thirteen games. On their arrival back home the team was outfitted in new uniforms—white with black vertical stripes. However, the new uniforms would not enhance the team's standing in the league. During the first ten days of August, Jimmie played right field and was frequently used as a pinch hitter. When playing right field he generally hit third in the lineup. It was during this interval that Providence observed its first Ladies Day at Kinsley Park. This observance was on August 7 when "several hundred women" were admitted to the game without charge. Ladies Day was proclaimed a success and it would become a regular feature among International League teams.[18]

On August 12, Byrd Lynn was hit on the foot by a foul tip and was forced to leave the game. This injury sidelined the catcher for the next four or five games, and manager Shaughnessy put Foxx behind the plate. The day after Jimmie returned to catching he hit a triple and scored a run. This prompted the local newspaper to report that Foxx "was working nicely behind the bat." After several days of rest Lynn was able to share catching duties and Jimmie divided his playing time between catching and right field. A milestone of sorts in Jimmie's career came on August 21 in a game against the Syracuse Stars. He was playing right field in a game which the Grays won 5–3. In this contest Jimmie was one for five, but this one hit was a drive over the left field fence off the Stars' southpaw "Wild Bill" Hallahan. This was Jimmie's first and only International League home run. It would not be his last look at Hallahan—in a few years they would be World Series opponents when the Athletics and Cardinals contested each other for the world championship.[19]

Two days later Al Grabowski of the Stars tossed a no-hitter against the Grays. In this game Foxx was 0 for one, and he also suffered a shoulder injury. In the fourth inning Grabowski walked Jimmie; and while attempting to steal second base Foxx "slid over the bag and injured his left shoulder severely."[20]

The following day it was reported that Dr. Knight had treated Foxx for a "dislocated shoulder" and "that the shoulder was so sore or painful that Jimmie could not use the arm at all ... and was carrying the arm in a sling."[21] This injury kept Jimmie out of the lineup for a week. He returned to action on August 30 and in a doubleheader against the Buffalo Bisons he was three for seven, having two singles and a double.[22]

Jimmie's performance in the game against the Bisons indicated that he had recovered from the shoulder injury. However, Connie Mack was not willing to risk further possible injury to his young prospect and he recalled him after the games on August 30. The *Philadelphia Evening Bulletin* announced that "Foxx waved good-bye to Providence on August 31 and would join the Athletics at home for their game against the Senators."[23]

During Foxx's tenure at Providence, from June 26 to August 31, he appeared in 41 games: seventeen as a catcher, ten as a right fielder, one as a center fielder, and three as first baseman. In eight games he served as a pinch hitter and in two others he was a pinch runner. His stats for the forty-one games were as follows: he went to bat 101 times, scored eleven runs, had thirty-three hits for forty-eight total bases. Among his hits were six doubles, three triples, and one home run. He stole three bases, was walked eleven times and he struck out sixteen times; his batting average was .327.[24]

In the closing weeks of the 1925 season Jimmie was with the Athletics. He went to bat only nine times but garnered six hits for an average of .667. He doubtless would have appeared in more games but he agitated his recently injured shoulder when he fell rounding a base; his spike caught on the bag and caused him to trip and fall.[25] Jimmie would not be optioned again; he would remain with the Athletics and the problem Manager Mack would have was where to play this versatile and hard-hitting youngster. His roommate, Mickey Cochrane, was Mack's experienced catcher and his batting average for the 1925 season was .331.[26]

After the close of the baseball season in 1925, Foxx returned to Sudlersville and during the fall and winter worked on the farm and hunted ducks and other small game. He accompanied the Athletics to spring training in February, 1926. His off-season work on the farm had helped him maintain his weight at around 175–180 pounds and although this was his second season with the Athletics, his salary of $2,000.00 was the same as Connie Mack had paid him in 1925.[27]

The shoulder which Jimmie injured late in the 1925 season had healed well before he departed for Florida in 1926. Foxx, however, would be prone to an assortment of injuries and illnesses throughout his career. During March he suffered an ankle injury which kept him from playing until mid–May. *The Sporting News* reported that Mack was disappointed at Jimmie's misfortune because he had planned on using him to spell Cochrane behind the bat. Jimmie spent most of the exhibition period and the early weeks of the season "warming up pitchers."[28] On May 18, in a game against the Detroit Tigers, Foxx pinch hit in the eighth inning for Bill Lamar, the left fielder, and received a base on balls. This was his first major league appearance in 1926. For the next three or four weeks Mack used Foxx for pinch hitting and occasionally would have him relieve his roommate Mickey Cochrane behind the bat. For example, on May 28 in a game with the Senators, Foxx and Cochrane each caught four innings. In this contest Foxx was two for three, with a triple and single. However, the Athletics lost 17–12. At other times Mack would try to utilize Foxx's speed by inserting him as a pinch runner, as in a game against the Red Sox when Jimmie was put in the game to run for outfielder Walter French.[29]

In a three-game series with the Tigers at Detroit in late June, Mack experimented for the first time with playing Foxx in the outfield. In these games Jimmie played right field, and he had five hits in thirteen times at bat. Foxx's first experience as a major league outfielder "proved to Mack

Jimmie Foxx, ca. 1926 (courtesy Sudlersville Memorial Library).

that he was a natural ball player," one who could play well at a variety of positions. One reporter wrote, "He covered right field as well as if he had been playing there all season."[30]

Throughout the latter half of the season Foxx was called upon mainly for pinch hitting duties. When Cochrane suffered a slight injury in late July, Jimmie and Cy Perkins shared catching duties for several games. John P. "Jack" Quinn, a veteran pitcher and spitballer, was with the Athletics in 1926. He recalled that Foxx was a fine catcher and that "he could handle the spitter without any trouble." Jimmie's first complete game as a major leaguer came at Cleveland on July 30, 1926. Cochrane had injured his hand and Perkins had been suspended for a game because of an argument he had with an umpire on the preceding day. Jimmie caught this game and the knuckleballer Eddie

Rommel was the pitcher. Foxx committed no errors, allowed no passed balls, and flawlessly handled the offerings of the veteran Rommel, who struck out two and walked one in a game the Athletics lost 4-1. One observer was much impressed with Foxx's catching and declared his "handling of Rommel's deliveries points to the certainty that he will become a top notch catcher."[31]

As the 1926 season wound down the Athletics settled into third place in the American League standings, behind the pennant-winning Yankees and the Cleveland Indians. Jimmie spent this season observing the older players, listening to Connie Mack, and talking with his more experienced teammates. The first full season in the majors was a learning experience for the eighteen-year-old youngster. During the season he participated in twenty-six games; he shared catching duties in twelve games, was a pinch hitter or runner in nine contests and patrolled the outfield in the other games. He went to bat thirty-two times and had ten hits for a batting average of .313. His play impressed Connie Mack sufficiently to increase his salary for the coming season by $500.00 to $2,500.00. At no time in the 1926 season did Mack use Foxx at first base as Shaughnessy had at Providence. All this time Mack had Jim Poole and Joe Hauser, who shared first base. Hauser had been the regular first baseman, but he was forced to sit out the entire 1925 season with a broken knee cap. He returned in 1926, and he shared the position with Poole, whom Mack had acquired to play first base in 1925. Neither of these men hit .300 in 1926.

When the Athletics assembled in Fort Myers, Florida, in February, 1927, for spring training several veteran players had been added to the roster. Eddie Collins, who had been a member of Mack's $100,000.00 infield from 1910 to 1914 and a teammate of Frank Baker, returned to the Athletics after an eleven-year stint with the White Sox. Also present was Ty Cobb, former outfielder and manager of the Tigers, who was with the Detroit club for twenty-one years and who had led the American League in hitting on twelve different occasions. Mack had signed these veterans after the close of the 1926 season. Nineteen-year-old Jimmie Foxx reported to spring camp in "the pink of condition" and ready to play wherever Mack assigned him. He had worked on the farm during the winter and had spent considerable time "boxing, running, and working out in a gym." He had heeded Connie Mack's advice "to watch his weight," which in October 1926 was near 185. When he reported to spring camp in February, 1927 he weighed 164.[32]

Foxx respected and admired the veterans who were now his teammates, and he was eager to learn from them. He talked with Collins, watched his infield play, and observed him at the plate. Jimmie later credited Collins with "teaching him confidence." Jimmie especially relished the opportunity to talk with Cobb and to "study him at close range." He was "the most relaxed hitter" that Jimmie had ever seen. Unlike Ruth, Cobb was a choke hitter; he did not hold the bat at the end and swing away aiming for home runs; most of Cobb's 4,000 plus hits were singles. Foxx called him a "master technician of hitting." "He was the only man I have ever seen," Jimmie wrote, who could hit through spaces between infielders with regularity." Cobb advised Jimmie to "get out in front of every pitch" and always be looking for the fast ball. He instructed him to never take his eyes off the ball; always be looking for the fast ball but be loose so he could adjust for a curve or change of pace. Cobb also counseled him that a hitter must have patience, to be willing to wait for a pitch "you like."

Mickey Cochrane asserts that Foxx learned much from talking with and carefully watching the play of Cobb, Collins, and another veteran whom Mack later signed, Tris Speaker. Jimmie also learned from others. A writer for the *Philadelphia Evening Bulletin* observed the teenager carefully and reported that during a game Foxx's "eyes and ears were open every moment" and that he was constantly "picking up catching traits from Cochrane and Perkins." He also talked with Joe Hauser and Jim Poole about the intricacies of playing first base. Connie Mack and coach "Kid" Gleason also instructed the youngster, and he received tips on outfield play from his teammate Al Simmons.[33]

In the spring exhibition games and during the early weeks of the season Foxx saw action as a pinch hitter and occasionally relieved Cochrane or Perkins for a few innings behind the plate. On May 8, in a game against the Indians, Jimmie pinch hit for the first baseman, Jim Poole, and tripled. The next day Mack started Foxx at first base; this was Jimmie's first appearance as a first baseman in the major leagues. Although he did not play the entire game at first base, this signaled the beginning of Mack's experiment with using Jimmie at the initial sack. For the next few weeks Mack used Foxx at first base for a few innings at a time, allowing him to slowly gain experience and confidence at the position. On June 6, Jimmie played the entire game at first base and although he made one error the Athletics won the game 4-1. Mack was so favorably impressed with Foxx's play at first that in mid–June he announced he would use Jimmie at first base in all games in which the opposition used a left-handed pitcher. Throughout the remainder of the 1927 season Mack alternated Foxx and Jimmy Dykes at first, and he disposed of Poole by releasing him to Baltimore. Dykes had been with the Athletics since 1919 and had played a variety of infield positions—mostly at second base but also at short stop, third, and first. When Foxx was not at first base he was used as a pinch hitter and on occasions relieved Cochrane or Perkins with catching chores.[34]

It seemed to make no difference to Foxx what position Mack asked him to play; wherever he played, he hit. And his hitting was attracting increasing attention from both the fans and Connie Mack. In the sixty-one games in which he participated, twenty were as a pinch hitter; in thirty-two games he played or shared first base with others, and his fielding average for these games was .975. The remaining games he served as catcher. More than one-third of his forty-two hits were for extra bases as he accumulated a batting average of .323. Three of those extra base hits were home runs. Jimmie's first major league home run came at Shibe Park in the second game of a Memorial Day doubleheader against the Yankees. The home run, however, was hit in a losing cause since the Yankees won both games. This first home run for Jimmie was hit off the veteran spitball right-hander, Urban Shocker. Shocker was one of the few hurlers remaining in the majors who was allowed to use this pitch. A week later and in a game against the Browns in St. Louis, Jimmie hit a line drive off Walter "Lefty" Stewart into the "upper deck in left field" for his second home run. Jimmie's third and final home run of the season came in a game with the White Sox in September. Dykes had pulled a muscle in his left leg and Foxx was inserted at first base for several games. In the first game of a three-game series with the White Sox, Foxx was one for three, his hit being a double. The next day the Athletics won an eleven-inning contest with the Sox 5-4, when Foxx's eleventh-inning single drove in the winning run. The following day the Athletics won by the same score but in regulation time. Jimmie's home run, with two mates on base, provided the margin of victory. This hit was described by one writer as "a terrific drive over the center field (468') wall—a lick of Ruthian might."[35] This was the first of Foxx's home runs which would be favorably compared with those of Ruth. By the close of the season Mack was becoming keenly aware that he would have to find more playing time for his hard-hitting and versatile youngster who was becoming increasingly popular with the fans. James Isaminger wrote in *The Sporting News* that Philadelphia fans were "demanding that Mack use Foxx against right-handed pitchers as well as against southpaws."[36]

Although the 1927 Athletics improved their standing in the American League by one place over their 1926 position, they finished second to the Yankees. Their share of the World Series revenue was $39,958.00 or $1,178.22 for each of the twenty-five men on Mack's roster. This sum was almost one-half of Foxx's regular salary of $2,500.00 and was quite a bonus for the young man. He used some of this money to purchase a Studebaker automobile, his first car.[37] He returned to Sudlersville in October and during the off-season worked on the farm with his father. On one occasion he spoke to the high school assembly; he related some of his experiences in the big league and urged the youngsters to "stay in school and get a good education."[38]

When Foxx arrived at the Athletics spring training camp at Fort Myers, Florida, in February, 1928, neither manager Connie Mack nor his teammates were aware of how fortunate they were that Jimmie was present and accounted for. About a week before he was to leave Sudlersville for camp, Foxx was involved in an automobile accident that destroyed his car. One evening while he was driving along a Maryland highway Foxx "went to sleep at the wheel," and his car veered off the highway into a ditch, snapping a telephone pole and nearly overturning the car. "Both front wheels were ripped off and the engine was smashed." The report of this accident related that Foxx had "a miraculous escape from death." Jimmie was shaken, suffered a few bruises, but no bones were broken, and in a week he was on the train to Florida. Foxx now weighed 176 pounds, about ten pounds more than a year earlier, but more nearly his customary weight. Also this spring the veteran outfielder, Tris Speaker, was in camp. Mack had signed Speaker during the off season and he would spend his last season in baseball with Mack and his friend Ty Cobb. Both Speaker and Cobb would retire at the end of the 1928 season.[39]

As in previous springs, Mack played Foxx at different positions: he shared catching duties with Cochrane and Perkins; at other times he, Hauser, and Dykes alternated at first base. However, when the season got under way he was spending more and more time at third base. Mack had to find some place for the youngster who, no matter where he played, hit over .300 and a large percentage of his hits were for extra bases. And despite his playing at various positions, his fielding average was never under .965.[40]

When the Athletics broke camp and began heading north, their fans would recognize a distinct difference in their on-field appearance: they had new uniforms. They no longer sported the white elephant emblem. Early in the twentieth century John McGraw had referred to the Athletics as the "white elephants of the American League." Connie Mack remembered this remark and seemingly thought of it as a compliment: he adopted it as a sort of nickname for the Athletics. And since 1918 the Athletics had worn the elephant symbol; it was the only marking on their uniform and it was placed on the left front side of the shirt. After ten years Mack decided to remove the elephant and cease using the term "white elephants" when referring to the Athletics. The new uniform replaced the white elephant with a large letter "A"; the letter "A" was also worn, for the first time in the team's history, on the front of the cap.[41]

In the first two months of the season Jimmie appeared in thirty-one games, playing some at first, at other times alternating at third, and relieving behind the bat. However, by late June he was hitting .407, second in the American League to Leon "Goose" Goslin of the Senators, who was leading the league with a .429. Bill Slocum of the *Philadelphia Evening Bulletin* wrote, Foxx "proved himself so valuable that he must be used every day."[42] Jimmie's fine play during the early months of the 1928 season was interrupted in late June when he suffered a finger injury and had to be removed from the lineup. For slightly more than a month, during mid-season, his participation was limited to pinch hitting and pinch running roles. By August he had recovered from his finger injury and Mack began to use him at third, shifting Dykes back to first, and benching Hauser, whom he would shortly sell to Cleveland. Dykes, who preferred the third base position, grumbled a bit about being shifted back to first. He later related an encounter he had with Mack about this. He says that in one game, when Foxx was playing third, a low line drive hit and bounced off Jimmie's shins for a hit. Dykes was confident he could have handled the ball and gotten the runner at first. Between innings he asked Mack, "So you think Foxx is a better third baseman than me, do you?" He recalled that Mack eyed him coldly and replied, "No, he isn't. But he can hit a darned sight farther than you can."[43] By early September Connie Mack had decided where he would play Foxx as a regular. He moved Jimmie from third to first and sent Dykes to third. He knew Dykes was "more at home at third base than anywhere else" and that "the agile Foxx," as he was referred to in *The Sporting News*, "could play a dashing game at first." And before the 1928 season closed Mack informed Jimmie that he would be the first baseman from now on. The apprenticeship was over.[44]

As in 1927, the 1928 Athletics finished second in the American League, again outdistanced by the Yankees, from whom they won only six of twenty-two games. For the 1928 season Jimmie appeared in 118 games, went to bat 400 times and hit for a .323 average. Fifty-two of his 131 hits were for extra bases, including thirteen home runs, and he was walked sixty times. Several of his home runs were noted for their distance and power. For example, in a game with the St. Louis Browns on July 21, Foxx hit one of John Ogden's curve balls over the top of the left field stands and out of Shibe Park. The *Philadelphia Evening Bulletin* reported that it cleared the top of the stands by twenty feet, carried beyond the park, and landed one hundred feet beyond on Lambert Street. An earlier home run, hit against Detroit and carried "over the wall near the new scoreboard" at Shibe Park, was described as "a truly Ruthian clout." At another time, when the Athletics lost to the Senators 7-2, two of the three hits the Athletics had in that game were by Foxx and one was a long-distance home run. Before the end of the season one baseball scribe declared that "Foxx is one of the most feared batters in the American League. ... he hits with the abandon of Ruth."[45]

Wherever he played during the 1928 season, Jimmie hit fifth in the lineup, behind Cochrane and Simmons. During his years with the Athletics, Foxx experimented with or used bats of various sizes. In an interview, published in the August, 1934, issue of *Baseball Magazine*, he stated that when he came to the Athletics he "sometimes used a bat that weighed forty-two ounces." However, he remarked that he "cut this down to forty and then to thirty-eight." He concluded by saying that last season, 1933, he "generally used a thirty-six ounce bat." He explained that he could "whip the thirty-six ounce bat through the air with a lot more snap than he could a forty-two ounce one." "And," he concluded, "it's the snap and velocity which drive the ball." Later, after he went to Boston, it was reported that Foxx used a thirty-four and one-half ounce bat and occasionally one weighing thirty-three and one-half ounces. His bat on display at the Baseball Museum in Cooperstown is thirty-four and one-half inches in length and weighs thirty-three and one-half ounces.[46]

Jimmie's improved showing in 1928 and Connie Mack's decision to use him as a regular at first base in 1929, was reflected in a substantial salary increase. His contract for 1929 was for $5,000.00, a two-thousand-dollar increase over what he received in 1928.[47]

After the close of the baseball season in October, 1928, Foxx participated in a series of barnstorming games with a group of major league players before he returned to his home in Sudlersville. The playing of barnstorming games in the fall after the close of the major league season had been an activity of various players for many years. These games were often played between different contingents of major league players, and they were played in cities away from the homes of major league clubs. Games were played in the Midwest, the South, and on the Pacific Coast. Barnstorming games gave people the opportunity to see major league players in action, it promoted baseball, and extended the popular appeal of the game. Such games also afforded the players an occasion to earn extra money to supplement their yearly salaries. In the early 1920s Commissioner Landis had formulated certain procedures for barnstorming major league players. Games were limited to the end of the season in October through November 10. Players who wished to participate in such contests had to have the approval of the commissioner, and not more than three players on each team were permitted from a team that had participated in the World Series of that year.[48]

In the fall of 1928 Foxx participated in a series of games between a contingent of major league players and a group of stars from the Negro major leagues. Although it would be nearly twenty years before a black player was permitted to play in the majors, throughout the 1920s and 1930s it was not uncommon for black and white major leaguers to contest each other in autumn barnstorming games. In these contests Foxx played against such black stars as Joe Williams, Josh Gibson, Satchel Paige, Joe Rogan, Judy Johnson, and others.[49] It appears that if the question of black players had been left to the stars of the American and National leagues, blacks would have been accepted into the majors much sooner than they were.

There was a tradition among baseball players, going back to the early years of the century, that after the close of the season and before winter set in they would spend a week or two hunting various game and fowl. Young Jimmie Foxx sought to continue this tradition. Early in his career he would invite teammates to join him in hunting geese, ducks, and other game on Maryland's Eastern Shore. On one occasion Grove and Cochrane visited him, and they spent several days hunting. At another time teammates Joe Boley, Mule Haas, and Lew Krausse were his hunting guests. One Sudlersville native recalls that frequently Jimmie's guests would stay at a tourist home in the village operated by Frank A. Tarbutton. Jimmie and his major league friends were popular with the townspeople of Sudlersville, and Foxx was considered one of the most prominent persons in the town.[50]

One suggested innovation for baseball which was made in the fall of 1928 failed to receive the support of team owners. This was the proposal to create the position of designated hitters. At a meeting of National League executives and owners in December, John Heydler, president of the National League, proposed that major league baseball adopt the idea of designated hitter. He claimed that having a designated hitter for the pitcher would "improve and speed up the game." He argued that baseball fans were "tired of seeing weak hitting pitchers come to bat." Although John McGraw and several others favored this suggestion, the majority were opposed to it. The American League owners and officials also disapproved of the suggestion. The concept, however, of the designated hitter was never completely forgotten. Forty-five years later it was revived and was adopted by the American League in 1973; the National League, which had raised the issue in 1928, refused to follow the American League and twenty-three years later still has no designated hitter.[51]

Late in life and in an interview with a sports columnist, Foxx recalled the straitened economic circumstances of being the son of a tenant farmer. He stated that "Christmas was nothing special" when he was a "kid." "We were dirt poor," he declared.[52] Perhaps an economically deprived environment had some influence on Foxx's use of money when he became more affluent and contributed to his propensity for excessive spending or his inability to manage finances. Throughout his major league career he would acquire the reputation as a free spender and a generous touch for assorted "friends," acquaintances, and businessmen. Jimmie's first significant purchase was a responsible and worthy one. In 1928 he bought a 172-acre farm and home in the Sudlersville area for his parents. He paid $3,000.00 down on a $10,500.00 estate. It was his aim to assist his father in making payments until the mortgage was cleared. Ten years later, with the property still not paid for and his parents becoming older, Jimmie was forced to sell the estate, and his parents moved into a small house in the village of Sudlersville.[53]

By the time of his twenty-first birthday, Jimmie was described as a prudent and competent young man as well as one of the rising stars of major league baseball. His purchase of the farm was described as an investment, which he would add to in years to come, and the place where he would eventually retire. He informed one sportswriter that "all of my people have been farmers" and that "he expected to be one too." The writer, Tom Doerer, applauded Foxx's sense of values and declared that he was quite a contrast to many of his peers; noting that the "primrose roadways and the glitter and glare of the white lights made no impression on him."[54]

Although Jimmie had a very good year in 1928 and knew that beginning the following season he would be the regular first baseman, his mind was not wholly focused on baseball during the 1928 season. Jimmie was in love and wanted very much to get married. The young woman whom he was in love with was Helen Heite of Dover, Delaware, the daughter of Mr. and Mrs. Charles A. Heite. Helen and Jimmie were the same age and had known each other for several years. She had been a high school athlete, playing side center or guard on the girls' basketball team. In an interview with Helen O. Mankin of the *Philadelphia Evening Bulletin*, she related that she first met Jimmie when she "was only a kid," had probably seen him at some high school sports function. Several years later (1927) they met formally through a mutual friend, were attracted to each other and began a courtship in the fall and winter of 1927–28. When Jimmie went south for spring training in 1928 he missed Helen, and they corresponded throughout the season. In one letter, during the summer, Jimmie wrote that he had "something for her." Several letters later he revealed he had purchased an engagement ring and wanted to give it to her. In a few days Helen telephoned him and informed him that she would accept the ring.[55] The engagement was not publicly announced and Foxx's teammates were not aware of it. However, in a conversation with a sportswriter in mid–August Jimmie revealed what the writer described as the three main aims or desires at this stage in the life of a twenty-year-old emerging baseball superstar. One was for the Athletics to win an American League pennant; the other was "to be as good a baseball player as his father was," and finally he confessed that he wanted to get married.[56]

At the close of the season and before the barnstorming games began, Jimmie went to Dover and gave Helen the ring, although they set no date for the wedding. Later that fall, when Jimmie returned to Sudlersville, they began seeing each other quite often and soon decided to get married. During the Christmas season they were invited to a formal dance in Centreville, Maryland—Helen and Jimmie together with her sister and boy friend. The evening of the dance, December 26, Jimmie and Helen decided to "elope." As she related it to Ms. Mankin, she, Jimmie, her sister and date, all dressed in formal attire, departed for the dance. However, they made one stop before arriving at the dance. They drove first to Church Hill, Maryland, where they stopped at the parsonage of a local Methodist minister whom they knew and were married. After the brief ceremony the four young people drove to the dance at Centreville. During the evening Helen told of the marriage to one of her girl friends, and in a short while everyone at the dance was aware that Helen and Jimmie were married. When the news became common knowledge the orchestra stopped playing, an announcement of the marriage was made, and the band played "here comes the bride." As the newlyweds danced, their friends and others yelled congratulations and best wishes. It was reported that the couple left shortly thereafter on a wedding trip.[57] Later they established their residence on Hillcrest Avenue in Elkins Park, a suburb of Philadelphia.[58]

Notes

1. *The Sporting News*, February 26, 1925; *Philadelphia Evening Bulletin*, February 11, 1925. Rommel would be with the Athletics through 1932; from 1938–1959 he served as an umpire in the American League.

2. *The Sporting News*, March 5, 19, 1925.

3. *Ibid.*, March 12, 19, 1925.

4. Charles C. Alexander, *Our Game, An American Baseball History* (New York: Henry Holt and Company, 1991), p. 120.

5. David Quentin Voigt, *American Baseball*, 3 volumes (Norman: University of Oklahoma Press, 1966–1983), II, p. 202.

6. David Q. Voigt, "Sex in Baseball: Reflections on Changing Taboos," *Journal of Popular Culture* (Winter, 1978), p. 392; A.H. Tarvin, "The Origin of Ladies Day," *Baseball Magazine* (July, 1934), pp. 368-69; Harold Winerip, "Opinions on Ladies Day," *Baseball Magazine* (July, 1939), pp. 343-44, 382; James Cruisinberry, "Women Fans and Their Effects on the Game," *Baseball Magazine* (November, 1949), pp. 405-406, 430; *The Sporting News*, February 27, 1930.

7. *The Sporting News*, June 4, 1925.

8. *Providence Journal*, June 2, 1925; Mark Shatzkin, editor, *The Ballplayers: Baseball's Ultimate Biographical Reference* (New York: William Morrow, 1990), p. 990.

9. Bob Hoxie, "The Farm System," in John Thorn and Peter Palmer, *Total Baseball* (New York: Warner Books, 1989), p. 662.

10. Peter Filichia, *Professional Baseball Franchises, From the Abbeville Athletics to the Zanesville Indians* (New York: Facts on File, 1993), pp. 186-87; *Providence Journal*, May 21, 23, June 5, 1925.

11. *Providence Journal*, June 23, 1925.

12. *Ibid.*, June 26, 1925.

13. *Ibid.*, June 26, 1925.

14. *Ibid.* June 30, 1925.

15. *Ibid.*, July 23, 1925.

16. *Ibid.*, July 24, 1925.

17. *Ibid.*, July 25, 26, 28, 1925.

18. *Ibid.*, August 8, 1925.

19. *Ibid.*, August 13, 17, 18, 22, 1925.

20. *Ibid.*, August 23, 24, 1925.

21. *Ibid.*, August 25, 1925.

22. *Ibid.*, August 31, 1925.

23. *Philadelphia Evening Bulletin*, September 1, 1925.

24. *The Sporting News*, February 4, 1926.

25. *Ibid.*, November 5, 1925; *Philadelphia Evening Bulletin*, March 9, 1926.

26. *The Sporting News*, November 5, 1925.

27. Jimmie Foxx, "I'm Glad I Was a Ballplayer," *Sport* (March, 1952), p. 78; *The Sporting News*, March 14, 1956.

28. *The Sporting News*, March 18, April 1, 1926.

29. *Ibid.*, June 3, 24, 1926.

30. *Ibid.*, June 24, 1926.

31. *New York Times*, July 31, 1926; Ira L. Smith, *Baseball's Famous First Basemen* (New York: A.S. Barnes and Company, 1956), p. 216; *Philadelphia Evening Bulletin*, June 4, 1953.

32. *Philadelphia Evening Bulletin*, February 23, 1927; *The Sporting News*, March 3, 27, April 14, 1927.

33. *Boston American*, December 17, 1935; *Philadelphia Evening Bulletin*, March 15, 1926, August 13, 1928; *Philadelphia Inquirer*, September 4, 1932; Boston *Globe*, March 26, 1936; Gordon S. "Mickey" Cochrane, *Baseball, the Fan's Game* (New York: Funk and Wagnalls Company, 1939), pp. 90–91.

34. *The Sporting News*, July 4, 11, August 11, September 5, 29, October 6, 1927.

35. *Ibid.*, June 9, 16, September 22, 1927.

36. *Ibid.*, June 16, 1927.

37. *Ibid.*, October 20, 1927; Dan Roderick's column, *Baltimore Evening Sun*, among undated clippings in Sudlersville Memorial Library, Sudlersville, Maryland.

38. *Queen Anne's Journal*, Centreville, Maryland, March 21, 1979.

39. *The Sporting News*, February 2, 9, March 1, 8, 1928.

40. *Boston Daily Record*, August 14, 1932.

41. Marc Okkonen, *Baseball Uniforms of the Twentieth Century* (New York: Sterling Publishing Company, 1991), pp. 57–58.

42. *Philadelphia Evening Bulletin*, July 8, 1928; *The Sporting News*, June 28, 1928.

43. Jimmie Dykes and C.O. Dexter, *You Can't Steal First Base* (Philadelphia: J.B. Lippincott Company, 1967), pp. 28–29.

44. *The Sporting News*, September 13, December 6, 1928; *Boston American*, December 18, 1935.

45. *The Sporting News*, May 10, December 20, 27, 1928; *Philadelphia Evening Bulletin*, July 21, August 13, 1928.

46. "The Secret of Jimmy Foxx's Slugging Power," an interview in *Baseball Magazine* (August, 1934), p. 394; Charles H.L. Johnston, *Famous American Athletes of Today*, fourth series (Boston: L.C. Page and Company, 1934), p. 56; *Boston Globe*, March 26, 1936; *Philadelphia Evening Bulletin*, September 17, 1961.

47. *The Sporting News*, March 14, 1956.

48. *New York Times*, October 6, November 2, 1922; Harold Seymour, *Baseball, The Golden Age* (New York: Oxford University Press, 1971), pp. 392–93.

49. John B. Holway, *Blackball Stars, Negro League Pioneers* (Westport, Conn.: Meckler Books, 1988), pp. 73, 117, 182; Donn Rogosin, *Invisible Men, Life in Baseball's Negro Leagues* (New York: Atheneum, 1985), p. 124.

50. George Herman Ruth, *Babe Ruth's Own Book of Baseball* (Lincoln: University of Nebraska Press, 1992, reprint of 1928 edition), pp. 262–63; *Wilmington State News*, September 10, 1981; *The Queen Anne's Record-Observer*, Centreville, Maryland, October 28, 1987; *Queen Anne's Journal*, March 21, 1979.

51. Rick Wolff, editorial director, *The Baseball Encyclopedia*, eighth edition (New York: Macmillan Publishing Company, 1990), p. 11; James Charlton, editor, *The Baseball Chronology* (New York: Macmillan Publishing Company, 1991), p. 248.

52. *Chicago Daily News*, December 24, 1963.

53. See xerox copy of deeds in Sudlersville Memorial Library; *Philadelphia Evening Bulletin*, December 28, 1928; *Washington Post*, October 24, 1987; F.C. Lane, "The Strong Arm Slugger of the Fighting Athletics," *Baseball Magazine* (September 1929).

54. Tom Doerer, "Jimmy Foxx and His Brilliant Future," *Baseball Magazine* (October, 1928), pp. 507, 520.

55. *Philadelphia Evening Bulletin*, July 31, 1929, September 23, 1930.

56. *Ibid.*, August 13, 1928.

57. *Philadelphia Evening Bulletin*, December 27, 28, 1928, July 31, 1929; *The Sporting News*, January 10, 1929.

58. *The Sporting News*, February 13, 1930.

Three

The Athletics, Their
Glory Years, 1929–1932

By 1929 the team that Connie Mack had been assembling for the past five years emerged as the dominant club in the American League. In this year the Athletics broke the Yankees' dominance, and during the next three years they won the American League pennant and two world championships. From the 1929 season Foxx was a regular in the Athletics' lineup, and his principal position was first base. However, he would occasionally appear at other positions; for example, in 1929 he participated in 149 games, 142 at first base and seven at third.

In February, Foxx's bride of two months accompanied him to Florida when he reported to the Athletics' spring training camp at Fort Myers. While Jimmie was working out with the team, Helen enjoyed the warm weather, sunshine, and water. Throughout the spring exhibition season Foxx was on a hitting rampage; he hit the ball often and long. *The Sporting News* reported "Foxx is now bombing the ball out of the park" and is "performing spectacularly at first base." One of Jimmie's memorable home runs was hit at Richmond, Virginia, in early April, as the Athletics were nearing the end of their exhibition season. The ball park in Richmond was located on Mayo Island, one of the larger islands in the James River. In an exhibition game against the Browns, Jimmie hit two home runs; one over the center field fence and the other to left field. The one to left field cleared the fence, went beyond the boundary of the island, and "splashed almost midway in the James."[1]

Jimmie's timely hitting continued after the regular season began. In the season's opener at Washington, on April 17, President Herbert Hoover was on hand to continue the tradition begun by William Howard Taft of throwing out the first ball of the season for the Senators. Foxx helped to ruin the opener for Clark Griffith and his Senators as he went three for four, with a double and a home run in a game the Athletics won 13-4.[2] Jimmie's hitting throughout the first half of the season was described as "spectacular" as he was constantly batting .400 or better. During this time he hit safely in twenty-two consecutive games and one scribe declared that Foxx had "created a reign of terror with the bat that few could match." Some of his hits amazed longtime observers of the game. For example, in a game at Boston on May 1, he hit what was described by *The Sporting News* as "one of the longest home runs ever seen." It was a blast "high over the left field fence," out of the park and over "a nearby factory building," that landed on the "tracks of the Boston and Albany railroad." Some speculated that Jimmie would succeed Babe Ruth as the premier power hitter in major league baseball. During this period of exceptional batting, one writer declared that Foxx could hit any pitch; slow ball, curve, change of pace, fast ball—they all looked alike to him. The reporter admitted that Jimmie might swing at a pitch and "miss it a mile," but the next time he saw it he might "knock it out of the park."[3] The exceptional play of Foxx prompted the editors of *Time* magazine to feature him on the cover of its July 29 issue.

Before the 1929 season was a month old, Foxx participated in his first public relations role on behalf of baseball and in support of the game's interest in young people. On May 1 he and his teammate, pitcher George Earnshaw, spoke to the student assembly at Northeast High School in Philadelphia. The press reported that the players were given an enthusiastic welcome by the 2500 students. At the assembly, which was to honor the school's outstanding athletes, Foxx and Earnshaw presented to the most valuable baseball player at the school a baseball autographed by members of the Athletics team. Foxx then addressed the student gathering and tried to emphasize to them the importance of education. He told them that when he was in school, he "took more interest in athletics than in books." This, he declared, "was a mistake, was no good." He told them, "I wish I had studied more … gone to college." "In these days," he continued, "a fellow needs all the knowledge he can obtain" since knowledge is "what life is all about."[4] Jimmie would return to this theme on other occasions in his career and later in life; it was a theme his mother had emphasized when he was a schoolboy.

In the midst of Foxx's early season hitting exploits and the Athletics' rise to the top of the American League, some local merchants and fans decided to show their appreciation for the efforts of the young first baseman and also to honor the recently wed couple by presenting them with a gift. Just prior to the game on June 10, Jimmie, Helen, and most of the spectators were surprised to see a truck enter the playing field at Shibe Park. In a brief ceremony Jimmie and Helen were presented a "new model Majestic radio set," a gift from the Majestic dealers in the Philadelphia area. The young couple, it was reported, were very pleased with "the high class radio set."[5]

Although Foxx's hitting fell below .400 during the second half of the season, he was leading the American League with a .381 average at the end of August. At this time the Athletics had a thirteen-game lead over the Yankees and were on their way to the American League title. The entire team was playing with zeal and confidence; even Connie Mack was quoted as saying that only an earthquake could prevent the Athletics from winning the pennant.[6] Throughout these weeks Jimmie's long-distance home runs continued to amaze fans and old-time sportswriters. One remarked that his hits were mainly line drives, rather than long fly balls as Ruth hit, and that many of Jimmie's drives hit the outfield barriers on the rise and deprived him of some home runs. Another commented that Foxx, who hit right-handed, was "supposed to hit to left field," but in a game at St. Louis in mid–August he hit two home runs, both clearing the right field pavilion on their flight out of the park. *The Sporting News* account of this game declared that "Jimmie Foxx is playing wonderful ball."[7] In one game near the end of the season, after the Athletics had clinched the pennant, Mack wanted to observe the play of George Burns, a veteran whom Mack had picked up. For this game Burns was on first and Foxx was shifted to third. And although Jimmie "covered third as if he had been there all season," the following games he was back at first. In the final days of the season Foxx was overtaken in the race for the batting title; Lew Fonseca of Cleveland came on to win the title with a .369 average, followed by Jimmie's teammate and roommate, Al Simmons, who hit .365. Jimmie's final average was .354, and his fielding average was .995.[8] Despite the slip in his batting average near the end of the season, Foxx finished with thirty-three home runs and 117 runs batted in. Veteran sportswriter Bill Dooley speculated that the "modest and unaffected" twenty-one-year-old Sudlersville youngster was "perhaps the most valuable player in the big leagues." He quoted "Kid" Gleason, one of the Athletics' coaches and a wise judge of baseball talent, as predicting "that in a couple of years Foxx will be recognized as the greatest baseball player who ever lived." Although 1929 was Jimmie's first year as a regular, devoting his time almost wholly to one position, first base, he was not enthusiastic about this position. In an article in the December, 1929, issue of *Baseball Magazine*, he confessed, "If I had my preferences, I'd rather catch behind the plate than do anything else." But, with "a wonder like Mickey Cochrane" in the lineup "there's no chance of anyone else replacing him." Foxx continued by comparing playing third base with first; although he claimed that third base "was a harder position" to play, it "appealed to him more than first." Playing first base he termed "a breeze" compared to the hot corner. Jimmie concluded by declaring he loved the game of baseball, no matter which position he played.[9]

The 1929 season was the one, it seems, that the fans and press were struggling for an identity for the young star of the Athletics. It should be emphasized, however, that Foxx was never bothered with this "problem." Jimmie would be given a variety of nicknames during his career. Connie Mack often referred to him as "Foxxie"; early in his career some of his teammates called him "the farmer boy," referring to his background and to the fact that he spent his off seasons on the farm and often proclaimed his love for farm life. But early in the 1929 season and because he was only twenty-one years old and had a new bride, some of the teammates and fans called him "the boy bridegroom." However, with his outstanding play at bat and in the field the press and others began referring to Jimmie as the "Maryland Mauler" or the "Sudlersville Slugger." By the close of the 1929 season few people were thinking of Jimmie Foxx as a "boy." As a baseball player he was acknowledged by his peers and the press as a man among men.

There were two developments in 1929, associated with major league baseball, designed to assist the fans in their knowledge and understanding of what was happening on the playing field. Both of these innovations were instituted by New York clubs and were afterwards adopted by other major league clubs. The Giants installed the first public address system in a major league park. An announcer would present the team lineups, inform the spectators as to who was batting, announce pitching changes or other lineup modifications—all designed to help the fans know what was going on. Previously, announcements of such information were made by persons using megaphones and walking back and forth in foul territory on each side of the playing field. The other innovation was introduced by the Yankees, who in 1929 were the first team to place numerals on the back of player uniforms. This allowed fans to identify players at a glance. In a few years all teams had followed this practice. The Athletics placed numerals on uniforms for the first time in 1931. Foxx's number for 1931 through 1934 was three; in his last season with the Athletics he wore number two. When he joined the Red Sox he wore number three throughout his tenure in Boston.[10]

As Jimmie's career began to attract increasing attention in 1929, both fans and the press became interested in his bride of less than a year. The couple were living in Philadelphia, and Helen often attended home games with the wives or girl friends of Jimmie's teammates. In July Rose Terlitz, a reporter for the *Philadelphia Evening Bulletin*, interviewed Helen and did a feature story on her. Ms. Terlitz described the young Mrs. Foxx as someone who appeared to be no more than "sixteen years old," small of frame, possessing dark hair and eyes, and an olive complexion. She "wore no cosmetics," had bobbed hair and Ms. Terlitz noted that there was "an air of deviltry pervading her entire make-up." Despite the appearance of immaturity, Ms. Terlitz declared that the young woman impressed her "as straight-thinking, clear-minded, and frank" a person as she had met in a long while. The reporter concluded that Helen Foxx was independent, self-assertive, and sincere in her statements. Helen revealed to her that sometimes when Jimmie was on the road she would drive to her family home in Dover, Delaware, to "break the lonesome spell."[11]

One can assume that during the closing weeks of the 1929 season Jimmie's thoughts and concentration were often not on baseball, even though he was performing in a spectacular manner. Earlier in the season it was discovered that Helen was pregnant, and her physician had informed her that she would give birth about the same time as the baseball season was closing. In

September and several weeks before the end of the season, Helen returned to her home in Dover to await the birth of their child. Jimmie would finish the season, participate in the World Series, which was scheduled to begin on October 8 with the Cubs in Chicago, and then go to be with her.

As the Athletics completed their last western trip and prepared to go to Chicago, Helen entered the Kent General Hospital in Dover, Delaware, where on October 2 she gave birth to a son, whom the couple named James Emory Foxx, Jr. She was in the hospital recuperating when the World Series began six days later. Although Helen would have liked to see Jimmie play in his first World Series, she was able to listen to the games on the radio. Since 1922 the World Series games had been broadcast to the nation and on October 8, the opening game in Chicago, Helen listened to it via radio in the "sun parlor" of Kent County General Hospital. She was overjoyed when in the seventh inning Jimmie broke a scoreless tie game with a home run off the Cubs' ace, Charlie Root. The Athletics won this contest 2-1, and afterwards Helen wired congratulations to Jimmie, saying she was very happy with the results of the game.[12] The Athletics also won the second game by a score of 9-3. In this game Foxx hit a three-run homer in the third, and the Athletics were never challenged. The teams then departed for Philadelphia where the next three games were scheduled. Twenty-one years later Foxx related, in a conversation with some young Phillie players who were soon to participate in their first World Series, how he felt the first time he played in a World Series game. He told them that it "is ok to be nervous" at such a time. He declared that he "was as nervous as a hen on a hot griddle" the first time he went to bat in a World Series game. He confessed that the first time one participated in a World Series "it gives one a kind of feeling you never forget."[13] The pep talk which Foxx, Dykes, and several other old-timers gave to the Phillies might have helped dispel their "nervousness," but unlike the 1929 Athletics, the 1950 Phillies lost the World Series to the Yankees in four straight games.

There was a break of one day between the completion of the first two games of the series in Chicago and the forthcoming games in Philadelphia. At this time Jimmie went to Dover to see his wife and son. He visited them briefly at the hospital and returned to Philadelphia for game three.[14] Guy Bush pitched Chicago to a 3-1 win in game three. The fourth game of this series was, in some ways, one of the most incredible games in World Series history. The Cubs, with Root again pitching, were clobbering the Athletics; they had an 8-0 lead going into the last of the seventh inning. Suddenly, when the Athletics came to bat the Cubs seemed to come apart; several walks, an infield hit, a home run by Mule Haas, and Hack Wilson's losing a fly ball in the sun permitted the Athletics to score ten runs in their half of the seventh. Lefty Grove came in and shut out the Cubs in the last two innings to preserve the Athletics' 10-8 win. The dispirited Cubs lost the following day and the Athletics were the world champions of baseball for the first time since 1913. Foxx hit .350 in the five-game series with the Cubs and his share of the World Series proceeds, $5,620.57, was more than his $5,000 salary for the entire season.[15]

Immediately after the final game of the World Series on October 14, a number of the Athletics, including Foxx, Simmons, and Grove, joined a group of American League players for a three-week barnstorming tour through the Midwest and on to the Pacific Coast. The group, called "Babe Ruth's All-Stars," featured the Bambino and included, among others, Bob Meusel of the Yankees, Earl Whitehill of the Senators, and Willis Hudlin of the Indians. The All-Stars were divided into two teams, and they played exhibition games in the cities they visited. The contingent that included Foxx was under the care and supervision of Ira Thomas, an executive with the Athletics.[16] The barnstormers played in Springfield, Illinois, Milwaukee and several other places before reaching the coast where they completed their exhibitions at San Francisco. While in California the American Leaguers also played several contests against a group of barnstormers from the Negro leagues. In a game against the black team, played on October 31 in San Francisco, Foxx, who was at first base for part of the game, moved from that position to the mound and pitched for several innings. Although the All-Stars lost this game 14-10, Foxx was three for three at bat, with two doubles and a single.[17]

When the barnstorming exhibition concluded, the *Philadelphia Evening Bulletin* reported that the players "made many friends for baseball," not only in the cities they visited but in towns along the railway route which they traveled. The *Bulletin* writer, traveling with the contingent, exclaimed that the tour resembled a political campaign. At many of the small towns through which the train passed, crowds would gather to see and greet the players. The train would stop briefly, and Foxx and others would appear on the platform at the rear of the train, talk with fans, sign a few autographs, receive the plaudits of the crowd, and bid them best wishes and good-bye. At the end of the eleven-game barnstorming tour it was reported that such activities were not only "good for baseball," but that the tour was very profitable for the players since Foxx, Simmons and others received "about $5,000.00 apiece" for this three-weeks exhibition.[18]

After the All-Stars returned to Philadelphia Jimmie departed for Dover to see his wife and son and then to Sudlersville, where his hometown people had arranged a welcoming "homecoming" reception for him. From early September, after the Athletics had clinched the American League pennant, friends and civic leaders in Sudlersville began planning for a celebration to honor their native son once the World Series was over. Throughout the month of September plans were formulated but the date was left open, to be decided after the Series and the barnstorming tour. The people of Sudlersville and the upper Eastern Shore of Maryland were proud of Foxx and the notoriety he had brought to the region. As one town spokesman exclaimed, "Sudlersville was just a small town minding its own business and trying to get along before

Helen, Jimmie and Jimmie Jr., ca. 1931 (courtesy Temple University Libraries).

Jimmie Foxx went to the Athletics and put it on the map" and made it "one of the best advertised little towns in the country." And, to show their appreciation, his hometown folks, together with friends, fans, and neighbors from Centreville, Chestertown, and elsewhere on the shore, decided to have a welcoming celebration and "testimonial banquet" for Jimmie and some of his invited teammates.[19]

One of the groups that played a leading role in organizing the reception-banquet was the Ladies Aid Society of the Sudlersville Methodist Episcopal Church, the church where the Foxx family were members. By mid–October plans were completed. The banquet would be held in Cox Memorial Hall in Sudlersville; the dinner would be prepared and served by the women of the Methodist Church. Alan S. Walls, a local businessman, would serve as toast-master; the Reverend C.W. Clark, pastor of the Methodist Church, would offer a tribute to his former parishioner. Connie Mack was invited, and it was expected that he would offer a few remarks. It was also decided that Jimmie would be presented a gift at the banquet. The welcome home and banquet were scheduled for the evening of November 13. On this pleasant autumn evening more than 200 "citizens, representing the political, agricultural, and religious life of the Eastern Shore" attended the banquet honoring Foxx. Cox Memorial Hall was "artistically decorated" for the affair, and music was provided by "a local orchestra." Those who had arranged the ceremony were disappointed that Connie Mack was not present. However, Mack sent his son and the Athletics' general manager, Earl, to represent him. Other Athletics who attended included Ira Thomas, Bing Miller, Rube Walberg, Max Bishop, and Ed Rommel. After the dinner and the tributes and speeches, Jimmie was presented a cedar chest; this was a gift from his former schoolmates and friends in Sudlersville. Jimmie gave a brief response, thanking everyone for arranging this "memorable occasion." Foxx would visit Sudlersville at other times, but he would not spend his off seasons at the farm. He and Helen and their young son would spend these months at their home in Elkins Park, Pennsylvania, a suburb of Philadelphia.[20]

For some years advertising agents had obtained contracts for certain outstanding baseball players to endorse certain products. One of the earliest of these advertisements featured baseball players' pictures on packages of tobacco products. However, Foxx's fine performance in 1929 led to his first endorsement of a different product. *The Sporting News* of October 17 presented a two-column, fourteen-inch-high advertisement featuring a photograph and commentary by Foxx for the Louisville Slugger baseball bats.[21] Endorsements for other products would appear later in his career.

For the first time since leaving home to play baseball, Jimmie did not return to Sudlersville for the 1929–30 off season. He and his family were living in the Philadelphia area and would visit occasionally. During the months of the late fall and winter of 1929–30 Jimmie worked in a local sporting goods store in Philadelphia, and he kept in good physical shape by working out in a gym and playing basketball with what one writer called "some of the big shots of the game." His local group was referred to as the "all stars." It seems to have been a rather informal group. Jimmie played center and for one game the all stars traveled to Chestertown, Maryland, to play the Washington College team. The collegians trounced them 54-26, and in this game Foxx scored only three points. Despite the unspectacular performance of the all-stars it was reported that during late 1929 Jim Furey, manager of the "world champion" Celtics in Philadelphia, wanted to sign Foxx to play for another team with which he was connected, the "Shamrocks." There is no evidence that Jimmie was tempted to try to pursue careers in two sports simultaneously.[22] After the winter of 1929–30 it seems that Foxx suppressed or abandoned his interest in basketball. His off-season athletic activities hereafter would consist of gym workouts, swimming, and golf, complemented by an occasional hunting trip.

For several years it had been the custom, following the close of the baseball season and after the official statistics had been compiled, for *The Sporting News* and the baseball writers association to select a major league baseball All-Star team. It was the general consensus that the players named to this team by the nation's "experts" comprised the elite of major league baseball. The All-Star team for 1929 was announced in December, and it included four members of the World Champion Athletics: the battery of Lefty Grove and Mickey Cochrane; left fielder and power hitter Al Simmons, and first baseman Jimmie Foxx. The other members of the team were Hack Wilson and Rogers Hornsby of the Cubs, Harold "Pie" Traynor and Burleigh Grimes of the Pirates, Travis Jackson of the Giants, and Babe Ruth of the Yankees.[23]

Despite the acclaim and recognition Jimmie had achieved in major league baseball, a veteran sport columnist for *The Sporting News* declared that none of this had affected Jimmie: he was "as modest and unassuming" in the fall of 1929 as he had been the day he first reported to Connie Mack. Jimmie was "still the likeable youngster" Frank Baker had recommended to the Athletics five years ago.[24]

Before Foxx and the Athletics headed south for spring training in 1930, Connie Mack "departed from his usual custom of offering one-year contracts to his players" by signing Jimmie to a three-year contract for $50,000 or $16,666.00 for each of the 1930, 1931, and 1932 seasons. Omitting Babe Ruth, whose salary was in a class apart, this was still a modest sum when compared with the salaries of Gehrig, Simmons, Cochrane, and Hornsby. Connie Mack, who often complained of his "high payroll," grossly underpaid Foxx during his years with the Athletics. At the same time Mack was paying Jimmie $16,000-plus a year, he was paying Simmons and Cochrane each a yearly salary of $30,000.[25]

In late January, just prior to Jimmie's heading south for a few weeks of golf and sun before the beginning of spring training, he was a dinner guest of the Philadelphia Service Bureau of Umpires. This organization was active in providing umpires for college and semi-pro teams in the area. Among those attending this function were major league umpires Bill McGowan, Eddie McLaughlin, and John Quinn. Judge Eugene Bonniwell served as toastmaster, and those who offered brief speeches included Foxx and Gerald Nugent of the Phillies.[26] A few days later the Foxx family departed for Fort Myers,

Florida, where Jimmie would enjoy three weeks of sun, water, and golf before reporting to camp.

The World Series victory in 1929 had strengthened the confidence of a team which in later years Jimmy Dykes would claim was probably the greatest baseball aggregation ever assembled.[27] Before spring training began, Foxx expressed to a reporter his belief that the Athletics would repeat their success of the previous year. He informed one writer that he thought the "Athletics would repeat as pennant winner." He explained that all the team previously lacked was confidence; their success of last year had remedied that situation, and now, Foxx asserted, "we know we can win." The sportswriters evidently felt the same way about the Athletics as Dykes and Foxx since they selected them to win the American League race, and the Cubs were picked to repeat in the National League.[28]

Although Foxx's hitting in the exhibition or Grapefruit League games did not attract the attention it did in 1929, he closed the spring games with a flourish. In the four-game "city series" with the Phillies, which concluded several days before the season opened, Foxx hit four home runs. The Athletics opened against the Yankees on April 15, and defeated them 6-2.[29] However, since the Athletics did not run away from the rest of the league, some commentators described them as being in a slump during the first part of the season. Despite this accusation they were leading the American League from mid-July on. One might argue that Foxx was in a slump of sorts during this time since in mid–July he was hitting about fifty percentage points below where he had been a year ago. In mid–July, 1930, he was hitting only .353, ninth in the league.[30]

During the period of this so-called slump, Jimmie hit several home runs which at a later date would be described as the "tape-measure" variety. That term had not been "invented" or "coined" in the 1930s. For example, in a game with the Tigers at Shibe Park on May 1, Jimmie hit two home runs. The one in the third inning was described as "a copyright Ruthian one," over the scoreboard in right center. It was explained that the scoreboard was "several feet higher than the wall," and it was very seldom that anyone ever cleared the wall. His eighth-inning home run was labeled "a truly gargantuan wallop"; it went out of the park over the left center portion of the stadium and into Somerset Street. It was noted that this was the fourth time Foxx had hit one out of the park, over the roof and into adjoining territory—and that he was the only person ever to accomplish this feat.[31] A week later, on May 8, in a game against the Cleveland Indians Foxx hit "another record home run." This one he "drove out of the park and through a second-story window of a dwelling house on Twentieth Street." Later that season in a game against the White Sox in Chicago, Jimmie unloaded another "Ruthian" type hit. On Friday, July 18, he became the first person to ever hit a baseball over the left field stands and completely out of Comiskey Park.[32]

From July on the Athletics led the American League and by mid–September they had won the American League title; their World Series foe this time was the St. Louis Cardinals.[33] The Series opened on October 1, and the first two games were played in Philadelphia. The first game featured a pitching duel between Lefty Grove and Burleigh Grimes, the last of the legal or legitimate spitball pitchers, who would retire in 1934. Although the Athletics were outhit 9-5, all of their hits were for extra bases, and each produced a run. The Athletics' first hit of the game was a triple by Foxx in the second inning and they went on to win the opener 5-2. However, Grimes struck out Foxx twice in this contest. In the second game George Earnshaw was the winning pitcher in a game the Athletics won 6-1. Games three, four, and five were in Sportsman's Park, St. Louis. In the first game at the Cards' home park the southpaw Bill Hallahan shut out the Athletics 5-0, although they had seven hits. The Series evened at two games each as the Cards won the following day 3-1. Foxx had a single in this game and Dykes' error at third base allowed the Cardinals to score two runs and win the game. The fifth game, and the last one played in St. Louis, featured a pitchers' battle between Earnshaw and Grimes. The score was 0-0 going into the ninth inning. The first batter, Cochrane, walked; Simmons was out on an infield pop-up; and the next batter was Foxx. In the seventh inning Grimes had struck out Foxx, making the third time in the Series he had accomplished this feat. Grimes' first pitch to Jimmie was a curve which Foxx hit into the left field bleachers to give the Athletics a 2-0 lead, a margin which Grove preserved in the bottom of the ninth. Foxx later declared that this game-winning home run off his nemesis Grimes was his "greatest thrill in baseball." Years later Grimes declared that he threw only two curve balls that entire game: one was the pitch on which he struck out Foxx in the seventh inning, and the other was the ball Jimmie hit for the game-winning home run in the ninth.[34]

The teams returned to Philadelphia where, on October 8, the Athletics won 7-1 to become world champions of baseball for the second consecutive year. Jimmie was the only regular on either team to hit safely in all six of the World Series games. He was seven for twenty-one, hitting .333 for the Series. For the second successive year the Athletics divided the winners' World Series revenue; each of the Athletics received $5,038.07. It was reported that the Foxx family would use some of this to purchase furniture for their home.[35] After the Series moved back to Philadelphia, but before it was concluded, Foxx and Grove did a bit of community service or public relations for the home team. The press had noted that there was a fifteen-year-old patient at the Camden County Tuberculosis Hospital who was a rabid baseball fan. This youngster had followed the series on the radio and his "idol" was Jimmie Foxx. One day Foxx and Grove visited this hospital and talked with the youngster. Before leaving, Jimmie presented him a baseball which he and his teammates had autographed.[36]

Unlike the 1929 World Series, which came at the same time Helen gave birth to the couple's first child, she was able to attend and watch Jimmie perform in the 1930 Series. It appears that she had become a genuine baseball fan. She told one interviewer that she attended most of the home games and that she "liked to see Jimmie play." She added that "if it wasn't his day," she "never commented about the game to him." She made friends with the wives of some of Jimmie's teammates, and she and "Dottie" Kuhn, fiancee of Al Simmons, would often go horseback riding together when the team was out of town. She enjoyed walking the course with Jimmie when he went golfing and expressed the desire to learn to use a gun so that she could join him in hunting ducks and rabbits. Although she was the mother of a young son, she explained that she enjoyed a great deal of freedom since she was assisted with housekeeping chores and the supervision of Jimmie, Jr., by a competent Negro maid named Ruby.[37]

The American League batting title in 1930 was won by Jimmie's colleague and away games roommate, Al Simmons, who hit .381. Foxx played 153 games in 1930 and all were at first base. He hit thirty-seven home runs, drove in 156 runs, and had a batting average of .335. His fielding average at first base was .990; Joe Judge of the Senators had the best fielding average for American League first basemen with .998. Lou Gehrig of New York was second; his average was .001 ahead of Foxx. When *The Sporting News* and the baseball writers of America selected their major league All-Star team for 1930, it included three members of the world champion Athletics: Cochrane, Grove, and Simmons. Foxx was replaced by the writers who selected Bill Terry of the Giants for first base. Terry led the National League in hitting in 1930 with an average of .401.[38]

Two days after the World Series ended most of the Athletics embarked on a barnstorming tour until November 1. One group, under the oversight of Earl Mack, departed for Milwaukee where they played a group of minor and major league players. For the next two weeks they toured the upper Midwest, playing games in cities of the Three-I-League (Indiana, Illinois, and Iowa) and the adjoining area. A second group of Athletics, including Foxx, Simmons, and Earnshaw, were under the direction of Ira Thomas. They made a tour of the South playing local teams which included some minor and major league players. Their itinerary included games in Georgia, Alabama, Mississippi, Louisiana, and Texas. In one of these exhibition games Foxx moved from first base to the pitcher's mound and pitched for several innings. Some of the barnstorming games also included contests against teams from the Negro League. For example, the contingent of which Foxx was a member played a contest against a group of All-Stars from the Negro Leagues in Baltimore; the Negro League All-Stars won this game 2-1.[39]

One of Jimmie's teammates on the Athletics during the 1928 and 1929 years was Ossie Orwold, a utility pitcher/outfielder from Decorah, Iowa, located in the northeastern portion of the state near the Minnesota border and approximately twenty miles west of the Mississippi River. A couple of weeks after the barnstorming activities ended, Jimmie accepted an invitation from Orwold to join him and a few friends on a hunting trip. While Foxx was visiting in Iowa the local school authorities in Decorah asked if he would be the speaker at a high school assembly. Jimmie accepted this invitation and was the principal speaker at an assembly in which he related some of his baseball experiences and emphasized the theme of the importance of young people acquiring a good education.[40] When he returned from Iowa, Jimmie remained at home with his wife and son from Thanksgiving until early January. These weeks constituted the first break or rest period for him since the opening of spring training last February.

Jimmie and Helen were eager to leave the wintry weather and enjoy the sun, water, and golf courses of Florida. Soon after the Christmas season and brief visits with the in-laws in Delaware and Maryland, the Foxx family departed via automobile from their home in the Philadelphia area for Fort Myers, where they had leased a house for the months of January, February, and March. In the weeks prior to spring training Jimmie kept in good physical condition by working out, swimming, and playing golf. He was relaxed and ready for the spring season when the Athletics opened camp in March.[41] However, this was not a good spring for Jimmie as he was hampered by illness and injuries. In March he came down with a serious cold, the team physician ordered him to bed, and it was several weeks before he was permitted to resume working out with the team. It was reported that for the first time in seven years Jimmie missed the opening exhibition game. Before he returned to the lineup as a regular he pinch hit several times.[42]

Shortly after Jimmie returned to regular play he received an injury that sidelined him for several weeks. In the second game of the season he fell, rounding second base and "tore a tendon in his left knee." This injury kept him out of the lineup until May 5; during this interval Phil Todt filled in at first base. On his return Foxx remained well and injury-free until the last month of the season. On September 9, in a game against the Senators, Heinie Manush accidentally stepped on Jimmie's right foot. Although this spiking incident did not break any bones in his foot, Jimmie's foot and ankle were so "seriously bruised" that he had to use crutches for several days "to get around." His foot healed sufficiently for him to return to the lineup ten days later on September 19. Despite Foxx's early-season illness and injuries the Athletics got off to a magnificent start and won all eleven games on their first western tour. Sportswriters picked them and the Cardinals to repeat as pennant winners for 1931.[43]

In June, Jimmy Dykes was injured and was out of the lineup for about three weeks. At this time Mack moved Foxx to third base and put Todt at first. When Dykes returned Foxx went back to first and remained there, except for one game. The one exception was in a game on August 1, when the right fielder, Bing Miller, became ill and had to leave the game. Mack sent Jimmie to replace Miller and put Todt on first. Despite the occasional minor injuries to key players, they occurred at different times and were of short duration. Such injuries did not seem to adversely affect the play of the Athletics. During the months of May, June and July they played .777 ball; by August 1, *The Sporting News* announced that they could win the American League title by playing .500 ball for the rest of the season. The season of 1931 was a landmark one for the Athletics; they became the first major league team in history to win more than 100 games in three consecutive seasons. Although the Athletics were having a great season, Foxx experienced "an extended batting slump" in 1931. For the first time in his major league career he would hit under .300 as he wound up the season with a .291 average. However, he drove in 120 runs and hit thirty home runs.[44]

While the Athletics were handily winning the American League pennant, the St. Louis Cardinals were repeating their 1930 performance in the National League. The World Series began on October 1, at Sportsman's Park in St. Louis. The Athletics won the opener 6-2 on the pitching of Lefty Grove and the home run–hitting of Al Simmons. The Cards came back the following day and won 2-0 as Bill Hallahan threw a three-hitter at the powerful Athletics. In these two games Foxx was three for six—all singles. Games three, four, and five were played in Philadelphia. The first of these contests was won by the Cardinals 5-2 as Burleigh Grimes bested Grove, allowing the Athletics only two hits, one of which was a home run by Simmons in the ninth, saving the Athletics from a shutout. In this game Grimes walked Foxx twice and got him on strikes once. In the fourth game of the Series and the second at Shibe Park, George Earnshaw shut out the Cards on two hits as the Athletics won 3-0. One of these runs was a sixth-inning home run by Foxx which Connie Mack described as the longest he had ever seen in a World Series game. It was over the left field roof and out of the stadium. The left field wall was 334 feet from home plate, the last row of grand stand seats was more than 100 feet from the wall and the roof above the seats was an added distance.[45] The next game featured Hallahan's second victory and gave the Cardinals a three-games-to-two lead as the Series shifted back to St. Louis. Game six was won by the Athletics 8-1 as Grove won his second Series victory. In the final and seventh game Grimes outdueled Earnshaw as the Cardinals won 4-2 to claim the world championship. The sensation of the 1931 Series was the Cardinals' rookie outfielder, John Leonard "Pepper" Martin. Martin had hit .300 in the regular season, but in the Series he hit .500, drove in five runs, and stole five bases. It was claimed that he "completely unsettled" the Athletics. Foxx hit .348 in the Series, more than fifty points above his season average. For the first time in three years the Athletics would not be dividing the winner's share of World Series proceeds. Each member of the team received $2,989.50 as the loser's share of the 1931 Series revenue.[46]

A number of the Athletics participated again in barnstorming activities for several weeks after the close of the season. One contingent, including Foxx, Cochrane and Ted Lyons of the White Sox, engaged in exhibition games at different cities from Milwaukee to San Francisco, where they boarded a ship for Honolulu. After several days in the Hawaiian Islands, one group of the players, under the guidance of Lefty O'Doul continued to Japan. The group of which Foxx was a member returned home.[47] Jimmie remained with his wife and two-year-old son in their home near Philadelphia. He worked out in a local gym and played basketball with a team composed mainly of his Athletics teammates. During the winter they visited families in Dover and Sudlersville and in late January departed for several weeks of sun, golf, and swimming before spring training began.[48]

The Athletics were a relaxed and confident group in the spring of 1932, and the Baseball Writers Association again picked them and the Cardinals to repeat as pennant winners. In the spring exhibition games Jimmie played a few games at third base, but mainly he was at first. Among the most publicized games of the Grapefruit League season was one between the Athletics and the world champion Cardinals. This spring the Cards had a talkative rookie on their roster who had been something of a sensation in the Texas League—Jay Hanna "Dizzy" Dean. Dean would win eighteen games for the Cardinals this season. However, in March he was quoted in the press as saying how he would like to pitch against the Athletics, and how he "would make 'em roll over" as if dead. Dean got his chance against Simmons, Cochrane, Foxx, and others in a mid–March game in Florida. Dean started this game for the Cards, but his tenure was brief. In the first inning four of the Athletics clipped him for home runs, including one by Foxx.[49]

Unlike 1931, Jimmie was not plagued by illness and injuries in 1932, and he got off to a strong start. During the first two months of the season he hit over .400. He asserted that he was "no longer waiting for a pitch" but was "going after anything that was near the plate."[50] Jimmie, however, was an exception this spring; while he was hitting over .400 only two of his teammates were batting .300. As a result the Athletics were struggling to keep up appearances. The Yankees were playing as though they were to reclaim the pennant they last won in 1928. By the end of June New York was leading the American League by seven and one-half games; the Athletics were in second place. This was the order in which the teams would finish the season and each Athletics regular would receive only $992.25 as his share of World Series revenue.[51]

In June, when the Athletics were in Cleveland for a series of games, Foxx and his teammates had an unusual and frightening experience. One night an apartment house near the hotel where the Athletics were staying erupted in a fire that was accompanied by a large explosion. Foxx, who was rooming with Simmons, declared that the explosion "lifted him out of the bed." When they looked out the window they saw the building ablaze and heard people

Babe Ruth and Foxx, ca. 1932 (courtesy Sudlersville Memorial Library).

screaming for help. Foxx and other Athletics dressed themselves, went to their hotel lobby and outside to witness the spectacular fire. Jimmie met Cochrane and, in the panic situation before the arrival of fire personnel, helped to rescue three young girls and a man from the burning building.[52]

The 1932 Athletics as a team were a disappointment to their fans, to themselves, and to Connie Mack. They were the same eight regulars and the same starting pitchers who had won three pennants and two World Series. What happened to cause them to end the season thirteen games behind New York? Some time later Jimmy Dykes, the Athletics third baseman, probably gave a valid explanation of why the Athletics had the season they did. He declared "the bitter truth was that we no longer had it, we no longer believed we were invincible. Our faith in ourselves was no longer there."[53]

Although the Athletics were replaced by the Yankees as the American League champions in 1932, they did set a major league club record for home runs in one season with 172. This was one more than the record formerly held by the Cubs and thirteen more than the American League record established by the Yankees in 1927.[54] Even though the Athletics faltered in 1932, Jimmie enjoyed a magnificent season. From the opening week of the campaign he began hitting home runs. By the first week in May he had hit nineteen; a month later he had twenty-six and the press was beginning to compare his hitting with that of Ruth when the Babe hit sixty in 1927. For example, *The Sporting News* of June 23 noted that Foxx's twenty-sixth home run came sixteen days ahead of Ruth's twenty-sixth in 1927 and when Jimmie hit number forty-one on July 28, it exclaimed that Foxx was now thirty-one days ahead of Ruth's record.[55] The press noted that his home runs were mostly exceptionally long drives rather than towering fly balls. During the summer it was reported that Jimmie's home runs in Philadelphia had cost Connie Mack and the Athletics $110.00 "thus far into the season to pay for broken windows in homes located on streets near Shibe Park."[56]

On July 10 the Athletics played one of the longest games in the annals of baseball, a four-hour-and-five-minutes contest against the Cleveland Indians. This was an eighteen-inning affair which the Athletics eventually won 18-17. In this contest Ed Rommel relieved Lew Krausse after the first and pitched seventeen innings in relief for the Athletics. Foxx was six for nine in this game; he had three home runs, three singles, and batted in eight runs. Years later Alva Bradley, owner of the Indians and a spectator at this game, declared it was a memorable contest and one of "my greatest diamond thrills."[57] Jimmie ended the 1932 season with a batting average of .364, fifty-eight home runs, and 169 runs batted in. Dale Alexander of Boston had a batting average of .367 and was proclaimed the batting champion although he played in thirty fewer games than Foxx and went to bat less than 400 times, or two hundred times fewer than Jimmie. Later the American League would require that one had to have a minimum of 400 times at bat to qualify for the hitting title, no matter what one's average.

Jimmie's pursuit of Ruth's home-run record of sixty for one season was not realized and he finished with fifty-eight. Several factors contributed to Foxx's decline in home-run hitting during August, a month which he entered thirty-one days ahead of Ruth's 1927 pace. His wife, Helen, became ill and entered the hospital in August, and although her illness was minor and her hospital stay was not lengthy, it was of great concern to Jimmie and probably affected his concentration on baseball. Also, it was during August that Foxx suffered an injury that rendered him less effective as a batter. One day he was

Foxx in A's dugout, ca. 1932 (courtesy Sudlersville Memorial Library).

doing some chores around the house, trying to hang a curtain in a window. He was using a step ladder and while he was trying to install a curtain fixture the ladder began to tilt and fall. When Jimmie tried to halt his fall he jammed a thumb and sprained a wrist.[58] Although this injury was not sufficient to keep him out of the lineup, it did affect his use of the bat. For several weeks he could not grip the bat tightly or hit with his normal wrist-snap swing. Also at the same time he further agitated the injured wrist when on one occasion he slid into second base trying to break up a double play.[59]

Perhaps the principal reason that Jimmie did not have more than fifty-eight home runs in 1932 was the fact that the playing conditions and rules had changed between 1927 and 1932. Between 1927 and 1932 several major league parks erected fences above the outfield walls. In St. Louis, Cleveland, and Detroit high screens were installed and balls hit into the screens were no longer home runs, but at most were usually doubles. Estimates vary for the number of times Foxx drove baseballs into the screen at St. Louis in 1932, from a low of five to a high of twelve. He also drove several hits into the screens in other parks—parks where there were none in 1927. The ground rule double, adopted by baseball officials in 1930, affected Foxx's home run total in 1932. In 1927 a hit that bounced into the stands was a home run, but with the 1930 rule modification, hits that bounced into the stands were no longer home runs, only "ground rule doubles." One sportswriter asserts that if the ground rule double had not been in effect in 1932, Foxx would have hit seventy home runs.[60]

The culmination of Jimmie's 1932 season was when the Baseball Writers Association of America chose him as the most valuable player in the American League. Since 1911 there had been sporadic efforts to establish a most valuable player award for each league. However, the practice of selecting such an individual was not completely agreed on by baseball authorities and put into permanent effect until 1931. In that year the responsibility for selecting the league's most valuable player was turned over to the Baseball Writers Association of America. This group of impartial professional sportswriters was considered the most likely to select the proper player. In 1931 they chose Lefty Grove as MVP for the American League and second baseman Frank Frisch of the Cardinals as MVP for the National League. In 1932 their selection for each league happened to be two men from the same city: Jimmie Foxx of the Athletics and outfielder Charles "Chuck" Klein of the Phillies. It was no surprise to baseball fans that when *The Sporting News* announced the major league All-Star team for 1932 it included three players from Philadelphia teams: Grove, Foxx, and Klein.[61]

In the fall of 1932 Jimmie did not go on a barnstorming tour. He remained at home with his wife and son, visited families in Maryland and Delaware, and worked out in a local gym. In November he was away for about a week on a hunting trip with Cochrane, Bing Miller, and Eddie Collins.[62]

By 1932 Foxx's achievements on the diamond had transformed the Maryland farm boy into something of a celebrity, and some in the press began referring to him as the "new King of Swat." However, it was also noted that he remained a modest, unaffected, and genial person, one who "had no dissipating habits" and was "not corrupted" by the bright lights of the city.[63] Jimmie was proud of his achievements in baseball, but he never talked about them. One scribe said that if a person did not know Jimmie he might think that he was the team's water boy. Another wrote that although Foxx had become the object of "fame, fawnings, and favors" he was embarrassed by the attention. Jimmie was portrayed by one interviewer as a person who enjoys the simple life: one who enjoys the outdoors, simple food, and a good night's sleep of eight to ten hours. Steak was his favorite food and milk his favorite drink. Although Jimmie weighed 180 pounds he was portrayed as a "light eater," consuming only one "solid meal" a day, dinner. For entertainment he and his wife enjoyed movies and his favorites were musicals. He could play bridge but "didn't care much for it." His reading consisted of the daily newspapers and an occasional western or mystery story. Among his leisure pursuits in the off season were hunting, bowling, and golf.[64]

With fame and prosperity Foxx had given more attention to his wardrobe and had become a rather meticulous dresser. One columnist for the *Philadelphia Evening Bulletin* described Jimmie as a "dressy dresser," one who wore "a soft light felt hat, light tan coat of a fine texture flannel, tan sweater, white silk tie with tiny red flowers, shirt of light green and pink stripes, brown and white striped flannel trousers, and brown and white shoes."[65] Jimmie's interest in his personal appearance was not limited to a fashionable wardrobe; he was also concerned about his physical appearance. This was reflected in his

Foxx with MVP trophy, 1933 (courtesy Sudlersville Memorial Library).

penchant for visiting the manicurist and having his "nails done." One Philadelphia reporter wrote that Jimmie "has a passion for getting his nails done" and declared he "bought more manicures than any other member" of the team.[66]

By this time Jimmie also had acquired a couple of additional nicknames. His consistent and frequent power hitting, together with his menacing appearance at the plate, had prompted some to affectionately refer to him as "the Beast." This term is associated with another moniker his teammate Mickey Cochrane gave him after Cochrane saw the movie "King Kong." This film featured a "beast" and other beasts who made a screeching sound somewhat like "iggai iggai." After seeing the movie Cochrane and a few other Athletics sought to give Foxx, the Beast, the nickname of "Ingagi." The press picked it up and for a few months some reporters occasionally used it in reference to Jimmie. However, after a brief time they ceased and the term was forgotten.[67]

In October, 1929, after a decade of unregulated Wall Street gambling and irresponsible speculation by the banking industry, the stock market collapsed. The nation was plunged into the most severe depression in its history, and one which would plague the country for the next ten years. Perhaps the nadir of the Depression was reached during the winter of 1932–33. At this time the nation's unemployment rate was in excess of twenty-five percent; more than 5000 banks had closed in the past two and one-half years, wiping out savings in excess of nine million dollars; and the national income had fallen to less than one-half of what it had been a few years earlier.

No segment of American society escaped the effects of the Great Depression—including major league baseball. Rising unemployment was reflected in declining attendance at games. In 1929 approximately ten million persons attended major league baseball games; by 1932 attendance had declined to approximately three and one-half million, and throughout the decade attendance would not recover to the 1929 level.[68]

The early reaction of baseball owners to the onset of the Depression included the adoption of a resolution to reduce player salaries, cut the player limit for each team from twenty-five to twenty-two, and to maintain admission prices at their former level.[69] The Philadelphia franchise in the American League was in a more precarious economic situation than most major league franchises. In the mid-twenties Shibe Park had undergone major renovations, and to accomplish this, Mack and the Athletics had borrowed heavily from local banks. It is estimated that this debt was more than $800,000.00, and much of it was outstanding in the early thirties. Also in 1930, '31, and '32 the Athletics had the largest payroll in major league baseball.[70] These two factors, together with declining attendance, presented serious problems for the Athletics' management. These problems were exacerbated by the fact that attendance at Athletics' games declined during 1930 and 1931, years they won the pennant and before the Depression became more severe. Connie Mack had experienced declining interest and attendance on the part of Philadelphia fans earlier when his teams dominated the American League (1911–14). His theory was that local fans became bored when a team was too successful and lost interest in its performance. He reasoned that if a team was strongly challenged for leadership, if it had to fight or struggle for each victory, the fans would flock to see the action. His response in 1914 had been to sell off his $100,000.00 infield, break up his team and rebuild. Some in Philadelphia were aware of Mack's attitude and his past actions, and in the spring of 1932 there was some speculation and a few rumors in the city that Mack would disassemble his current team.[71]

Jimmy Dykes, one of the mainstays of the Athletics at this time, tends to support the views of Mack. He explains the attendance decline in 1931 as the fans' attitude of "what's the use of watching 'em when we know they're going to win?" In 1932 it was "what's the use of watching 'em when they're out of the race?"[72] Lack of support by the fans was disastrous for Mack and his large payroll. In 1932 major league baseball losses amounted to over $1.2 million and practically all clubs except the Yankees and Cubs ran a deficit. With declining attendance, bank notes coming due, and a roster filled with high-salaried players Connie Mack decided that his only recourse to save the franchise was to sell some of his players.[73] The break-up of the Athletics began during the time of the 1932 World Series, when it was announced that Al Simmons, Jimmy Dykes and Mule Haas had been sold to the Chicago White Sox for a sum of $100,000.00. At the same time it was noted that Roger Cramer and Ed Coleman would replace Simmons and Haas in the outfield and that the youngster, Frank "Pinky" Higgins, would take over third base from Dykes.[74]

A year later (1933) when the Athletics finished in third place, Mack sold to the new owner of the Red Sox, the millionaire businessman Tom Yawkey, pitchers Grove and Walberg and second baseman Max Bishop for $125,000.00. At about the same time he announced the sale of catcher Mickey Cochrane to the Tigers for $100,000.00, indicating that he was doing Mickey a favor since the Tiger management wanted him to also serve as field manager. Mack's last sale of 1933 was when he sent pitcher George Earnshaw to the White Sox for $25,000.00. Despite rumors throughout 1934 and later that Foxx and others were going to Boston, Connie Mack constantly denied that he would sell "Foxxie." Meanwhile the Athletics wound up in fifth place in the American League in 1934 and thereafter were last or next to the bottom throughout the decade.[75] Although Mack emphasized that the economic condition of the club forced him to dismantle the Athletics, both Dykes and Foxx later expressed the opinion that by 1932 the Athletics were a satiated ball club. These men claim that "the pennant no longer held a challenge for the team"; winning was "no longer exciting"; therefore, Mack's only recourse was "to take the team apart and start to rebuild."[76]

The Athletics were dismantled, and the Philadelphia franchise weathered the Depression; however, time would reveal that Connie Mack would never assemble a third group of players who would be able to claim the American League title.

Notes

1. *The Sporting News*, April 11, 1929; Philadelphia Evening Bulletin, July 31, 1929.

2. *The Sporting News*, April 25, 1929.

3. *Ibid.*, May 9, June 6, July 4, 1929; *Philadelphia Evening Bulletin*, June 19, 1929.

4. *Philadelphia Evening Bulletin*, May 2, 1929.

5. *Ibid.*, June 11, 1929.

6. *The Sporting News*, July 25, August 15, September 5, 1929.

7. Assorted clippings, August 29, 1929, Foxx files, Baseball Library, Cooperstown, New York; *The Sporting News*, August 22, 1929.

8. *The Sporting News*, September 5, October 10, 1929, January 10, February 13, 1930; *Philadelphia Inquirer*, September 4, 1932.

9. *The Sporting News*, October 10, 1929; Jimmie Foxx, "A Master Batter Discusses His Craft," *Baseball Magazine* (December, 1929), p. 327; Jimmie Foxx, "I'm Glad I Was A Ballplayer," *Sport* (March, 1952), p. 78.

10. Bob Broeg and William J. Miller, Jr., *Baseball from a Different Angle* (South Bend, Ind.: Diamond Communications, Inc., 1988), p. 246; Mark Stang and Linda Harkness, *Rosters* (Smyrna, Ga.: n.p., c. 1991).

11. *Philadelphia Evening Bulletin*, July 31, 1929.

12. *Ibid.*, October 9, 14, 1929; *The Sporting News*, October 10, 1929; Nick Curran, "How World Series Broadcasts Were Started in 1922," *Baseball Digest* (October-November, 1964), p. 47.

13. *Philadelphia Evening Bulletin*, October 3, 1950.

14. *Ibid.*, October 11, 1929.

15. Bob Broeg, *Super Stars of Baseball* (St. Louis: The Sporting News, 1971), p. 84; *The Sporting News*, October 31, 1929.

16. *Philadelphia Evening Bulletin*, October 21, 1929; *The Sporting News*, October 24, 1929.

17. John B. Holway, *Blackball Stars, Negro League Pioneers* (Westport, Conn.: Meckler Books, 1988), pp. 182, 227; *Philadelphia Evening Bulletin*, November 29, 1929.

18. *Philadelphia Evening Bulletin*, November 5, 14, 1929.

19. *Ibid.*, September 13, 1929; *The Sporting News*, October 3, 1929.

20. *Philadelphia Evening Bulletin*, November 4, 14, 1929; *The Sporting News*, November 21, 1929.

21. *The Sporting News*, October 17, 1929.

22. *Ibid.*, December 12, 1929; *Philadelphia Evening Bulletin*, December 7, 1929; assorted clippings (1929), Foxx files, Baseball Library, Cooperstown, New York.

23. *Philadelphia Evening Bulletin*, December 4, 1929; *The Sporting News*, December 5, 1929.

24. *The Sporting News*, October 24, 1929.

25. *Ibid.*, February 26, 1931; *Boston Herald*, January 18, 1958.

26. *The Sporting News*, January 30, 1930.

27. Jimmy Dykes and C.O. Dexter, *You Can't Steal First Base* (Philadelphia: J.B. Lippincott Company, 1967), pp. 207-208.

28. *The Sporting News*, February 13, April 17, 1930.

29. *Ibid.*, April 17, 24, 1930.

30. *Ibid.*, May 8, July 10, 1930.

31. *Ibid.*, May 8, 1930.

32. *Ibid.*, May 15, July 24, 1930.

33. *Ibid.*, September 11, 26, 1930.

34. *New York Times*, June 18, 1945; see Bill Libby, *Baseball's Greatest Sluggers* (New York: Random House, 1973), p. 53.

35. *The Sporting News*, October 16, 23, 1930.

36. *Philadelphia Evening Bulletin*, October 11, 1930.

37. *Ibid.*, September 23, 1930.

38. *The Sporting News*, December 11, 1930, January 1, 1931.

39. *Ibid.*, October 16, 1930; Holway, *Blackball Stars*, p. 112.

40. *The Sporting News*, November 20, 1930.

41. *Ibid.*, January 15, 22, 1931.

42. *Ibid.*, April 2, 1931.

43. *Ibid.*, April 16, 30, May 14, 28, September 24, 1931.

44. *Ibid.*, June 18, 25, July 30, August 6, 20, October 1, November 19, 1931; Donald Honig, *Baseball in the 30's* (New York: Crown Publishers, Inc., 1989), p. 32.

45. *The Sporting News*, October 15, 1931.

46. *Ibid.*, October 15, November 5, 1931.

47. *Ibid.*, October 13, 20, 1932.

48. *Ibid.*, October 29, 1931, January 28, February 11, 1932.

49. *Ibid.*, March 17, April 14, 1932.

50. *Ibid.*, May 19, 26, 1932.

51. *Ibid.*, November 24, 1932.

52. *Philadelphia Inquirer*, July 7, 1932.

53. Dykes and Dexter, *You Can't Steal First Base*, pp. 60-61.

54. *The Sporting News*, September 29, 1932.

55. *Ibid.*, May 12, June 23, August 4, 1932.

56. *Ibid.*, July 21, 1932.

57. *Ibid.*, January 13, 1944; *Philadelphia Evening Bulletin*, July 11, 1932.

58. Francis Stann, "The Day Foxx Tried to Hang a Curtain," *Baseball Digest* (November, 1961), p.70.

59. *New York Times*, September 18, 1961; assorted clippings, February 9, 1933, in Foxx files, Baseball Library, Cooperstown, New York.

60. Jimmie Foxx as told to Austen Lake, *Boston American*, December 21, 1935; Libby, *Baseball's Greatest Sluggers*, p. 53; Thomas Meany, *Baseball's Greatest Players* (New York: Grosset and Dunlap, 1953), p. 88; "The Threat to Babe Ruth's Home Run Record," *Literary Digest* (August 12, 1933), p. 20; *Philadelphia Evening Bulletin*, April 15, 1933.

61. Rick Wolff, editorial director, *The Baseball Encyclopedia*, eighth edition (New York: Macmillan, 1990), pp. 17, 19; *The Sporting News*, January 26, 1933.

62. *Philadelphia Evening Bulletin*, November 2, 1932.

63. *Ibid.*, May 27, 1932; Richard C. Crepeau, *Baseball America's Diamond Mind, 1919–1941* (Orlando: University Presses of Florida, 1980), p. 99.

64. *Philadelphia Evening Bulletin*, June 2, 1932; *The Sporting News*, July 1, 1932.

65. *Philadelphia Evening Bulletin*, June 2, 1921; *The Sporting News*, July 1, 1932.

66. *The Sporting News*, January 15, 1931, November 3, 1921.

67. *Ibid.*, November 3, 1932.

68. Charles C. Alexander, *Our Game, an American Baseball History* (New York: Henry Holt and Company, 1991), pp. 140, 159; Wolff, ed., *The Baseball Encyclopedia*, p. 5.

69. *The Sporting News*, December 17, 1931, January 21, 1932.

70. *Ibid.*, October 28, 1943; Harvey Frommer, *Baseball's Greatest Managers* (New York: Franklin Watts, 1985), p. 193.

71. *The Sporting News*, June 20, 1932.

72. Dykes and Dexter, *You Can't Steal First Base*, p. 61.

73. Alexander, *Our Game ...* , p. 159; Frommer, *Baseball's Greatest Managers*, p. 193; Connie Mack, *My 66 Years in the Big Leagues* (Philadelphia: John C. Winston Company, 1950), p. 16.

74. *The Sporting News*, October 6, 1932; Bruce Kuklick, *To Every Thing a Season: Shibe Park and Urban Philadelphia, 1909–1976* (Princeton: Princeton University Press, 1991), p. 62.

75. Kuklick, *To Every Thing a Season*, p. 62.

76. *Boston American*, December 21, 1935.

Four

The Decline of the
Athletics, 1933–1935

Jimmie's three-year contract, which set his salary at $16,666.00 a year, ended with the close of the 1932 season, and he had to negotiate new salary terms with Connie Mack for 1933. Professing hard times and noting that Commissioner Landis agreed to a reduction in his own salary from $65,000.00 to $40,000.00, Mack made an initial offer of $11,000.00 to Foxx—a 30-percent cut in salary. Jimmie refused this offer and negotiations extended for several meetings until Jimmie signed for approximately the same as he had received in 1932, $16,300.00.[1] Baseball officials not only sought to reduce salaries as a reaction to the Depression, they also employed more players as managers. Among the player-managers of the 1930s were Rogers Hornsby, Bill Terry, Jimmy Dykes, Joe Cronin, Charlie Grimm, Mickey Cochrane and Frank Frisch. It should be noted that although baseball owners and management were experiencing economic problems, admission prices remained what they had been in the mid and late twenties.[2]

Before heading to Florida and spring training, Foxx attended a farewell banquet that some Philadelphia friends gave for Jimmy Dykes, who was departing for Chicago. A few days after this affair Jimmie, Cochrane, Grove, and Lew Krausse left Philadelphia via automobile for Florida. They were eager to have several weeks of golf and swimming before spring camp opened on March 1. It appears that Helen and Jimmie, Jr., did not accompany Foxx; she was probably busy at their new home near Atlantic City, New Jersey.[3]

When spring training began Jimmie greeted the new season with a specific goal in mind: it was to hit sixty-one home runs. He declared, "If I got fifty-eight last year without trying for the record, I should do better than that this season." His other objectives were "to drive in 150 runs and have 200 hits." Manager Connie Mack shared Jimmie's objectives and said that he expected Foxx to break Ruth's mark this year. He observed that "Foxxie" was "getting better all along."[4]

However, before the season opened a shadow fell over the aspirations of

Lou Gehrig, Foxx, and Babe Ruth, ca. 1932 (courtesy Sudlersville Memorial Library).

both Foxx and Connie Mack. Near the end of the spring exhibition season, in a game with the Cardinals, Jimmie suffered a spike wound on his left leg in a collision with Card catcher Jimmy Wilson. This wound was in the same area of his leg as the one Foxx suffered several years earlier when Heinie Manush of the Senators spiked him. The day after the injury Mack sent Foxx back to Philadelphia. He was accompanied by Dr. Frank Baird, a team physician, who entered Jimmie in Graduate Hospital as soon as they reached Philadelphia. Foxx was in the hospital for several days for treatment and observation, and he did not return to Florida. He remained in the city until the season opened, and he did not accompany the team to Washington, where they opened the season on April 12. He was advised by his physician "to remain out of activity for the sake of safety."[5] When the Athletics opened at Shibe Park on April 20,

Foxx's injury had healed sufficiently for him to be in the lineup. In the home opener against the Senators Jimmie went three for three with two home runs and a single. He drove in five runs as the Athletics won 6-1.[6]

Six weeks later in a game with the Tigers, Lynwood "Schoolboy" Rowe defeated the Athletics 10-1. The Athletics' run was scored in the second inning by Foxx and resulted in his second injury of the young season. Foxx was on base and scored on a hit, but he twisted his left knee as he sought to elude the Detroit catcher when he crossed home plate. Foxx had to leave the game, but the club trainer informed the press that Jimmie's injury was "not serious" and that he would be "back in several days."[7] Despite these early season injuries, Foxx's batting eye did not seem to be affected. Through May he was hitting around .360. He also had taken time for some public relations activities on behalf of baseball. For example, on one occasion near the end of May he accompanied magistrate Atkinson Costello to the Episcopal Hospital to visit a fifteen-year-old fan who was stricken with infantile paralysis. Jimmie gave the youngster an autographed baseball and promised to try to hit a home run for him.[8]

It may be noted that two or three features of the game were a bit different from what they had been in 1932. One change involved the number of umpires assigned to work each game. Previously a game was handled by two umpires—one behind the plate and the other in the field. However, at the winter meeting of baseball executives, it was decided to add a third umpire for each game, beginning in 1933. This would provide for two umpires in the field and one behind the plate and perhaps eliminate or lessen arguments over calls on the bases. The three-man umpire crew would work games until 1952, when major league authorities inaugurated the four-man umpire force to work games.[9] Another aspect of the game's environment that was different in 1933 resulted from Congressional legislation. Shortly before the season opened Congress repealed the Eighteenth Amendment to the Constitution. This permitted the sale of beer in ball park grandstands for the first time. A final feature, peculiar to the Athletics, involved their batting order. Previously Foxx had hit fifth in the batting order, behind Cochrane and Simmons, but with the departure of Simmons, Mack moved Foxx into the cleanup slot where he would remain.[10]

Through the month of June Foxx remained healthy, played regularly, and hit .368, with twenty-four home runs. He was honored in a ceremony held at Shibe Park on June 12 prior to the regularly scheduled game. At this time a representative of the Baseball Writers Association of America presented to Jimmie a silver cup and a plaque, which proclaimed him the American League's Most Valuable Player for 1932.[11] On July 6, there was a pause from the regular season play as major league baseball inaugurated the first of what became the annual All-Star game. The All-Star game was the brainchild of Arch Ward, sports editor of the *Chicago Tribune*. He conceived of a game between star players from each league as having a wide appeal and fulfilling two

Foxx with Connie Mack, ca. 1933 (courtesy Temple University Libraries).

purposes. One was that the game would be a part of Chicago's celebration of the city's World's Fair; it would also be a charity event, with proceeds going to the Association of Professional Baseball Players. This association was formed in 1924 by baseball players and financed by them to help the "sick, maimed, and indigent of the profession." The fee was five dollars a year and membership was open to major and minor league baseball players. Prior to 1933 this organization obtained some revenue by occasionally sponsoring old-timer games. By the early thirties it had a membership of more than 7,000.[12]

During the winter of 1932–33 Ward presented the idea of an All-Star game to the club owners, league presidents, and Commissioner Landis. All were sympathetic to the idea and gave it their approval; civic leaders, the press, and World's Fair officials in Chicago also were enthusiastic for the All-Star game. After consultation among all involved, it was decided that the game would be played on July 6, in Comiskey Park. League authorities chose two of the game's elder statesmen and most successful managers—Connie Mack and John McGraw—to serve as managers for the American League and National League teams. Later that summer and after baseball officials decided that the All-Star game would be an annual affair, it was agreed that managers of the teams which won the American and National League pennants in the preceding year would serve as managers of the All-Star teams. In the spring of 1933 it was announced that the members of both teams would be chosen by the baseball fans of the country, who were asked to mail their choices to *The Sporting News* in St. Louis.[13]

Foxx was chosen as one of the twenty members of the first American League All-Star team. On July 6, the inaugural All-Star game was played in Chicago before 49,000 fans. However, those who had voted for Jimmie were disappointed since he sat on the bench for the entire game. Foxx, who was headed for the American League triple crown and his second consecutive MVP award, watched Lou Gehrig play first base for the full nine innings. Connie Mack explained he did not use Jimmie because he "did not want to break up a winning combination" by replacing players in a game the American League won by a score of 4-2.[14] Foxx fans, however, would see him participate in later contests since he would be chosen for the first nine of the American League All-Star teams.

After the All-Star break, league play resumed, and although Foxx continued with his superb play, the Athletics were faltering. By the end of July Jimmie was leading the league in hitting, but Connie Mack had concluded that "the Athletics were out of the race this year."[15] The team finished the season in third place, behind the Senators and Yankees. Foxx concluded the 1933 season as the triple crown winner in the American League; he hit .356, had forty-eight home runs, and 163 runs batted in. Nine of the 163 runs he batted in came against Cleveland on August 14 and established an American League record for a single contest. In this game he also hit for the cycle—having a home run, triple, double, and single.[16] On six different occasions he hit two home runs in a game. In a doubleheader at St. Louis he hit four home runs and in a game against the Yankees on June 8 he hit three home runs off their southpaw ace, Vernon "Lefty" Gomez. The following day, June 9, in his first time at bat against the Yankees, he hit a home run, thereby tying a major league record of four consecutive home runs.[17] Jimmie also led the American League in strikeouts, with ninety-three; this was three more than the "Sultan of Swat," Babe Ruth. It was no surprise that Jimmie was chosen by *The Sporting News* and the Baseball Writers Association of America for membership on the 1933 major league All-Star team. Shortly after the close of the base-ball season, and for the second consecutive year, Jimmie was chosen by the baseball writers of America as the Most Valuable Player in the American League.[18]

In addition to his magnificent performance in 1933, Jimmie found time during the season to participate in baseball public relations activities. For example, on May 23 he and George Earnshaw gave brief talks and presented sports awards to students at an assembly at Philadelphia's Northeast High School. At another time Foxx was the guest speaker at a sports banquet in Pleasantville, New Jersey, honoring the local American Legion boys baseball team.[19]

From the summer of 1933, when the Athletics were struggling to remain in the first division, there were rumors and speculation in the press that Mack was going to sell other players. One rumor was that Foxx would go to the Red Sox and Cochrane to Detroit. Mack denied all rumors, called them "foolish," and asserted that both men would be with the Athletics in 1934. Mack con-tinued to deny all rumors of player sales and trades until mid–December when it was announced that Grove, Bishop, and Walberg had been sold to the Red Sox for $125,000.00, that Earnshaw was going to the White Sox, and that Cochrane had been sold to the Tigers for $100,000.00.[20]

The annual autumnal barnstorming contests in which Foxx usually par-ticipated was shortened by a foot injury he suffered in early October. One account is that the injury occurred before the end of the season, during the last western trip of the Athletics. It seems that Foxx and some teammates were clowning around when he injured a toe, and although it caused swelling, Foxx continued to play through the last game of the season. Another account of this injury is that his foot was fractured during a post-season barnstorming contest when he fouled a pitch off his foot. At that time his foot was x-rayed and the fracture was discovered. His physician taped the foot and ankle and instructed Jimmie to rest his foot and leg. A few days after the doctor treated his leg, Jimmie went to his home near Atlantic City for a rest and to give leg. his injury time to heal.[21] By the end of October the injury was healed suffi-ciently so that Foxx was able to join Grove, Cochrane, and Miller for a hunt-ing outing in the Sudlersville area.[22]

Foxx was in Sudlersville on November 7 for a very special occasion. Civic, business, and religious leaders of the town, in cooperation with the Commu-nity Betterment Club, held a formal "welcoming home" ceremony to honor a local son who was now the homerun king of major league baseball and the Most Valuable Player in the American League. This affair was held in Cox Memorial Hall, and a number of dignitaries and friends from the area and beyond were invited. Among those who attended the festivities were Connie and Mrs. Mack; teammates Cochrane, Walberg, Bing Miller, and Mule Haas; Jimmie's first manager, "Home Run" Baker; and American League umpire, Bill

McGowan. Others in attendance were Mayor Wallace Woodford of Dover, Delaware, and Senator Dudley G. Roe.[23]

It was reported that people began assembling at Cox Memorial Hall around 6:30 P.M. and by 7:30 the place "was packed" with "friends, relatives, and admirers from the Eastern Shore, Delaware, and Pennsylvania." Shortly after seven o'clock the assemblage moved to the banquet area for the meal and testimonials. The menu included Maryland turkey, Virginia ham, cranberries, sweet potatoes, hominy, and all the "trimmings from fruit cups to mints." Mayor Woodford and Senator Roe praised Jimmie as an athlete who, despite his many honors, continued to be modest, friendly and unassuming. Senator Roe spoke warmly of Foxx's parents and the training they had given him as a youth. Connie Mack referred to Jimmie as "my boy" and declared that no one in baseball, including Babe Ruth, could hit with the power of Foxx. He described Foxx as a team player, as one who was more interested in winning than in compiling individual statistics. Mack concluded his remarks by expressing the belief that one year Jimmie would break Ruth's record of sixty home runs. Before the evening concluded around eleven P.M., the baseball guests kindly autographed programs, baseballs, place mats and other items for anyone in the group who wished autographs.[24]

Although several articles by Foxx and interviews with him had been published in newspapers and magazines in previous years, 1933 marks the publication of a book by Jimmie. *The Sporting News* of May 25, 1933, announced the appearance of a book, *How I Bat*, by Jimmie Foxx. This was a forty-eight page book in a sport series edited by Bill Cunningham of the *Boston Post* and several of his associates. It was published by the Courier-Citizen Publishing Company. The book consists of a brief foreword and eight chapters, titled as follows: (1) Laying A Batting Foundation; (2) Keep Your Eye on the Ball; (3) Developing an Individual Style; (4) The Science of Choosing a Bat; (5) Picking up the Fine Points; (6) Riding Over the Rough Spots; (7) Studies in Batting Psychology; and (8) A Summary of Batting Mechanics.

In this book Foxx emphasized that there was no one correct form or style for hitting. He noted that each of the great hitters—Ruth, Simmons, Hornsby, Cobb, and others—had his own individual stance in the batter's box. Some took a long stride into the pitch when they swung, others hit flat-footed; some stood far back in the box, others tended to crowd the plate. Some, like Ruth and Simmons, held the bat at the end of the handle, while Cobb was a choke hitter. Jimmie stressed that a hitter should be comfortable with his own style and not try to copy another. Batting style was not as important for good hitting, Jimmie declared, as having or developing strong hands, wrists and forearms—especially the wrists, because they provide "the powerful snap" of the bat as it connects with the ball.[25] Equally as important as physical strength, he asserted, was coordination or timing between eyes and muscles, or rhythm as he called it. Coordination was essential if a batter was to connect properly with the pitch.

Natural strength or talent, together with muscle-eye coordination alone, was not sufficient for being a skillful batter. Jimmie also stressed the need for one to continually practice hitting. "You can never get too much practice," he wrote. Foxx possessed all of the natural attributes of an athlete and he also loved the game of baseball, but perhaps no one practiced hitting any more than Jimmie. Practice helped to develop and tone muscles, and it also helped one's eye and muscle coordination. In writing about eye coordination Jimmie quoted Cobb and informed readers that perhaps there was no more important aspect of the game than always keeping one's eyes on the ball. Practice, he claimed, would enable one to keep an eye on the ball from the time it left the pitcher's hand until it made connection with the bat. He noted that all of the good hitters had this skill. "Learning to watch the ball," he said, "is one of the prime rules of successful hitting."[26]

Also important for a hitter was the type or size of bat which one used. Jimmie asserted that the most important thing about the size of bat was to select one that "felt good," that one could easily handle, one that had "balance" and when swung seemed to almost be an extension of one's arms. He noted that some men such as Babe Ruth used a heavy bat—40/42 ounces—but he emphasized that size of bat did not mean that one was a more powerful hitter. Power hitting, he asserted, resulted from the use of a "comfortable" bat, correct timing, and wrist-snapping of the bat to meet the ball. Whatever bat the hitter used, Foxx cautioned that the hands and arms should be kept "fairly well away from the body." This allowed the batter better control of his swing. In addition to selecting a "comfortable" bat, Foxx advised one to be relaxed and not "tense up" in the batter's box. And again he used his ex-teammate, Ty Cobb, as an example. He called Cobb "the most relaxed batter he had ever seen." He was as loose as if he had "ball-bearing joints."[27] If a hitter has a slump, as Foxx experienced in 1931 when he hit only .291, he advised that one should not "fuss and fume" but try to keep relaxed and not alter one's natural style of batting. The slump will pass, he maintained, and the breaks will soon come your way.[28]

Foxx summarized his narrative on hitting by describing his own form. He stated that he stood fairly close to the plate, about eight inches away, and kept his feet still until ready to swing. Then he took a short stride into the pitch as he swung, with his wrists giving the bat a "last quick flick." He always held the bat (which for most of his career was a 37/38-ounce model) at the end of the handle and made a complete follow through, although he had a minimum back swing. He relates that he never tried for home runs but only sought to make a solid connection with the ball. He maintained that if one had proper timing or coordination and "hit the ball solid it would travel." Jimmie also advised batters to "study the habits and delivery" of opposing pitchers. While waiting for one's time to bat, he urged hitters to carefully observe pitchers; to note differences, if any, in their motion or manner of delivery; to try to discern their "best pitch"; and note any changes in the delivery of various pitches.

Although he advised the careful study of pitchers, Foxx cautioned that the batter should not be a "guess hitter," trying to guess what the next pitch would be. If one developed eye-muscle coordination, he declared, one would be ready for any pitch, whether curve, fast ball, change of pace or knuckler.[29] Jimmie's narrative account of *How I Bat* was accompanied by a number of photographs and illustrations. The publisher announced that the next book in the series would be *How I Pitch* by Lefty Grove.

Near the end of the 1932 season the Foxx family had moved from the Philadelphia area to a home in Margate City, New Jersey, a suburb of Atlantic City. Whether this move was at the suggestion of his wife, Helen, or whether the family simply wanted to be near the beach is uncertain. But as Foxx had become more affluent the family's lifestyle had become quite different from that of the unpretentious farm boy. How much this transformation was influenced by Helen or simply by the changing sense of values of Foxx himself is difficult to ascertain; perhaps both were responsible. This change was observed when the family departed their home in January, 1934, for Florida. It was reported that when the family left, they were accompanied by their maid and chauffeur.[30] Their destination in Florida was not Fort Myers, the site of the Athletics' spring camp, but Miami Beach. They would vacation there for a month before moving to Fort Myers.

This winter, as the previous one, Jimmie was going south without having signed a contract for the coming year (1934). A season earlier he had experienced a bit of hassle with Mack before he finally signed for approximately the same salary he had received for each of the three previous seasons. The press reported that during the fall Mack had offered Jimmie a contract but that he wanted to cut the triple crown winner's salary to $11,000.00. It was also reported that Foxx wanted a salary increase and was "demanding" $25,000.00. Despite the disparity in these figures, it was assumed that Foxx's hold-out would be resolved and he would be in the lineup by opening day on April 17. Foxx and Mack conferred several times about salary and on one occasion Mack increased the Athletics' offer to $15,000.00 and included a bonus clause; if the team drew 900,000 fans Jimmie's salary would be increased. Foxx refused this suggestion and confided to one reporter that he "might sit out the season and farm."[31]

During the period of contract negotiations and hold-out, a Philadelphia wrestling promoter, Ray Fabiani, sought to persuade Foxx to change sports and become a professional wrestler. He declared that Jimmie had "the ideal build for a matman" and offered him a contract of $30,000.00 a year to sign with him.[32] This suggestion had no appeal for Foxx, who shortly agreed to terms with Connie Mack.

Throughout his negotiations with the Athletics, Mack adamantly denied rumors that he was going to sell Foxx and insisted that Jimmie would play for the Athletics in 1934. After several additional conferences and only a day or

Foxx catching, ca. 1934 (courtesy Sudlersville Memorial Library).

two before spring training began, Foxx signed a one-year contract for a reported $18,000.00. Jimmie accepted this when Mack, in his most fatherly manner, explained to him that he simply was unable to pay him any more. Jimmie declared that he "was delighted to be under contract," and the press noted that throughout the weeks of negotiations Jimmie and Connie Mack were always friendly, cordial, and respectful of each other.[33]

Prior to the opening game of the 1934 season, state and local legislation in Pennsylvania had assured that the coming season would be somewhat different from previous ones. The 1934 season would mark the appearance of major league baseball games on Sunday in the state of Pennsylvania. Sunday games in major league cities date from the opening years of the century in Chicago, St. Louis, and Cincinnati, where such games were usual as early as 1905. Gradually the practice expanded, and by 1920 Sunday baseball was played in Detroit, Cleveland, Washington, and New York. The only states which continued the "blue law opposition" to major league baseball on Sunday were Massachusetts and Pennsylvania. Following several years of agitation and political activism by citizens of Boston, the Massachusetts legislature, in 1929, approved Sunday baseball in that state, leaving only two major league cities where Sunday baseball was prohibited—Pittsburgh and Philadelphia.[34]

For nearly ten years Connie Mack and others had sought to have the Sunday ban on baseball lifted. On one occasion in 1926 and in connection with the sesquicentennial observance of the Declaration of Independence, Mack sought to test the legality of the 1794 statute under which the courts declared such activities as professional baseball to be illegal on the Sabbath. Late in the summer those who sponsored and operated the sesquicentennial affairs were "running a deficit," and the city government decided to permit some of the businesses associated with the celebration, which had formerly been prohibited to operate on Sunday, to remain open. The city officials made this decision after receiving a favorable opinion from the state supreme court.[35] At this same time Connie Mack decided to test the ban on Sunday baseball games and on August 22 the Athletics and White Sox played the first Sunday major league baseball game in the state of Pennsylvania. In legal proceedings following this game, the courts upheld the ban on Sunday baseball games by declaring they were a violation of the eighteenth-century statute.[36]

Supporters of baseball in Pittsburgh and Philadelphia continued to agitate for Sunday baseball or for legislation to permit local option to decide the issue. At one time Ben Shibe and Connie Mack talked with the press and to officials in Philadelphia and Camden, New Jersey, about the possibility of playing Sunday games in New Jersey.[37] While rumors of these talks were in process a local option measure was introduced in 1931 in the Pennsylvania legislature. This measure, if passed and implemented, would permit baseball to be played after 2:00 P.M. on Sundays. There was considerable opposition to this proposal and it did not pass. However, it was revived two years later and passed in 1933. Local option was almost immediately approved in Pittsburgh and Philadelphia, and major league baseball games were played during the 1934 season. The law specified that games might be played on Sunday between 2:00 and 6:00 P.M. The first game in Philadelphia was a city contest just prior to the opening of the season between the Athletics and the Phillies, on Sunday, April 8, 1934.[38] Mack expressed hearty approval of the lifting of the Sunday ban and declared it would help alleviate some of the team's economic problems.[39] Thus, some might claim that one of the effects of the Depression was to remove the restrictions against Sunday baseball in the last holdout area of the major leagues.

Foxx reported to camp the day he signed his contract and played throughout the exhibition season. The Athletics opened at home against the Yankees before a crowd of 14,400, "the smallest opening crowd in memory," one observer noted. In this contest Foxx hit two home runs—one into the right field stands and the other over the left field roof and out of the park—but the Athletics lost 11-5. The following day attendance was 5,500 and for the third game of this series it was reported that "only a quorum was present." In an attempt to attract more fans the Athletics made a slight modification in admission charges. For the 1934 season the price of box seats was reduced from $2.20 to $1.65; however, general admission for bleacher and grandstand seats remained unchanged at fifty-five cents and $1.10 respectively.[40]

Although the Athletics were off to a slow start in 1934, Foxx was hitting well. On April 16, in a game against the Senators in the nation's capital he hit a home run with the bases full, but the Athletics lost 7-6. By the end of May he was hitting .336 and had twelve home runs. One of these home runs had attracted considerable attention in the press. It was hit off Ted Lyons of the White Sox in a game at Comiskey Park on May 18. It was the first ball ever hit into the center field bleachers at Comiskey. The center field wall was 436 feet from home plate and Foxx's blast was over the wall and up into the bleachers, landing in the seventh row of seats.[41]

Throughout June there was increasing publicity for the second annual All-Star game, which was played on July 10 at the Polo Grounds in New York before 48,363 fans. As in the first of these contests, the fans voted for players who would participate. However, the managers would arrange the lineups and name their pitching choices. Foxx was again chosen for the team, and this year manager Joe Cronin of the Senators put him in the lineup, but at third base. Lou Gehrig, the league's leading hitter and on his way to a triple crown winning season, was at first base. Although the American League won this game 9-7, the hero or the most noteworthy participant in this game was the Giant pitcher and screwball artist, southpaw Carl Hubbell. Hubbell was the starting pitcher for the National League; he worked for three innings and was relieved by Lon Warneke of the Cubs. The National League jumped to a 4-0 lead after three innings, and Hubbell gave a pitching exhibition which has remained unmatched in All-Star history. He not only shut out the American League hitters for three innings, but for one stretch he struck out in succession five of the league's best hitters—Ruth, Gehrig, Foxx, Simmons and Cronin. Foxx claimed that he was the only one of the five to so much as touch Hubbell for a foul, saying that before he struck out, he hit "a long foul" off the lanky screwballer. Foxx and his teammates had less trouble with Hubbell's successors, Warneke and Van Mungo, who allowed the American League nine runs in innings four, five and six. For the game, Jimmie was two for five, having a double and a single.[42]

A few days prior to the All-Star game there was, for the second consecutive year, a ceremony at Shibe Park honoring Foxx. This affair was held before the game between the Athletics and White Sox and Jimmie was presented two awards. One was a silver plaque, presented by Harry Roberts, a representative of the Baseball Writers Association of America, which designated Foxx as the MVP of the American League for 1933. The other award was presented by Judge Harry S. McDevitt on behalf of *The Sporting News*. It was a desk set and a plaque which declared Foxx the outstanding baseball player in America during 1933, an honor determined on the basis of a nationwide vote conducted by *The Sporting News*.[43]

Throughout the second half of the season Foxx continued to have a good year, but the Athletics fell to seventh place in the American League standings. Their one moment of notoriety was in a game with Mickey Cochrane's pennant-winning Tigers at Shibe Park on August 29. The Tiger ace, "Schoolboy" Rowe, had won sixteen consecutive games, a season record shared with several others, and he was going for his seventeenth straight win. The Athletics thwarted his effort by knocking him out of the box in the seventh inning and winning the game 13-5.[44] Jimmie finished the 1934 season with a .334 average, forty-four home runs and 130 runs batted in. Except for nine games, he spent the season at first base. In September, when Frank "Pinky" Higgins injured a thumb, Foxx was shifted to third base, and Lou Finney took over first. *The Sporting News* reported that Jimmie played third base as if it were his home and that opposing players in Boston, New York, and Detroit "marveled at his work at third base."[45]

From March to October there were occasional rumors and speculations reported in the press that 1934 was Foxx's last year with the Athletics, that Connie Mack was going to sell him to another team, purportedly to Tom Yawkey of the Red Sox who had made an offer for Jimmie.[46] Mack ignored or denied all of these rumors and in mid–September announced that Foxx was not and never had been for sale and that he would be with the Athletics in 1935. A few days later another announcement was made by the Athletics' front office. It stated that Jimmie Foxx had just signed a three-year contract, and beginning in 1935 he would serve as captain of the team. It was also announced that Jimmie would shift positions next season and would catch instead of playing first base. First base, it was explained, would be taken over by Lou Finney or the incoming rookie from the Texas League, Alex Hooks. No mention was made of Foxx's salary in the announcement, although it was rumored to be $18,000.00 a year.[47]

During the early years of the Depression some teams began to charge a fee for a certain group of patrons whom baseball owners had sought to attract to the game by designating a certain day of the week when they were admitted without charge—female fans. By 1925 many minor league clubs and a few of the major league teams had adopted the practice of observing Ladies Day. Certain days of the season, usually a Monday but occasionally a Friday, were designated Ladies Day, and on these days female fans were admitted to games without charge. The idea of having a Ladies Day dated back to the 1890s when the Cincinnati Reds experimented with and later established the practice. However, most major league franchises refused to follow their example until the 1920s, when the St. Louis clubs, the Tigers, and several others inaugurated the practice in their parks. When first begun, some argued that baseball was male entertainment and that the environment at baseball parks was unsuitable for ladies. It was claimed by some that the language used by male fans was "not polite," that the fans were sometimes raucous and were uncouth with their use of tobacco. Others maintained that the custom of Ladies Day was "good for baseball." It would create new fans, increase interest in the game and even improve the environment at baseball parks.[48] By 1930 Ladies Day was an established practice in many major league cities, and public opinion was that it created new fans and interest in the game. However, by 1934 certain teams which observed Ladies Day began to levy a charge for admission rather than admit the ladies free. For example, in St. Louis and Detroit, baseball management continued to observe a number of Ladies Days throughout the season, but they instituted an admission charge of twenty-five cents or about one-half the regular price for bleacher seat admission.[49]

The economic effects of the Depression in the early thirties on major league baseball prompted club owners and league officials to seek various sources of revenue. One possible source was from a practice that had been around for at least twelve years: the radio broadcast of baseball games. The first radio broadcast of a play by play major league game was on August 5, 1921, by station KDKA in Pittsburgh of a contest between the Pirates and the Phillies. A year later the entire World Series, between the Yankees and Giants, was broadcast, and every Series since that date (1922) has been broadcast in its entirety.[50] From 1922 to 1934 the World Series games were broadcast, but major league baseball received no revenue from this activity. The broadcasts were arranged by the network, usually the red or blue National Broadcasting Company affiliate and the local station. However, in 1934 major league officials and Commissioner Landis announced that World Series games would be broadcast, but that the network would have to pay major league baseball for the privilege of broadcasting the games. This announcement did not dampen the ardor of would-be sponsors. The Ford Motor Company paid major league baseball $100,000.00 for the right to sponsor radio broadcasts of the 1934 games between the Cardinals and Tigers.[51] The decision by the baseball establishment to sell the right to broadcast the World Series games set a precedent that would continue.

Although the World Series games had been broadcast since 1922, there was considerable controversy in the 1920s and 1930s concerning the propriety of broadcasting regular season games. Whether to permit a team's games to be broadcast was a decision left to local management or ownership. Some owners such as W.K. Wrigley of the Cubs were enthusiastic about the new medium, and in 1924 Wrigley's team became the first major league franchise to broadcast its games. Shortly thereafter the Chicago White Sox followed Wrigley's example.[52] A number of other clubs followed suit. In 1926 the Tigers, Cardinals, and Browns allowed their games to be broadcast, and in 1929 Cleveland fans were permitted to hear radio broadcasts of Indians' games. By this date all major league clubs in "the west" except the Reds were allowing the broadcast of their games.[53] None of the major league clubs in the eastern portion of the nation had given permission for their games to be broadcast by 1929.

The controversy over the advisability of allowing the broadcast of games was structured in economic terms. Those who favored the broadcast of games argued that it was "good for baseball," that it stimulated interest in the game, especially among women and youths, and created new fans who, in turn, would come to the park to see the players they had heard about on the radio. Radio, it was maintained, would create new paying customers, which was "good for baseball."[54] Those unsympathetic to the radio broadcast of games were generally found in the metropolitan areas along the eastern seaboard from Washington to Boston. Baseball spokesmen in these areas maintained that radio broadcast of games would have a deleterious influence on the game. One commentator who opposed the broadcasting of games declared that baseball and radio "mix no better than oil and water" and that the announcers "talk too much" and most of them know "nothing about the game." Some reasoned that if one could hear the games on radio "for free" why would they pay to come to the ball park? Radio might stimulate interest, they reasoned, but at the same time it would lessen attendance.[55] Such arguments persisted despite the fact that attendance in Chicago and St. Louis increased in the late twenties. Among those in the forefront of opposition to the radio broadcast of games was *The Sporting News*. Typical of the view of this publication was an editorial in the August 29, 1929, issue, titled "On the Air." The argument against the broadcast of baseball games was summed up in the following terms: "God made some things," the editor declared, "to be seen and not heard and some things to be heard and not seen. A ball game is to be seen and not heard." This sentiment would be repeated and with the suggestion that broadcasters be kept from all of the parks.[56]

Despite the skepticism and opposition throughout the 1920s to the broadcasting of major league games in the eastern cities, the sentiment toward radio changed after 1929 and in the summer of 1932 it was reported that all of the clubs, except the Senators, were permitting the broadcast of their home games. However, the decline in attendance in 1932 and 1933 prompted owners in St. Louis to discontinue the radio broadcast of games from Sportsman's Park, and in 1934 baseball owners in New York, the principal center of opposition to radio broadcast of games, and where the owners evidently were in complete agreement with the sentiments of the editor of *The Sporting News*, entered into an agreement that after the current season no games of the Yankees, Giants, or Dodgers would be broadcast during the next five years.[57]

In 1934, the first year that the owners and Landis sold the privilege of broadcasting the World Series games, a new innovation in radio broadcasting of baseball began in a city which had been the last hold-out against radio in the west—Cincinnati. In this year Larry MacPhail, a successful minor league baseball executive, assumed management of the Reds for the franchise owner Powell Crosley. MacPhail was an innovator as well as a competent baseball executive. He persuaded Crosley, who owned a radio station in Cincinnati, that broadcasting of games would create interest and bring fans into the park. MacPhail hired an experienced announcer and a man thoroughly acquainted with the game, Walter "Red" Barber, to broadcast the games. MacPhail inaugurated the practice of broadcasting all away games as well as home games to keep up interest.[58]

Despite some continued opposition to the broadcasting of games and after more than fifteen years of reviewing and evaluating the practice, by the close of the 1930s baseball magnates accepted the radio broadcast of games. When the 1939 season opened, there was, for the first time, regular radio broadcast of games in every major league city. No doubt the precedent established by Landis in the 1934 World Series of obtaining revenue by broadcasting helped influence local owners, who by this time were also receiving revenues from sponsors for the privilege of broadcasting local games and advertising their products.[59] The five-year ban on the broadcasting of games in the New York area was broken by Larry MacPhail, who in January, 1938, became the general manager of the Dodgers. When he came to the area one of his first announcements was that he would not be a party to any agreement to deny baseball to the public and that Dodger games would be broadcast in 1939.[60]

In 1934 MacPhail had also introduced Reds fans and major league baseball to the practice of purchasing season tickets, offering purchasers a reduced admission for games. In this same year MacPhail became the first major league executive to charter an airplane for team travel. Both of these practices would later be adopted by other clubs and become standard operating procedures. However, air travel would not become the regular mode of team travel until 1946 when the Yankees entered into a charter arrangement with United Airlines for transportation.[61] After he went to Brooklyn, MacPhail installed one of the first organs in a major league baseball park, and he employed Gladys Gooding to play it; it became a feature at Ebbets Field and would be copied by others. In this instance, however, "The Red Head" was following, not establishing a practice. A short while before, the Cubs management had installed the first organ in a baseball park and employed Ray Nelson to operate it for the entertainment of the fans.[62]

Baseball had long been an active participant in what has been described as the American sense of mission—the effort to share with peoples of the world some of the elements of the most sophisticated and advanced culture that society has created. Among those elements of their culture which Americans have diligently tried to extend to others have been their concept of democracy, Christianity, capitalism and baseball. From 1874 to the outbreak of World War II, baseball owners and spokesmen, on numerous occasions, sought to promote baseball in Europe, the Middle East, Australia, Japan, and Latin America by sending contingents of players and officials to these areas to perform and engage in public relations activities.[63] One of the most impressive of these foreign tours was the one arranged by executives of the Philadelphia Athletics, which toured the Far East in the fall of 1934. Although games were played in Shanghai and Manila, this tour focused its interest and activities on Japan.

Japan, more than any area outside the United States, espoused the game of baseball. After the early 1850s, when Japan was forced to open its doors to foreign trade, customs, and investments, together with granting extraterritorial rights to foreigners, certain Western practices and values were introduced into the country. One of these was baseball. Sport historians designate two American school teachers, Horace Wilson and Albert Bates, as responsible for introducing the game to the Japanese in the early 1870s. Other Japanese learned of baseball from Americans in the foreign enclaves of certain port cities, where Americans would organize teams and play each other as well as compete with teams formed by American sailors stationed in those ports. Baseball was also promoted by some Japanese who had studied in the United States, become familiar with the game, and tried to popularize it when they returned home. Missionaries of certain American denominations formed teams composed of Japanese youths to compete with each other. One historian has written that the Japanese quickly developed a "passion for baseball" and by 1890 numerous high schools and colleges in the country had organized teams and were competing against each other as they were in the United States. Also, in some cities "amateur athletic clubs" formed teams and competed.[64]

Between 1878 and 1900 baseball teams from a number of American colleges and universities toured Japan and played against various college and club teams. Among the American university teams that visited Japan were those from the universities of Chicago, Indiana, Illinois, Wisconsin, California, Washington, Stanford and Harvard. In 1905 the first contingent of Japanese university baseball players visited the United States and played teams at Stanford, the University of California and the University of Washington. The first group of professional players to visit Japan was in 1908 when an executive of the A. J. Reach and Company, a Philadelphia sporting goods manufacturer, sponsored a group of minor league and several major league players to travel to Japan. Between November 21 and the end of December they played nineteen games against Japanese teams of collegians and amateur players in Toyko, Yokohama, and Kobe without suffering a single loss. The first contingent of American major league players to visit Japan was in the fall of 1913 when Charles Comiskey, president of the Chicago White Sox, and John McGraw, manager of the New York Giants, accompanied their teams on an around-the-world exhibition tour. Several games were played in Tokyo, Yokohama, Kobe, and Nagasaki before the teams departed for Shanghai. It was reported that the Japanese showed great interest in the American professionals and that "the games drew well."[65]

The first contingent of professional baseball players to visit Japan after the World War was in 1921 and 1922. These groups were organized by Herb Hunter, a former major league infielder with the Cubs and Cardinals. His 1922 group, designated the All-Americans, included Herb Pennock, Luke Sewell, Riggs Stephenson, Casey Stengel, Frederick "Irish" Meusel, and Waite Hoyt. Hunter's All-Americans had the approval of Commissioner Landis and the presidents of the American and National Leagues. Between November 5 and mid–December, the All-Americans played eleven games against Japanese teams in various cities, winning all except one game. Hunter arranged another exhibition tour in 1931. This group had the blessings of major league baseball, *The Sporting News*, and others. It also had a partial Japanese sponsor, the *Yomiuri Shimbun*, a Japanese newspaper whose owner, Matsutaro Shoriki, was a major booster of baseball and who would play a leading role in organizing the first professional baseball league in Japan in 1936. This team of Hunter's All-Stars included Lou Gehrig, Lefty Grove, Mickey Cochrane, Frank Frisch, Al Simmons, Lefty O'Doul, and others. The All-Stars won all seventeen games played in Japan, and although they won handily they attracted considerable interest; more than 50,000 fans attended a game in Tokyo. This tour tended to strengthen the relationship between Japanese baseball and major league baseball in the United States. On this tour Lefty O'Doul, the Brooklyn outfielder, made acquaintances which prompted an invitation the following year for him to come to Japan in the off season and serve as a baseball coach or instructor for Japanese youth. When he returned in 1932 he was accompanied by two colleagues who were also employed to instruct Japanese players—pitcher Ted Lyons of the White Sox and catcher Morris "Moe" Berg of the Senators.[66]

Perhaps the culmination of these American exhibition baseball tours to Japan was in the autumn of 1934. Under the leadership of John D. Shibe, vice-president of the Philadelphia Athletics, planning for a tour of American baseball All-Stars began in the fall and winter of 1933. This tour was also partially supported and highly publicized by the Japanese newspaper magnate and baseball promoter, Matsutaro Shoriki. This group of players consisted of the premier stars of the American League, and their designated "manager" was Babe Ruth, a name synonymous throughout the world with the best of American baseball. By mid-summer 1934, most of the arrangements for the tour were completed and the players selected. Connie Mack agreed to accompany the team which included Ruth, Gehrig, Foxx, Hornsby, Earl Averill, Moe Berg, Charlie Gehringer, Pinky Higgins, Ben Chapman, and others. John Quinn, an American League umpire, accompanied the group and served as an umpire.[67]

After the close of the 1934 season a portion of the All-Stars who were going to Japan played barnstorming games at several places in the United States and Canada prior to departure from Vancouver on October 20. The barnstorming group was under the supervision of Earl Mack of the Athletics. Connie Mack and the non-barnstorming players joined the others in Vancouver.[68] This tour included players and their wives and was envisioned as something of a grand vacation experience. Mrs. Lou Gehrig, in her memoir *My Luke and I*, described the experience and the impact it had on the American contingent.

Foxx was one of the group who departed at the close of the season to barnstorm their way to Vancouver prior to the journey to Japan. One of these games was against a group of Negro League All-Stars in Jamestown, North Dakota. In this contest, which the American League lost, Foxx was held hitless by the Negro pitcher "Papa" Chet Brewer. He was not impressed by Foxx but remarked that on this occasion "Foxx was filled up with some of that Canadian beer," and this impaired his hitting. This is one of the earliest mentions of Foxx's imbibing alcoholic beverages.[69]

Several days later, on October 8, a morning and afternoon doubleheader was played against a group of minor leaguers, the North Dakota All-Stars, at Winnipeg, Manitoba. In the morning game Foxx was hit in the head by a pitch from "Lefty" Barney Brown. He was knocked unconscious and was taken immediately to the hospital. One early report was that the injury was so serious Foxx "might never play ball again." However, the *Winnipeg Free Press* reported that Foxx would remain in the hospital for a day or two so that the doctors might observe his condition and x-ray his head. Jimmie was released from the hospital four days later, on October 12. The physician who attended him declared that Foxx suffered a concussion but no fracture of the skull, that he was now in "good condition" and could resume the journey to Vancouver and on to Japan.[70] When Jimmie was released from the hospital, he and Helen joined the others in Calgary, where the All-Stars had scheduled another contest. After crossing Canada they played exhibition games in Seattle (October 18) and Vancouver (October 19) before sailing for the Orient on the "Empress of Japan."[71] The beaning which Jimmie suffered in Winnipeg was one of the rare occasions in his career that he was "hit by a pitcher." It was later noted that Foxx was hit by a pitched ball probably less than any other dangerous hitter; one account lists him being hit thirteen times in a twenty-year career.[72]

The All-Stars arrived in Yokohama on November 2. Eleanor Gehrig recalls that in every city where they played the Americans were welcomed by immense crowds. She says that the players and their wives were entertained and treated as very special guests and were given gifts in every city they visited. From November 2 until the first week in December the American League All-Stars played eighteen games against teams of Japanese high school, university and club players. The Americans did not lose a game; Babe Ruth hit thirteen home runs and the All-Stars attracted more than 750,000 fans to see them perform.[73]

Foxx had recovered sufficiently from being beaned to be able to play in most of the games. He generally played third base or caught, but in one game he relieved the pitcher and held the opposition in check for several innings. In another game before approximately 50,000 spectators in Tokyo's Meiji Stadium, Foxx hit a ball which he claimed was the longest hit of his career. It was, out of the stadium and observers and newsmen estimate that it travelled at least 600 feet. It was reported that even Ruth and Gehrig were amazed at this blast from Foxx's bat.[74]

In these exhibition games Foxx went to bat sixty-nine times and had eighteen hits, seven of which were home runs; his batting average was .286. Gehrig hit .314 with six home runs and Ruth led all hitters with .408 and thirteen home runs.[75] *The Sporting News* reported that the Japanese were impressed by Jimmie's versatility. The affable slugger was also popular with the fans. He and Helen were given numerous gifts and souvenirs. When they returned home it required two large bags to contain the presents they had been given. Included among the gifts were "exquisite objects of the ivory carvers art," colorful pajamas, kimonos and "silken pillows."[76]

The All-Stars left Japan on December 2, and, after brief stops in Shanghai and Manila, Foxx and most of the contingent returned to Vancouver on the "Empress of Canada," arriving on January 2, 1935. It seems that only the Gehrigs, who were recently wed, did not return at this time but continued on an around-the-world trip.[77] The baseball tour was considered a successful public relations affair for both the sport and diplomacy. Bill Dooley, columnist for the Philadelphia *Record*, declared that the tour to Japan "did more to cement friendship between the United States and Japan than all of the windy platitudes of politicians." The expenses of all the players and their wives were paid by the sponsors and it was reported that John Shibe "made a little money on the venture."[78]

One aspect of the 1934 expedition which was later the subject of considerable interest was the role of Moe Berg, a catcher for the Cleveland Indians. Berg was a competent catcher but certainly not of All-Star quality. However, he was familiar with Japan, having served as an instructor there in 1932 and was fluent in the Japanese language. He served as interpreter for Connie Mack and others in the American delegation. It appears that on this trip Berg was also serving as an intelligence agent for the United States government. On one occasion, disguised as a Japanese citizen wearing a large flowing garment, he entered a hospital, ostensibly to visit the wife of a friend. He went to the top of the hospital, one of the taller buildings in Tokyo, took pictures of the city from as many different vantage points as possible, and then returned to his hotel room. It was claimed that these pictures were later very valuable in assisting Major General James H. Doolittle and American airmen when they conducted the first Allied air raid on Tokyo on April 18, 1942. This 1934 excursion to Japan was the last appearance of American baseball players in that country until 1949.[79]

Several years later Berg and Foxx would be teammates with the Red Sox and for a time they roomed together on road trips. It might seem that these two men would be the most unlikely pair to room together. Berg was a graduate of Princeton University, had studied at the Sorbonne, had a law degree from Columbia, was fluent in six languages, and wrote a Ph.D. dissertation on the Sanskrit language; Foxx was a farm boy who never finished high school. Each, however, had a common and lasting interest—baseball. One reporter who covered the Red Sox was intrigued by the idea of the scholar and the farm boy being roommates and declared that to hear Foxx and Berg converse about the game of baseball "one would never know who had the Ph.D. and who never finished high school."[80] On matters pertaining to baseball Jimmie was articulate and knowledgeable.

When the players returned from the Orient the *Philadelphia Inquirer* welcomed Foxx and his wife and reported that Jimmie seemed to have no ill effects from the beaning he experienced in October. It was also noted that he would "rest up" a while before going to Florida, and Jimmie and Helen returned to their home in Margate City, New Jersey. One day in mid–January he was a guest of one of the prosecutors at the trial of Bruno Hauptman, the accused kidnapper of Charles Lindbergh's son. This trial, which received tremendous publicity and national press coverage, was held in Flemington, New Jersey, and attracted many "celebrities."

On January 23 Foxx had an appointment with Dr. Herbert Goddard, a nose and throat specialist in Philadelphia, to have a tonsillectomy and to correct a troublesome nasal obstruction which was "interfering with his normal breathing." The operations were performed in Goddard's office, and although Jimmie did not enter a hospital, he was confined to his room at the Drake Hotel for about a week and was under the care and observation of his physician. An account of the operations by Ray Bell in the *Philadelphia Evening Bulletin* indicates that Jimmie was conscious throughout the operations, since he was given only a local anaesthetic. The tonsillectomy was completed in less than two minutes, while it required twelve minutes for the physician to chip "several large pieces of bone from Foxx's nose." Following the operations Jimmie was placed in bed in the doctor's office where he remained for some time before he returned to his hotel.[81]

Jimmie remained in Philadelphia for a little more than a week, returned to his home, then departed for Miami, where he served as an instructor for three weeks in Max Carey's baseball school. For fifteen years, from 1910–1925, Carey was an outfielder for the Pirates. In 1926 he went to Brooklyn; he managed the Dodgers his last two years in the major leagues, 1932 and 1933. This was Carey's first year of operating a baseball instructional camp for youngsters. The camp opened with seventy boys, but within a couple of days the enrollment increased to ninety-six. Instructions included lectures and demonstrations by various major league performers. The camp was in operation for five weeks and Jimmie's association with it was during the first three weeks. During the course of the camp, instructors included Foxx, Paul Waner of the Pirates, and Hank Greenberg and Jo Jo White of the Tigers.[82]

Jimmie interrupted his stint at Carey's baseball school in mid–February to attend, as an invited guest, a banquet of the New York chapter of the Baseball Writers Association of America. Among the other guests were Tom Shibe, president of the Athletics, and manager Connie Mack. Foxx remained in

Miami with Carey's school until he reported to the Athletics training camp on March 1. In addition to his instructional duties in the school he had played much golf, exercised daily, and often went swimming. This year Jimmie was more relaxed and in a better frame of mind than the year before, when he was a hold-out and was involved in negotiations with Mack over salary terms. He was satisfied with his three-year contract, signed in 1934, and he reported to camp "fit and ready to go."[83]

Despite the fact that Foxx was seemingly in good health and at the peak of physical condition there was much speculation in the press and among his peers about how shifting from first base to catching would affect his performance in 1935. Cy Peterman, a sport columnist for the *Philadelphia Evening Bulletin,* viewed the shift to catching as an excellent move and as one that would "transform the team." Foxx, he explained, "knows more about baseball than most players," and he had experience as a catcher; "players respect his judgment more than anyone on the team," and he also had the confidence and "implicit faith" of manager Mack. Others were not as optimistic about Mack's change. For example, it was noted that Foxx had "done practically no catching" since 1927 and that he was a very good first baseman. The eight-year layoff from catching, it was feared, would render Jimmie liable to injuries such as split fingers or jammed thumbs.[84] William C. Duncan, in a story in *The Sporting News,* was convinced that Mack was making a serious mistake in shifting Foxx to catching. He declared that catching would have an adverse effect on Jimmie's hitting because "catching saps one's strength" and places greater "tax on one's arms and legs." He believed that Mack should have acquired someone else to catch and left Foxx at first base "where he had developed into a finished performer." Among Jimmie's peers who voiced concern about his shift in positions was player-manager Bill Terry of the Giants and Giants catcher Gus Mancuso. Terry, a first baseman, said Mack was making a mistake in moving Jimmie to catching. He declared "it will hurt his hitting," and he predicted Foxx would "get hurt." Mancuso seconded Terry's views, noting that catching was more demanding than playing first base.[85]

Foxx was keenly aware of the press comments concerning his move from first to catcher. He was persuaded, however, that the shift "was best for the team," and he expressed the hope that Mack would "find a catcher" and that the change would be for only one season. He was aware that fans would have a tendency to compare him to Mickey Cochrane, one of the great catchers. He told one reporter that he was "going to do his best for Connie and the club" but admitted, "I'll be no second Cochrane, but I'll give it everything I have in 1935."[86] Perhaps the speculation concerning the ill effects catching might have on Jimmie's hitting prompted Connie Mack to sign, before the end of February, the veteran catcher Charley Berry as a back-up and possible replacement for Foxx in the event Jimmie became injured.[87]

There were two Foxxes at the Athletics spring camp in 1935. The other was Jimmie's nineteen-year-old brother, Sammy Dell. Sammy was a left-handed pitcher who had played semipro baseball on the Eastern Shore the past two seasons. He was a large youngster, standing 5'11" and weighing approximately 195 pounds. Jimmie had suggested that Connie Mack take a look at him, and the manager had invited Sammy for a tryout. *The Sporting News* reported that he worked a few innings in several games during March and showed "a lot of stuff, including a fast ball." However, doubt was expressed that he would "make the grade with the Athletics this year."[88] Sammy did not "make the grade"; he was not offered a contract and apparently abandoned any interest in pursuing a career in professional baseball.

Throughout the spring exhibition season Jimmie performed diligently as catcher. The rookie, Alexander Hooks, whom Mack had acquired from Tulsa, where he hit .340 last season was at first. By the end of the Grapefruit League season Mack was proclaiming the experiment with Jimmie a success. He told one reporter that Foxx was "brilliant behind the bat" and that his expert handling of pitchers would "make the Athletics a pennant contender this year." He asserted that Jimmie's leadership as team captain and catcher was "superb" and that his spirit and commitment would "appreciably improve the entire team."[89]

The 1935 season opened with Foxx behind the bat and he hit safely in the first eight games. In games at Washington he hit two long home runs into the left center stands, the "deepest portion" of Griffith Stadium. It was also reported that Foxx was "catching as if that were the only position he ever played." By May 9 he was hitting .386, second only to Hornsby's league-leading .390. In a game at Cleveland on May 4 he equalled a major league record for the second time in his career when he scored five runs in a single game. During the first week of May Pinky Higgins, the Athletics' third baseman, sprained his right ankle and Mack moved Foxx to third and put Berry behind the plate. After a few days Higgins returned to third and Jimmie went back to catching.[90] By the end of May Foxx was hitting .399, but the rookie first baseman was having a problem—he was hitting only .227. The first week in June Mack moved Berry to catching and sent Foxx back to first base where he remained for the rest of the season. By late June Jimmie was hitting .350 and "was playing the best ball of his career at first." However, the Athletics were floundering and had fallen to the second division in American League standings.[91]

The annual All-Star game was played at Cleveland in 1935. This year the rival managers, Cochrane and Frisch, selected team participants. Permitting managers to choose the squads was an aberration and after this one game the selection of team members was returned to the fans.[92] The game was played on July 8, and manager Cochrane chose his former roommate, Jimmie Foxx, to play third base. A record attendance of 72,000 witnessed the game, which for all practical purposes was won in the first inning. When the American

League stars came to bat, the first two hitters were outs, then Lou Gehrig walked. This brought Foxx to the plate. The count reached three and two when the National League catcher called for a curve. Gordon Cobbledick, sports editor of the *Cleveland Plain Dealer*, described what happened next. "It was a sweeping curve that southpaw Bill Walker threw." It "broke over the heart of the plate, waist high." "Almost leisurely," he wrote, Foxx's "powerful arms came around for the swing. Two hundred pounds of brawn pivoted on a pair of stocky legs and—crack! Almost as one, the 72,000 leaped to their feet ... Arching slightly as it flew toward left field, the ball carried some 340 feet into the tenth row of the stands."[93] The final run in the American League's 4-1 victory came in the fifth inning when Cleveland outfielder Joe Vosmik singled and came home on a drive through the infield and over second base by Foxx. Jimmie's final time at bat was in the ninth when Dizzy Dean was pitching for the Nationals. Trying to be too careful with the "Margate Mauler," as one scribe referred to Foxx, Dean walked Jimmie. Foxx's "cousin" Lefty Gomez of the Yankees received credit for the third consecutive American League win in the All-Star contests.[94]

Although Jimmie was referred to as the "Margate Mauler" by the press at the All-Star game, he and the family had moved from this New Jersey town and at the time their residence was 474 Kenwood Road in Drexel Park, Pennsylvania, a suburb of Philadelphia.[95]

Foxx experienced a hitting slump following the All-Star game, and by mid–August he was hitting .327 with nineteen home runs.[96] It was during this time that team captain Foxx had his first experience at managing a team. On July 12 Connie Mack had to go to Harrisburg for a hearing before the pardoning board and testify on behalf of one of his former players. Mack turned direction of the team over to Foxx, and Jimmie was manager for a day, in a game with the St. Louis Browns. He selected George Bleaholder to pitch for the Athletics, and Bleaholder responded by blanking the Browns 9-0. Foxx went three for four in this contest, all singles.[97] Since this would be the only major league game Foxx would ever manage, his record as a major league manager is 1.000. There was some speculation that by making Foxx team captain and permitting him to direct the team when he was absent, Mack was grooming Jimmie for a manager's position, possibly a future manager of the Athletics. Two of Mack's former stars, Jimmy Dykes and Mickey Cochrane, were now successful major league managers with the White Sox and Tigers. Some thought Jimmie would possibly be the next to assume managerial responsibilities. It soon became obvious that Mack never considered such a position for his first baseman.[98]

During the first half of the season, baseball witnessed the end of an era. On June 2, 1935, Babe Ruth announced his retirement from the game. Ruth had been released by the Yankees earlier in the year, and a short while later was signed by the Boston Braves to a three-year contract as assistant manager.

Ruth was disappointed that no one in major league baseball offered him the opportunity to manage, and he refused to consider a position in the minor leagues. After a rather unspectacular spring with the Braves, but following one last glorious game at Pittsburgh where he hit three home runs, the Babe announced that he was through.[99]

In the summer of 1935 baseball owners made a modification in the playing area. This change did not interfere with the game but was a safety measure for outfielders. George Selkirk, an outfielder with the Yankees, suggested that if a five- or six-foot cinder path were installed in front of the outfield walls or fences, it would warn players pursuing fly balls and prevent them from colliding with the wall and injuring themselves. The suggestion of Selkirk received a favorable response from club officials, and in a short time "warning tracks" were installed in all parks.[100]

An exhibition game which the Athletics played against Bridgeton, New Jersey, on July 29, afforded Foxx the opportunity to demonstrate his versatility as a baseball player. Everyone knew Foxx was competent as a catcher, first baseman, third baseman and outfielder. Some knew that in barnstorming games and during the 1934 post-season tour of Japan that Jimmie had occasionally taken the mound and pitched several innings and that he had a good curve and a rather lively fast ball. In the game against Bridgeton Mack permitted Jimmie to pitch the ninth inning. He struck out two batters and allowed one run to score in a game that the Athletics won 8-3.[101]

Throughout July and August the Athletics were struggling to stay in fifth or sixth place. Their chances, however, for such a modest position received a setback on August 28. In a game with the Tigers Foxx was involved in a collision at first base with the Tiger outfielder, Pete Fox, bruised his right shoulder, and had to leave the game. He was replaced by Lou Finney, and although Jimmie was out of the lineup for only a few games, his shoulder remained sore and this affected his swing. Despite this injury, Foxx soon returned and continued to play. In a doubleheader against the pennant-winning Tigers on September 7, Foxx played the role of spoiler in the second game. In this contest, which the Athletics lost, Jimmie ended Eldon Auker's no-hit bid with a double in the eighth inning.[102]

As the Athletics fell to last place in the American League, Connie Mack became despondent and berated the team for its "lack of hustle." *The Sporting News*, in noting that this was the first time the Athletics had finished last since 1921, seemed to agree with Mack. It reported that the team had "no one to blame but themselves" for their poor showing.[103]

Foxx ended the miserable 1935 season with a better record than the Athletics. He hit .346, had thirty-six home runs, and batted in 115 runs; his fielding average was .997.[104] Jimmie tied Hank Greenberg of the Tigers for home run honors with thirty-six. In his autobiography, published in 1989, Greenberg attributed Foxx's depriving him of the home run crown to the anti–Semitic attitude of a certain unnamed catcher for the Washington Senators. Greenberg claims that he later learned this catcher was informing Foxx of what pitch was coming and this gave Jimmie an advantage in the home run derby and permitted Foxx to tie him.[105] Jimmie's .346 batting average placed him third in the American League in this category. Buddy Myer of the Senators won the batting title with an average of .349 and the Indians' outfielder, Joe Vosmik, was second with .348. Some years later in his book *My Turn At Bat*, Ted Williams alleged that Foxx tried to back into the batting title by sitting out the final games of the 1935 season, hoping that he would thereby edge out Myer and Vosmik. Dominic DiMaggio, in his book *Real Grass, Real Heroes*, repeated Williams' erroneous assertion.[106] A check of box scores reveals that Foxx played in the closing games of the 1935 season. In the final game of the season, which was in Washington and the Senators won 11-8, Foxx was three for four, with two home runs and four runs batted in. Meyer was four for five in this game.[107] To imply that Foxx was trying to win the batting title by "sitting on his average" is incorrect and casts aspersions on one of the game's greatest hitters.

The 1935 season witnessed the inauguration of night baseball in the major leagues. Experimental night games date back to the 1880s; however, the first league of organized professional baseball to adopt the practice was the Western Association in 1930.[108] Within the next several years night baseball was introduced into other minor league cities. In 1932 Indianapolis and Columbus, Ohio, of the American Association installed lights and began night baseball in that league. At this time Larry MacPhail was the general manager of the Columbus Red Birds. A short time later, when he became general manager of the Cincinnati Reds, he was eager to have night games in that city. Powell Crosley, the team owner, approved of the idea and MacPhail then sought permission from the National League to install lights and inaugurate night baseball in Cincinnati. At the winter meeting of the National League owners and executives in December, 1934, MacPhail and the Reds were able to persuade the league to allow them to play seven games under the lights; this would be one home game with each of the other teams in the league.[109] Although the National League owners were almost unanimous (there was one abstention) in approving the proposal to permit the Reds to play at night, American League owners scoffed at the idea and refused to even discuss it at their meeting. Connie Mack, on one occasion, referred to night baseball as "only a fad," and Clark Griffith of the Senators declared that night baseball was "bush league" and "just a step above dog racing." He was of the opinion that "high class" baseball could not be played under lights and expressed the conviction that baseball was made to be played in the fresh air and sunshine. Others were convinced that night baseball would contribute to player injuries and adversely affect the performance of all players. *The Sporting News* asserted that baseball should not be "treated as a novelty" and that the game "needs no outside attraction" such as arc lights. Baseball, the editor affirmed, was a sport for "the sunlight."[110]

After receiving approval of the National League executives, lights were installed at Crosley Field in Cincinnati, and the first night baseball game in the major leagues was played on May 24, 1935, between the Reds and the Phillies. More than 20,000 fans, about ten times the regular attendance at Reds' games, were present when President Franklin D. Roosevelt, in Washington, D.C., pressed a switch to illuminate the park. It was an exciting game which the Reds won 2-1.[111] From its beginning, night baseball was a popular and successful feature in Cincinnati. The seven night games drew more than 130,000 fans, a greater attendance, *The Sporting News* reported, than several clubs drew for the entire season.[112] The acceptance of night baseball by other owners was not immediate and, for example, did not occur in New York until 1938 when MacPhail was general manager of the Dodgers. He persuaded club officials that night baseball would be as popular in Brooklyn as it was in Cincinnati. Lights were installed at Ebbets Field, and the first night game for the Dodgers was on June 15, 1938, against the Reds. The game was a sellout, and the fans witnessed one of the most spectacular feats in baseball. The Reds' Johnny Vander Meer pitched his second consecutive no-hit game; four days earlier he had no-hit the Boston Braves.[113]

With the proven success of night baseball in Cincinnati and Brooklyn other owners modified their views concerning the practice. The American League, which earlier had opposed night baseball, voted at their winter meeting in 1937 to permit teams to schedule night games but limited such contests to seven per club. By this time Connie Mack had become more sympathetic to night baseball, and his neighbors, the Phillies, were eager for the installation of lights in Shibe Park. Together the two teams cooperated; lights were installed, and in 1939 the first night game in the American League was played in Philadelphia on May 16. The Athletics lost this game to the Indians 8-3. Other teams followed suit and by 1941 nine of the sixteen major league ball parks had installed lights. By this time even *The Sporting News* was supporting night baseball. In one editorial it castigated those owners who continued to refuse to install lights. The editor declared that night games were the "answer to attendance problems" and asserted that "only the blind, stubborn, and bull-headed continue to hold out against" night baseball.[114] Although a majority of clubs had installed lights by 1941, league officials continued to limit the number of nocturnal contests to seven home games a season.[115]

After the conclusion of the major league season in October 1935, the barnstorming season began for a number of players. Barnstorming was allowed from the close of the season until early November, and it afforded players an opportunity to earn extra money and also to experience a different environment. Dizzy Dean, for example, claimed that he earned over $19,000 from barnstorming games in the early- and mid-thirties.[116] In 1935 one barnstorming contingent was organized and supervised by Earl Mack, an executive for the Athletics. Designated the American League All-Stars, this group consisted of players from a variety of clubs. Among these All-Stars were Foxx, Higgins, Eric McNair, and Charlie Berry of the Athletics; Rogers Hornsby, manager of the Browns, was named manager of the team. In September, after all arrangements were made, it was reported that this group would play several exhibition games against Texas League players as they journeyed to Mexico. In Mexico they would play a series of games against a contingent of Mexican All-Stars.[117] As on the 1934 tour to Japan, it was noted that player wives would accompany the team to Mexico. However, it seems that Helen did not accompany Jimmie to Mexico.

Most of the All-Stars departed for Mexico City from St. Louis on the Missouri Pacific train. Three games were scheduled for cities in Texas and in Monterey, Mexico, prior to the team's arrival in Mexico City.[118] Foxx, however, did not leave with the group; he attended some of the World Series games between the Cubs and Tigers and on one occasion was the guest of the golfer Walter Hagen. He also participated in a Masonic charity benefit game in Trenton, New Jersey (Foxx was a member of the Trenton Masonic lodge), before leaving Philadelphia to join his teammates in Mexico. After the benefit appearance Foxx flew to Mexico City. The report of his flight to Mexico made no mention of his wife; she probably remained at their new residence in Drexel Park with Jimmie Junior.[119]

The American League All-Stars played seven games against the Mexican All-Stars, or Aztecs as they were called in the press. Games were held in Mexico City and several towns in the nearby area. At the opening game United States Ambassador to Mexico Josephus Daniels was present and threw out the first pitch. The Americans lost only one game in the series and attendance at each contest ranged from 10,000 to 13,000.[120] Foxx played at various positions in these contests; in two of the games he appeared as a pitcher, going five innings on one occasion. He was also charged with the one loss suffered by the American Leaguers. In other games he participated as first baseman, third baseman and catcher. For the series Jimmie hit only .200, including two home runs.[121] While Earl Mack's contingent was in Mexico City a group of Negro League barnstormers, principally the Pittsburgh Crawfords, arrived there for several exhibition games with the Mexicans. A three-game series between the Crawfords and the American League All-Stars was arranged. These contests were played the last two of days of October. The first one ended after eleven innings in a 6-6 tie. The American Leaguers won the remaining games 11-1 and 7-2. In the games against the Crawfords Foxx was two for four; one of his hits was a double. *The Sporting News* reported that Foxx and Hornsby were the "most popular" players of the American League group and declared that these two were "besieged" at every game by autograph seekers.[122]

Mack and others termed the Mexican trip "a success." They were impressed by the interest of Mexicans in baseball and declared that the game was "growing in popularity" there. Hornsby expressed the opinion "that baseball has a great future in Mexico," but he added that their "facilities need improving."[123] It might be noted that Mack's All-Stars were one of two major league contingents to visit Latin American areas in the fall of 1935. At the same time the American Leaguers were in Mexico, Branch Rickey of the Cardinals was shepherding a collection of National League players to Cuba for a series of exhibition games.[124]

By the end of the Athletics' dismal season, rumors were rife that Foxx and possibly Pinky Higgins and outfielder Roger "Doc" Cramer were going to be sold. One rumor had Jimmie going to the White Sox, but most of the speculation had him going to Boston. As usual Connie Mack denied all rumors concerning Foxx and declared he did not think he would make a single off-season deal.[125] During the same time that the press was speculating about where Foxx would play next season, Jimmie was the featured speaker at the Lackawana County Sporting Legion banquet. At this occasion, held on December 3, Foxx entertained the audience by talking about his experiences in Japan the year before. A reporter present at the banquet declared that at no time did Foxx intimate that he would not be with the Athletics next season. Publicly Mack remained silent or denied all rumors concerning the sale of Foxx. However, during these weeks he informed Jimmie that he would be leaving Philadelphia before the 1936 season.[126]

On December 10, 1935, the *Philadelphia Inquirer* and the *Boston Globe* announced, simultaneously, that the Red Sox had acquired Foxx and pitcher Johnny Marcum from the Athletics for an estimated $250,000.00. With the sale of Foxx, the last member of Mack's 1929 and 1930 championship teams left Philadelphia. Although Jimmie said that he "was sorry to be leaving Philadelphia," he told a reporter for the *Boston Globe* that there was no other city "to which I'd rather go than Boston." At the same time he mentioned that although he was presently under a three-year contract, he expected Yawkey and general manager Eddie Collins to make some adjustments in his contract, since he would be giving up "other interests in Philadelphia which increased his income." These other interests included serving as an occasional commentator on a radio sports broadcast, which paid him $2,000.00 a year. A week after Christmas Foxx was in New York and while there he talked with Yawkey about a contract for the coming season. Several days later it was reported that Jimmie had signed a one-year contract with the Red Sox for $25,000.00, a $7,000.00 increase over his 1935 salary. This would more than compensate him for the loss of radio income which he was giving up.[127]

On the same day that the press announced the sale of Foxx to the Red Sox, there appeared in the *Boston American* the first of twelve articles, which were obviously designed to introduce Foxx to the fans and others of the Boston area. The first article appeared on December 10 and the last one on December

22; they appeared under the byline of Jimmie Foxx as told to Austen Lake, the sports editor of the *American*. Lake described the series as "telling the story of the rise and success of the slugging baseball star." The articles condensed much of the contents of Jimmie's book, *How I Bat*, but several of them also presented considerable biographical data on Jimmie.

When it was announced that Jimmie was going to Boston, Red Sox manager Joe Cronin was "delighted that Foxx was coming to Boston" and said that his addition to the Red Sox lineup would make them "a real contender for the American League pennant." After the Christmas holidays Foxx went to Boston where he was the guest of honor at two functions. One of these was an "elaborate welcome to Boston" for Foxx, given by the Red Sox and held at the team's headquarters. This affair "lasted from early noon until well along toward evening." That evening Jimmie was the honored guest at the annual father-son banquet given by the Temple Ohalia Shalom Brotherhood, which was attended by approximately two thousand persons. Foxx, Eddie Collins, Bob McQuinn, and others were present. Collins introduced Jimmie, who spoke briefly, telling stories about his trip to Japan and "trying not to openly predict great things for the Red Sox." It was reported that Jimmie received a warm and cordial welcome from everyone he met in Boston. After this visit Foxx returned to his home in Drexel Park to relax before heading for Miami to again serve as an instructor in Max Carey's baseball school.[128]

Notes

1. Assorted clippings, February 19, 1933, in Dell Foxx scrapbook #1; assorted clippings, Nanci Canaday item; Lowell Reidenbaugh, *Cooperstown, Where Baseball's Legends Live Forever* (St. Louis: The Sporting News, 1983), p. 83.

2. *The Sporting News*, May 25, 1933.

3. *Ibid.*, February 4, 11, 1933.

4. *Philadelphia Evening Bulletin*, March 27, 1933; *The Sporting News*, April 6, 1933.

5. *Philadelphia Evening Bulletin*, April 10, 1933; *The Sporting News*, April 20, 1933.

6. *The Sporting News*, April 27, 1933.

7. *Ibid.*, January 1, 1933; *Philadelphia Evening Bulletin*, May 27, 1933.

8. *Philadelphia Evening Bulletin*, May 26, 1933.

9. Charles C. Alexander, *Our Game, an American Baseball History* (New York: Henry Holt and Company, 1991), p. 185.

10. Robert Gregory, *Diz: Dizzy Dean and Baseball During the Great Depression* (New York: Viking, 1992), p. 98; *The Sporting News*. April 17, 1933.

11. *Philadelphia Inquirer*, June 12, 1933; *The Sporting News*, July 6, 1933.

12. *The Sporting News*, April 14, 1931, June 1, 1933; Lee Lowenfish and Tony Lupien, *The Imperfect Diamond: The Story of Baseball's Reserve System and the Men Who Fought to Change It* (New York: Stein and Day, 1980), pp. 107-108; Harold

Seymour, *Baseball, The Golden Age* (New York: Oxford University Press, 1971), p. 393.

13. Peter Levine, editor, *Baseball History, an Annual of Original Baseball Research* (Westport, Conn.: Meckler Books, 1989), p. 55; James Charlton, editor, *The Baseball Chronology* (New York: Macmillan, 1991), p. 228.

14. *The Sporting News,* July 13, 1933.

15. *The Sporting News,* July 20, August 3, 1933.

16. *Ibid.,* August 24, 1933.

17. *Philadelphia Inquirer,* July 2, August 14, 1933; *The Sporting News,* December 7, 1933; Charlton, ed., *Baseball Chronology,* p. 272.

18. *The Sporting News,* October 5, 1933, January 4, 1934.

19. *Philadelphia Inquirer,* May 23, November 15, 1933.

20. *The Sporting News,* August 24, November 9, December 21, 1933.

21. Assorted clippings, October 12, 26, 1933, in Foxx files, Baseball Library, Cooperstown, New York; *Philadelphia Evening Bulletin,* October 19, 1933; *The Sporting News,* November 2, 1933.

22. *Philadelphia Evening Bulletin,* November 4, 1933.

23. *The Sporting News,* November 16, 1933.

24. *Ibid.*

25. Jimmie Foxx, *How I Bat* (New York: Courier-Citizen Publishing Company, 1933), pp. 5, 7.

26. *Ibid.,* pp. 10, 15.

27. *Ibid.,* p. 23.

28. *Ibid.,* p. 37.

29. *Ibid.,* pp. 46–47.

30. *The Sporting News,* January 18, February 15, 1934.

31. *Ibid.,* February 22, 1934.

32. *Philadelphia Inquirer,* February 24, 1934.

33. *The Sporting News,* January 18, February 22, March 8, 15, 29, 1934; assorted clippings, March 8, 1934 in Foxx files, Baseball Library,Cooperstown, New York.

34. Alexander, *Our Game,* p. 25; William Curran, *Big Sticks: The Batting Revolution of the Twenties* (New York: William Morrow and Co., Inc., 1990), pp. 39–40; David Quentin Voigt, *American Baseball,* 3 volumes (Norman: University of Oklahoma Press, 1966–1983), II, pp. 88, 166; *The Sporting News,* October 30, December 1, 1929.

35. *The Sporting News,* August 26, November 4, 1926.

36. *Ibid.,* July 29, August 26, 1926, November 15, 1928.

37. Bruce Kuklick, *To Every Thing a Season: Shibe Park and Urban Philadelphia, 1909–1976* (Princeton: Princeton University Press, 1991), p. 72.

38. *Ibid.,* p. 71; *The Sporting News,* February 12, 1931, November 16, 1933; Charlton, ed., *Baseball Chronology,* p. 277.

39. Kuklick, *To Every Thing a Season,* p.72.

40. *The Sporting News,* April 19, 26, 1934.

41. Assorted clippings, May 19, 1934, in Foxx files, Baseball Library, Cooperstown, New York.

42. *The Sporting News,* July 5, 19, 1934.

43. *Philadelphia Inquirer*, July 2, 1934.

44. Charlton, ed., *Baseball Chronology*, p. 280.

45. *The Sporting News*, September 13, December 6, 1934.

46. *Ibid.*, March 29, September 6, 20, 1934.

47. *Ibid.*, October 11, 1934; *Philadelphia Inquirer*, October 2, 1934; Frank C. Lane, "The Greatest Individual Punch in the American League," in *Baseball Magazine* (March, 1934), pp. 437-39.

48. A. H. Tarvin, "The Origin of 'Ladies Day,'" in *Baseball Magazine* (July, 1934), pp. 368-69; James Crusinberry, "Women Fans and Their Effect on the Game," *Baseball Magazine* (November, 1949), p. 405; Bob Broeg and William J. Miller, Jr., *Baseball from a Different Angle* (South Bend, Ind.: Diamond Communications, Inc., 1988) p.10; *The Sporting News*, February 27, 1930; David Q. Voigt, "Sex in Baseball: Reflections of Changing Taboos," in *Journal of American Culture* (Winter, 1978), pp. 392-93.

49. *The Sporting News*, May 17, 1934.

50. Al Rainovic, "Baseball's First Radio Broadcast" in *Newsletter National Baseball Hall of Fame and Museum* (July, 1984); Nick Curran, "How World Series Broadcasts Were Started in 1922," in *Baseball Digest* (October, 1964), pp. 47-49.

51. Voigt, *American Baseball*, II, p. 147; Gregory, *Diz ...*, p. 208.

52. Red Barber, *The Broadcasters* (New York: The Dial Press, 1970), p. 89; Alexander, *Our Game*, p. 140; N.J. Abodaher, "Baseball via the Ether Waves," in *Baseball Magazine* (November, 1929), p. 551.

53. Abodaher, "Baseball via the Ether Waves," p. 551.

54. For example, see: Harry Hartman, "In Defense of Baseball by Radio," *Baseball Magazine* (October, 1930), p. 506.

55. James M. Gould, "Is the Radio Good for Baseball?," *Baseball Magazine* (July, 1930), p. 341.

56. *The Sporting News*, August 29, 1929, December 17, 1931.

57. Barber, *The Broadcasters*, p. 93, 127; *The Sporting News*, September 1, 1932.

58. Barber, *The Broadcasters*, p. 51.

59. Red Barber and Robert Creamer, *Rhubarb in the Catbird Seat* (Garden City: Doubleday and Company, 1968), p. 32.

60. Barber, *The Broadcasters*, p. 177.

61. *Ibid.*, pp. 8, 126; *The Sporting News*, February 23, 1933; Richard Goldstein, *Spartan Seasons, How Baseball Survived the Second World War* (New York: Macmillan, 1980), p. 277.

62. Don Warfield, *The Roaring Redhead, Larry MacPhail—Baseball's Great Innovator* (South Bend, Ind.: Diamond Communications, Inc., 1987), p. 139; Charleton, ed., *Baseball Chronology*, p. 315.

63. David Q. Voigt, *America Through Baseball* (Chicago: Nelson-Hall, 1976), p. 94f; Sid Mercer, "Foreign Tours Date back to '74," in *Baseball Digest* (November, 1943), p. 21; Arthur Bartless, *Baseball and Mr. Spalding, The History and Romance of Baseball* (New York: Farrar, Strauss and Young, 1951), p. 59f; Donald Roden, "Baseball and the Quest for National Dignity in Meiji Japan," *American Historical Review* (June, 1980), p. 512.

64. Robert Whiting, *You Gotta Have Wa* (New York: Vintage Books, c. 1990), pp. 27-29; Roden, "Baseball and the Quest ...," pp. 518-20.

65. Robert Obojski, *The Rise of Japanese Baseball Power* (Radnor, Penn.: Chilton Book Company, c. 1975), pp. 3, 8, 12; Whiting, *You Gotta Have Wa*, pp. 34, 39; Voigt, *America Through Baseball*, p. 96.

66. Obojski, *The Rise of Japanese* ... , pp. 17, 19; Whiting, *You Gotta Have Wa*, pp. 43-44, 46; Louis Kaufman, Barbara Fitzgerald, Tom Sewell, *Moe Berg: Athlete, Scholar, Spy* (Boston: Little Brown and Company, 1974), p. 5

67. *The Sporting News*, December 28, 1933, August 30, 1934.

68. *Philadelphia Inquirer*, October 17, 1934.

69. John B. Holway, *Black Diamonds, Life in the Negro Leagues from the Men Who Lived It* (Westport, Conn.: Meckler Books, 1989), p. 19.

70. *Philadelphia Evening Bulletin*, October 12, 1934; *Winnipeg Free Press*, October 11, 12, 1934.

71. *Winnipeg Free Press*, October 12, 15, 1934; *Philadelphia Evening Bulletin*, October 12, 1934; Obojski, *The Rise of Japanese* ..., p. 23.

72. *Philadelphia Evening Bulletin*, January 28, 1951; *The Society for American Baseball Research Bulletin* (March, 1993), p. 6.

73. Eleanor Gehrig and Joseph Duros, *My Luke and I* (New York: Thomas Y. Crowell Company, 1976), pp. 192-95; Whiting, *You Gotta Have Wa*, p. 42; *The Sporting News*, December 6, 1934; Charlton, ed., *Baseball Chronology*, p. 282.

74. Assorted clippings, November 22, 1934, in Foxx files, Baseball Library, Cooperstown, New York; assorted clippings, March 28, 1984 in Dell Foxx Scrapbook #2; Obojski, *The Rise of Japanese* ..., p. 24; *Philadelphia Inquirer*, June 21, 1970; *The Sporting News*, February 7, 1935; Charles Einstein, editor, *The Second Fireside Book of Baseball* (New York: Simon and Schuster, 1958), p. 202.

75. Obojski, *The Rise of Japanese* ..., p. 26.

76. *The Sporting News*, January 17, February 7, 1935.

77. Gehrig and Durso, *My Luke and I*, p. 192.

78. *The Sporting News*, January 17, 1935.

79. Kaufman et al., *Moe Berg*, pp. 83-84; Obojski, *The Rise of Japanese* ..., p. 29.

80. Dom DiMaggio with Bill Gilbert, *Real Grass, Real Heroes: Baseball's Historic 1941 Season* (New York: Kensington Publishing Corporation, 1990), p. 97; undated Foxx Files, *Boston Herald*.

81 *Philadelphia Inquirer*, January 15, 1935; *Philadelphia Evening Bulletin*, January 16, 24, 1935.

82. *Philadelphia Inquirer*, February 7, 8, 1935; assorted clippings, February 18, 1935, in Foxx files, Baseball Library, Cooperstown, New York; *The Sporting News*, March 7, 1935.

83. *The Sporting News*, February 14, March 7, 21, 1935.

84. *Philadelphia Evening Bulletin*, January 31, 1935; assorted clippings, January, 1935, in Foxx files, Baseball Library, Cooperstown, New York.

85. *The Sporting News*, February 7, 1935; assorted clippings, March 9, 1935, in Foxx files, Baseball Library, Cooperstown, New York.

86. *The Sporting News*, February 7, 1935.

87. *Ibid.*, February 14, 1935.

88. *Ibid.*, February 1, 22, March 3, 21, 1935.

89. *Ibid.*, March 7, 21, 28, 1935.

90. *Ibid.*, April 25, May 9, 16, 1935.

91. *Ibid.*, June 20, 1935; *Richmond, Virginia News-Leader*, June 6, 1935.

92. Gregory, *Diz ...*, p. 332; *Cleveland Plain Dealer*, July 8, 1935.

93. *Cleveland Plain Dealer*, July 9, 1935.

94. *Ibid.*

95. *Ibid.*, July 7, 1935.

96. *The Sporting News*, August 15, 1935.

97. *Ibid.*, July 18, 1935.

98. See, for example, *Philadelphia Inquirer*, December 10, 1935.

99. *The Sporting News*, February 28, 1935; Charlton, ed., *Baseball Chronology*, p. 285.

100. Charlton, ed., *Baseball Chronology*, p. 285.

101. *The Sporting News*, August 1, 1935.

102. *Ibid.*, September 5, 12, 1935.

103. *Ibid.*, September 12, October 3, 1935.

104. *Ibid.*, December 19, 1935.

105. Hank Greenberg, *The Story of My Life* (New York: Times Books, 1989), p. 77.

106. Ted Williams, *My Turn at Bat: The Story of My Life* (New York: Simon and Schuster, 1969), p. 83; DiMaggio and Gilbert, *Real Grass ...*, p. 144.

107. See *Richmond, Virginia Times-Dispatch*, September 30, 1935; *New York Times*, September 22-29, 1935.

108. *The Sporting News*, April 14, 1931, January 24, 1935; Warfield, *The Roaring Redhead*, p. 57.

109. Frank C. Lane, "The Romance of Night Baseball," in *Baseball Magazine* (October, 1930), p. 483; Warfield, *The Roaring Redhead*, p. 30; *The Sporting News*, December 20, 1934.

110. *The Sporting News*, January 16, 1930, February 2, 1935; Warfield, *The Roaring Redhead*, p. 59; Levine, ed., *Baseball History ...*, p. 57.

111. *The Sporting News*, May 30, 1935; Levine, ed., *Baseball History ...*, p. 57.

112. *The Sporting News*, September 12, 1935; Larry MacPhail, "The Triumph of Arc Lights" in *Baseball Magazine* (September, 1936), pp. 445-56.

113. Warfield, *The Roaring Redhead...* , p. 72.

114. Charlton, ed., *Baseball Chronology*, pp. 282-83, 303, 304; *The Sporting News*, July 6, 1939.

115. Kuklick, *To Every Thing a Season*, p. 76; Levine, ed., *Baseball History ...*, p. 58.

116. Gregory, *Diz ...*, p. 304.

117. *The Sporting News*, September 26, 1935.

118. *Ibid.*, October 10, 1935; assorted clippings, October 11, 1935, in Foxx files, Baseball Library, Cooperstown, New York.

119. *The Sporting News*, October 10, 1935.

120. *Ibid.*, October 31, 1935; *New York Times*, October 11, 1935.

121. *The Sporting News*, October 31, November 7, 1935.

122. *Ibid.*, October 31, November 7, 1935.

123. *Ibid.*, November 7, 14, 1935.

124. *Ibid.*, November 7, 1935.

125. See *Ibid.*, September 10, 17, 26, October 17, November 7, 1935; *Philadelphia Inquirer*, December 1, 1935.

126. *Philadelphia Inquirer*, December 4, 10, 1935; *Boston Globe*, December 10, 1935; assorted clippings, late 1935, Nanci Canaday item.

127. *Boston Globe*, December 10, 1935; *Philadelphia Inquirer*, December 11, 1935; assorted clippings, January 3, 1936, in Foxx files, Baseball Library, Cooperstown, New York; *Philadelphia Inquirer*, January 8, 1936.

128. *The Sporting News*, December 12, 16, 1935, January 2, 9, 1936; *Philadelphia Inquirer*, December 7, 1935.

Five
The Red Sox Years, 1936–1942

With the purchase of Foxx, Marcum, McNair, and Cramer in December, 1935, Tom Yawkey hoped his dream of having a championship team in Boston would soon be realized. Yawkey, a millionaire businessman whose family had baseball connections going back to the opening decade of the century, purchased the Red Sox in 1932. Since that time the press estimated that he had spent more than a million dollars for players, including $250,000.00 to Clark Griffith for his nephew-in-law, Joe Cronin, whom he purchased to manage the Red Sox.[1]

After the return of Earl Mack's All-Stars from Mexico, Foxx spent the winter with his wife and son at their home in Jenkintown. They visited relatives in Delaware and Maryland during the Christmas season, and Jimmie went on a brief hunting trip in the Sudlersville area. He worked out diligently at a Philadelphia health club, lost a few extra pounds, and sought to get in "good shape" before the Red Sox opened spring camp at Sarasota, Florida.[2] On one occasion he went to Atlantic City, where he was the honored guest at the annual All-Sport Dinner of the Atlantic City Tuna Club. On January 30, Jimmie traveled to Baltimore to attend a testimonial dinner-dance in honor of his former teammate, Max Bishop. Bishop was leaving the area to become the playing manager of the Portland, Oregon, club in the Pacific Coast League. Foxx served as toastmaster at this function, which was attended by over 400 persons and was held at the Southern Hotel. The principal speaker was Maryland's Attorney-General, Herbert O'Conner, although Harry W. Nice, Governor of Maryland, also offered a few remarks. Among Bishop's peers attending the dinner were Grove, Ed Rommel, Rube Walberg, Orioles' owner Jack Dunn, and others. After a dinner that included roast turkey, brussels sprouts, and sweet potatoes, but before the dancing began, the toastmaster took over. Jimmie praised Bishop as "a smart player" who "knows plenty of baseball," and he predicted that he would "be a successful manager." Several others also made brief comments on behalf of Bishop.[3]

97

During the first week of February Foxx suffered what was probably his first experience with sinus trouble. This condition, one assumes, was associated with his being hit in the head by a pitched ball the previous year in Winnipeg. This was the beginning of a condition which, over the years, would become increasingly worse and would be a significant factor in determining the length of Jimmie's baseball career. For several days he was under the care of a physician and was confined to his home. However, he was feeling well enough to address the Norristown Rotary Club on February 6. Three days later he was the guest at a farewell party arranged by Al Horowitz of the *Philadelphia Evening Bulletin* and a few other friends. This affair was a Sunday-night dinner held at the Ritz-Carlton Hotel in Philadelphia. A few days after the party Foxx departed for Miami, where he served again as a part-time instructor in Max Carey's baseball school.[4]

Spring training went well for Jimmie; he was in fine physical condition and his weight was down to 180 pounds. In the second exhibition game of the spring, a contest against the Reds, Foxx showed that he was ready for the season to begin. He went three for four, including a long home run. Although Foxx was eager for the season to open, he had more than baseball on his mind this spring. Helen was pregnant with their second child, and she did not accompany Jimmie to Florida. She remained home in the Philadelphia area, expecting to give birth later in the spring.[5]

When the Red Sox returned to Boston for the season opener, there was speculation in the press that this would be "a great year" for the team. Some were predicting that Foxx would break Ruth's season home-run record of sixty, and others declared Jimmie would be the difference in making Boston a pennant winner.[6] Foxx was chosen to be team captain of the Red Sox, a role he had performed for the Athletics. Cronin had him hitting cleanup, his regular and familiar position, and his uniform was number 3, the same he wore at Philadelphia. In the Red Sox opening game, against his former team, the Philadelphia Athletics, the Red Sox won 6–4; Foxx was three for five with a double and a triple.[7]

Although Jimmie was hitting .324 after the first month of the season, it was observed that he was off to a slow start. However, by the end of June he was hitting .345 and had twenty-two home runs, including perhaps the longest home run ever hit in Comiskey Park. On June 6, Foxx hit a ball that cleared a ninety-two-foot-high wall located 352 feet from home plate. The ball traveled out of the park and landed on a playground across the street from the stadium, approximately 550 feet from where Jimmie hit it.[8] Foxx's batting average increased about twenty points following the birth of his second son on May 26 at the Germantown Hospital in Philadelphia. This son, who weighed seven pounds and ten ounces, was named William Kenneth. The *Philadelphia Evening Bulletin* for that day reported that mother and son were doing well.[9]

In mid–May *The Sporting News* reported that Foxx would soon be doing radio commentary on certain sports programs as he had in Philadelphia. This, however, seems to have been a very brief activity since there was no further mention in the press of his radio program. Perhaps the Red Sox's management believed that they were paying Foxx sufficiently so that he did not need outside income and suggested that he focus his time and attention on playing the game. Jimmie was also active in public relations appearances in Boston. For example, on one occasion he, Grove, and several others devoted an off-day to visiting crippled children in the Robert Brent Brigham Hospital in Roxbury. They talked with the children, gave them autographed pictures of the Red Sox team, and signed autographs for them.[10]

The 1936 All-Star game was played on July 7 in Boston at the home park of Boston's entry in the National League, the Braves or, as the team was known from 1936 to 1941, the Bees. In the winter of 1935–36 the owners of the team, seeking a new identity for the club, dropped the nickname Braves and conducted a contest for a new moniker. The result was to change the name of the team from Braves to Bees. For the next few years the team was often referred to by the press and others by either name. In April, 1941, at a stockholders' meeting, the name Bees was abandoned and Braves again became the official name of the team.[11] Foxx was selected as a member of the American League All-Star squad. The starting pitchers were Grove and Dizzy Dean. Jimmie did not start but played the last three innings at third base. He had a single for two times at bat in a game the American League lost 4-3. Carl Hubbell was the winning pitcher in the National League's first victory in the All-Star competition.[12]

The second half of the season was an excruciating experience for those Red Sox fans who only a few months earlier had such high hopes for their team. The Yankees ran away with the pennant, and the Red Sox faithful saw their team slide from third place and begin struggling unsuccessfully with the Indians for fourth place. During this time the fans began "riding" the players, including Foxx, whose performance was improving all the while.[13] It was during these weeks of fan frustration with the Red Sox that Yawkey and the Sox set what would become a precedent for team travel. On July 30, after a game with the Browns in St. Louis, the entire team, with five exceptions who were given the option of taking the train, flew on the American Airways flagship, The Texan, to Chicago in one hour and forty minutes. Foxx was among those who flew and were enthusiastic about this method of travel.[14]

The 1936 season witnessed the appearance of two remarkable rookies in the American League, young men who would have exceptional careers and eventually enter baseball's Hall of Fame. One was Joseph Paul DiMaggio, a twenty-one-year-old outfielder for the Yankees who would hit .323, including twenty-nine home runs. The other was a seventeen-year-old pitcher for the Cleveland Indians, Robert William Andrew Feller. He made his first start on August 23 against the Browns and struck out fifteen batters.[15]

During the last month of the season the Red Sox brought up some younger players from the minors and shifted a few of the veterans from their regular positions. Foxx, who was always ready and willing to play any position, went to third for one game and to left field for sixteen games. His replacement at first was Ellsworth "Babe" Dahlgren, recently with Syracuse of the International League. Foxx continued to hit in the cleanup position and, as one observer reported, "Dahlgren will never hit hard enough to keep Foxx in the outfield."[16] The Red Sox finished the season in sixth place with seventy-four wins and eighty losses. Foxx ended the campaign with an average of .338, fifty points below the league leading mark of Luke Appling, the White Sox shortstop. Foxx had forty-one home runs, eight behind the league leader, Lou Gehrig, and one less than Hal Trotsky, first baseman for the Indians. Foxx also drove in 143 runs and set an American League record for strikeouts with 119, making this the sixth time in his career that he had led the league in this category.[17]

When the baseball season ended Jimmie returned to his family in Jenkintown. When he went to Boston in 1936 the family did not accompany him. He and Helen had recently purchased a home in the suburbs of Philadelphia, and she and the boys lived there; Jimmie rented living quarters in Boston. This would be the family arrangement throughout Jimmie's career in Boston. Helen and the two boys would live in their home in Pennsylvania where she had a maid to assist her with household chores and the children. Jimmie, Jr., would soon be placed in a boarding school at Germantown and later at Riverside Military Academy in Georgia. Foxx visited with Helen and the boys when the Red Sox came to Philadelphia, but his association with the family was limited, except during the off season.[18]

Shortly after the close of the baseball season (1936), Jimmie made a brief and unexpected return to the Eastern Shore. He and several of his Red Sox buddies were enticed there to participate in what was known locally as the "Dorchester County Baseball War." There were two semi-pro baseball teams in Cambridge, Maryland: one was sponsored by Albanus Phillips, owner of Phillips Packing Company, an establishment that featured canned vegetables. The other team was sponsored by Joe Fowler, the owner of the local Coca Cola franchise. Each autumn, after the close of the local baseball season, the "Phillips Delicious" and the "Coca Cola" teams engaged in a seven-game series to determine the Cambridge city champion. During this series it was not unusual for each team to recruit "visiting" players to assist the regulars. In 1936 the Phillips team won the first two games and this prompted Fowler to recruit some players from acquaintances in the International League. The Coca Cola team handily won the next two contests. Fowler's hiring of Triple A League players infuriated Phillips and prompted him to contact his friend, Jake Ruppert, owner of the Yankees, and seek assistance. Ruppert suggested that he telephone Jimmie Foxx, a native of the area, adding that Jimmie might be able to help him. Phillips' call to Jimmie, and his offer of $300.00 per game, elicited a favorable response and the promise to bring several others with him for the game on October 4. The Phillips lineup for that game included major leaguers Foxx, Roger Cramer, Billy Werber, Max Bishop, Frank Hayes and Jimmy DeShong. They easily defeated the Coca Cola contingent 8-2. Over 3,000 fans saw Jimmie hit a 450-foot home run over the left field fence. Phillips won the final game 2-0 and was proclaimed city champion for 1936. After participating in the Dorchester County baseball "war," Foxx and several other Red Sox players were invited by Tom Yawkey to his island estate near Charleston, South Carolina, where they were his guests for a hunting trip.[19]

Among the newspaper clippings in the Foxx files at the Baseball Library at Cooperstown, New York, is one which indicates that possibly Jimmie Foxx was unique among baseball players of his day. In September, 1936 a commercial flower breeder and grower, Stanley Johnson of Cheltenham, Pennsylvania, a suburb of Philadelphia, announced that he had produced a new and different variety of dahlia. This plant featured a large "copper-red" colored flower and was named "The Jimmie Foxx Dahlia." It was noted that in recent months this flower had won three prizes at flower shows sponsored by the American Dahlia Society.[20]

On January 3, 1937, Jimmie, his wife, and their two sons departed Philadelphia via train for Sarasota, Florida. Foxx wanted to escape the winter weather, swim, play golf, and have plenty of time to get in condition before the Red Sox's training camp opened. They took the train to Charleston, where they picked up Foxx's automobile, which he had left at Yawkey's home. One of Yawkey's employees met the Foxx family at the railroad station with Jimmie's car, and the family then drove to Sarasota.[21] Although Cronin was satisfied with Foxx's performance in 1936, Jimmie was disappointed with it and also with the overall play of the Red Sox. He was determined to "get in the very best condition possible" for the upcoming season. Regular workouts in the gym were supplemented by the daily playing of golf. Jimmie had become an avid golfer. He was introduced to this sport by some of his teammates in the late twenties, and he quickly became a patron of the game. Most of his golfing was limited to the early months of the year when he would go to Florida prior to the opening of spring training. On one occasion he was accorded recognition in the press when he made an eagle on the sixteenth hole of the Fort Myers, Florida, course. It was claimed that his was the first eagle ever recorded on that hole. In this year (1937) Jimmie participated in the professional baseball players' golf tournament, held on January 8, at Venice, Florida. The low score for this event was turned in by Rick Ferrell, a catcher for the Red Sox. Ferrell posted a 74; Jimmie shot a 78, the same score as Rick's brother, Wes. Other scores included a 79 for Paul Waner and 81 for Dizzy Dean.[22]

The weeks that Jimmie was golfing and enjoying the sun and water with his family he was also in contact with Red Sox general manager Eddie Collins concerning his 1937 contract. Earlier Foxx had refused to sign when the Sox had proposed a $5,000.00 reduction from his 1936 salary. The negotiations with Collins were amiable and were finally concluded with Foxx receiving what the press estimated was the same salary he had in 1936, $25,000.00.[23] Foxx and other baseball stars might have their incomes supplemented by endorsing certain products. Throughout this decade the R.J. Reynolds Tobacco Company obtained the endorsements of many prominent athletes from various sports for Camel cigarettes. Camel advertisements, featuring prominent sport personalities, were displayed in newspapers, on highway billboards, and heard on radio commercials. It was claimed that Camels would "settle the nerves" or give one "healthy nerves" or that they would "aid digestion" and "give one a lift." In February Foxx was featured in a Camel advertisement; Dizzy Dean, Lou Gehrig, and Carl Hubbell were among other major league players who also endorsed Camels. For such endorsements, according to Dean, each player received a fee of $250.00.[24]

During spring training the Red Sox were more relaxed than they were a year earlier. Joe Cronin, manager of the Sox, said that the team was "tight in 1936," that everyone was expecting too much from them and, he declared, "We flopped." Only Foxx and Rick Ferrell hit .300 in 1936. "This year," Cronin informed a reporter,"I really think we'll do better."[25] The optimistic sentiments of Cronin and others were darkened by the illness of Jimmie Foxx before the opening game of the season. In the last week of March Jimmie became ill, his temperature reaching 101 degrees. The team physician confined him to his hotel room and diagnosed his ailment first as the flu, but later as pneumonia. Foxx missed the closing games of the exhibition season, and Mel Almada filled in at first base for the Sox. After about ten or twelve days Jimmie seemingly had recovered, although he was weak and lethargic. When the Red Sox were returning to Boston to prepare for the season opener, they passed through Philadelphia, and Jimmie stopped to see his physician, Dr. Herbert M. Goddard. Foxx was suffering severe headaches and the pain above his eyes was affecting his sight and hitting. Goddard's examination revealed that Jimmie was still running a temperature and that his sinuses were infected. He committed Jimmie to the Jewish Hospital in Philadelphia on April 16. Ten days later, and after missing the opening games in Boston, Foxx was released from the hospital to join the Red Sox. While he was ill Jimmie lost twelve pounds.[26]

Jimmie sought to explain to a reporter how the sinus infection troubled him when he tried to play. "When it was real bad," he said, "I'd go blind every time I moved suddenly or took a heavy step." "You see," he continued, "my lower sinuses, down under my eyes, would be filled most of the time, and the upper ones would be empty. So when I moved suddenly ... the top ones would begin to fill up and it would be like someone dropped a black curtain in front of me." "Sometimes," he related, "things would go black when I was running out a hit, or when I would run over to cover first base ... or after bending down to field a roller." "But," Jimmie explained, "it happened most of the time at the plate. I take a ... step toward the pitcher when I swing on the ball .... Well the shock of landing at the end of that step would often make those upper sinuses begin to fill, and I'd be standing up there like a guy trying to hit a ball at midnight."[27]

Foxx returned to the Red Sox lineup on April 30 and in his first game of the season he was two for four, having a single and a home run and driving in three runs. Although the Red Sox as a team were performing better than a year earlier— they were in third place on July 1—Foxx was having a miserable start, hitting only .260 and fifteen home runs at the All-Star break. Although Jimmie was experiencing one of his worst seasons, he was selected by the manager as a member of the All-Star squad. The game was played in Washington, and although the American League won 6-3, Foxx sat on the bench except for the time when he grounded out as a pinch hitter for Tommy Bridges in the sixth inning.[28]

The spring of 1937 witnessed a noteworthy

A batting pose, ca. 1937 (courtesy Sudlersville Memorial Library).

achievement by one of the major league's premier pitchers. At the close of the 1936 season the Giants' southpaw ace, Carl Hubbell, had won sixteen games without a single loss. When the 1937 season began he continued this string of victories until May 27, when he won his twenty-fourth consecutive victory. His monumental achievement ended at twenty-four, but he went on to win twenty-two and lead the National League hurlers for the season.[29] Early in the 1937 season baseball fans and others were shocked when the career of perhaps the American League's most brilliant catcher came to a near tragic end. On May 25, in a game at Yankee Stadium, New York pitcher Irving "Bump" Hadley beaned Mickey Cochrane. Cochrane suffered "a triple fracture of the skull" and was rushed to the hospital. Although Cochrane recovered, six weeks later he announced that he "was through as a player."[30] The ending of this magnificent thirteen-year major league career by a pitch that nearly killed Cochrane, prompted baseball owners and officials to consider some form of protective headgear for batters. Some years earlier, in 1920, when Carl Mays, another Yankee pitcher, fractured the skull of Roy Chapman, the Cleveland shortstop, with a pitch that resulted in Chapman's death, there had been some discussion of protection for batters. However, nothing was done and commentators usually dismissed this tragedy with the observation that Chapman had been crowding the plate and froze when the pitch came toward him.

Although major league baseball was slow to respond to the need for protective headwear for batters, there was some experimentation with protective devices in the minor leagues. In the mid-thirties players for Des Moines and Cedar Rapids in the Western League experimented with wearing polo helmets while at bat. These proved to be cumbersome, heavy and generally unsatisfactory. *The Sporting News* commented that although some protection for hitters was necessary "the polo helmet was not the answer" and declared that "they have no place in baseball."[31] In 1940 when the Dodger outfielder, Joe Medwick, was beaned and suffered a severe concussion, some major league owners began to seriously consider the use of a protective device or helmet for batters. Larry MacPhail of Brooklyn sought the advice and assistance of two orthopedic surgeons at the Johns Hopkins University. From consultations with these men, MacPhail had the Spalding Manufacturing Company modify a few of the protective caps worn by jockeys. These caps were constructed slightly larger then the usual size caps, to allow the insertion of a protective piece of material. The Dodgers introduced the use of helmets in the spring training season of 1941. They were made obligatory for the exhibition season and for Dodger farm teams throughout the season. Once the major league season opened, the Brooklyn players had the option of using the helmet or not. However, *The Sporting News* advocated making the use of helmets mandatory and urged the league presidents and owners "to take action to see that helmets will be used."[32]

In the meanwhile, Frank Shaughnessy, president of the International League and Edward Rainey of the A.G. Spalding Company, designed and produced a batting helmet. It was light, weighing only seven ounces, and it fit "snugly over the head." It was made from "hard fiber, rubber knobs, and steel bands." The helmet was adopted as official equipment in the International League in 1939, but its use was optional. One of the first players to use it regularly was Buster Mills of Newark. In the summer of 1941 the New York Giants made plastic helmets available, and some players used them. It was not until 1958 that major league officials made the wearing of helmets by batters a requirement, and after 1971 the helmets included ear flaps for added protection to the batter.[33]

Foxx's hitting improved slightly during the last half of the season, but the play of the Red Sox lapsed and they finished the season in fifth place in the American League standings. Their disappointed fans expressed themselves by staying away from Fenway Park. The Red Sox were the only American League team to suffer attendance loss in 1937; they drew 32,000 fewer than in 1936. Foxx's statistics for this season were a batting average of .285, representing the second time in his career that he had failed to hit .300. He had thirty-six home runs, drove in 127 runs, and led the league's first basemen in fielding with an average of .994.[34]

Throughout September Foxx continued to play, despite the fact that for this entire month he was bothered by sinus headaches that impaired his vision. This condition became so severe that in mid–September Jimmie went to see an eye specialist and was fitted with glasses. When discussing his eyesight problem, Jimmie told one reporter, "It's been plenty tough at the dish. ... Some days I would see as many as three balls coming at me. The wonder is I did not get hit. As a rule I picked out the middle one and took a cut at it." Foxx was examined and glasses were prescribed; however, he never wore them while playing. This was not the first time that physicians had prescribed glasses for Jimmie; later he revealed that he had worn glasses to read since he was a schoolboy.[35]

After the close of the season there was some speculation in the press that the Red Sox would trade or sell Foxx. Some baseball writers and others believed that Foxx "was finished" or "on his way out of baseball" and that the 1937 season had been a valid test of his ability.[36] Yawkey denied all rumors and speculation concerning Foxx's leaving Boston and after a month of rest and relaxation, he invited Jimmie, Grove, and the recently acquired Pinky Higgins to accompany him on a deer hunting trip to Wyoming. It was reported that although Foxx preferred to hunt small game, he shot a deer, an elk, and an antelope while on the hunting excursion in Wyoming.[37] After the group returned from the West, Foxx spent the remainder of the off season at home. He hoped to regain his health by working out at the gymnasium, playing some basketball, and trying to keep in condition before departing for Florida early in 1938.

Foxx arrived in Florida a month before training camp opened in March. His doctors had advised him that rest and sun should remove any lingering effects the sinus infection might have had on his eyesight. He and others were concerned that some years earlier persistent sinus trouble had brought to a close the career of George Sisler. In the pre–World War II years, before scientists produced antibiotics to combat sinus infections, victims often experienced recurring headaches, fever, and impaired eyesight. Jimmie and the Red Sox management hoped that his sinuses would be healthy and that he would not experience another season like the past one. In addition to taking in the sun and golf, Jimmie was scheduled to be a visiting instructor in Jimmy Wilson's baseball school in Bradenton. This school was scheduled to open in mid–February and was to have as instructors Paul Waner, Lefty Gomez, Dizzy Dean, Foxx, and others. However, about a week before it was supposed to open, the school was canceled. It seems that Jimmie then participated as a visiting instructor at a baseball instructional school operated by Billy Webb in St. Petersburg.[38]

While in Florida, Jimmie was also negotiating with Eddie Collins concerning his 1938 contract. After what was, for Foxx, a poor season, the Red Sox suggested that he take a $5,000.00 salary cut from what he was paid in 1937. Following several conversations Foxx signed for a slight reduction, at a salary of $23,000.00.[39] When he reported to the Sarasota training camp on March 1, Jimmie declared that he "felt fine" and predicted that he was going to have one of the best seasons of his career. He worked diligently in camp and was at first base when the exhibition season opened on March 13. In this game against the Reds, Foxx offered a preview of things to come by hitting a powerful home run.[40]

Jimmie and the Red Sox got off to a good start in 1938. After the first six weeks the Sox were leading the American League, and Jimmie was hitting .351. Jimmie was feeling well and he was also using a lighter bat, a thirty-four-ounce model. In early June he was hitting .365 and was leading the league in home runs with eighteen and in runs batted in with sixty-nine. However, about this time Foxx experienced a flare-up of sinus headaches and fever. Although his condition was painful Jimmie continued to play. At this time the Red Sox had several starters out because of injuries, and Foxx felt that for the "best of the team" he should try to ignore or minimize his pain.[41] It was during this time that the St. Louis Browns came to Fenway for a series. In a game on June 16, Foxx, who, according to one sportswriter, should have been home in bed, was playing first base. That day Foxx's sight was so impaired that he later confessed he could not see the ball when he was in the batter's box. The Browns' pitchers, however, were not aware of this. In a game which the Red Sox won 12-8, Foxx went to bat six times and did not swing at a single pitch. The visiting pitchers threw him "nothing good," and he walked six consecutive times, establishing a modern major league record.[42]

Foxx and the Red Sox were thankful that the sinus flare-up was not as serious as a year earlier. Jimmie's condition improved and he continued in the lineup. By the end of July he was hitting .363 with twenty-six home runs and ninety-seven runs batted in. The press remarked that Foxx was having a better season than "his banner year of 1932." Foxx was selected for the American League All-Star squad, and the game was played in Cincinnati on July 6. Foxx started at first base but was replaced by Gehrig in the fifth inning. He played the last four innings of the game at third. In this game, which the National League won 4-1, Foxx had a single in four times at bat. The winning pitcher, "no hit" Johnny Vander Meer, struck Jimmie out one time, but not until after he had hit a long ball into the left field stands which was slightly foul.[43]

Jimmie continued to hit throughout the second half of the season, but the Red Sox's early lead in the American League was brief. They were overtaken by the Yankees, who won the pennant by ten games. The Red Sox finished second, their highest since 1918, the year they won the American League pennant. The Red Sox faltered, but Foxx continued his amazing comeback. On two occasions he hit home runs with the bases full to bring his season total of grand slam home runs to three. During the season, on nine different occasions, he hit two home runs in a game, breaking a record held jointly by Babe Ruth and Hack Wilson. In a game at St. Louis on September 20, Jimmie equalled the American League record for extra base hits in a single inning when, in the sixth inning, he had a triple and a home run. *The Sporting News* lauded Foxx on his comeback and fine play and declared that he "was looking five years younger than he was last season."[44] Foxx escaped a serious injury on August 5, when the Red Sox were in Detroit for a game with the Tigers. Running after a high foul fly off the bat of Rudy York, Foxx "turned his right foot." Jimmie said he "felt something give way." Cronin immediately had physicians examine and x-ray his foot to determine the extent of Jimmie's injury. The x-rays revealed that no bones were broken but that he had sprained the ankle. Foxx was advised to rest for several days, advice which he ignored. He continued to play and suffer with the injured muscle.[45]

Throughout September Foxx was in a three-way battle with Cecil Travis of the Senators and Earl Averill of the Indians for the American League batting title. In the last week of the season he forged ahead and finished the season with an average of .349 to win his second batting title. He hit fifty home runs and thereby became the only righthanded batter and the second player in the history of the game to hit fifty or more home runs in more than one season. Jimmie, however, was not the home run champion in 1938; Hank Greenberg, first baseman for the Tigers hit fifty-eight, tying Foxx's 1932 high. Foxx did lead in runs batted in, with 175 and his slugging average of .704 was the highest in the American League. He also led the league in base on balls with 119. The Red Sox's second-place finish in the American League meant that the team would share in the World Series receipts, with each Red Sox player receiving more than one thousand dollars. The *Boston Globe* reported that Foxx also received $500.00 for winning the batting title. These "bonuses" would seem to negate the salary cut Foxx agreed to at the beginning of the season.[46]

In recognition of Foxx's remarkable comeback and his spectacular performance in 1938, the Baseball Writers Association of America chose him, for the third time in his career, as the American League's Most Valuable Player. Foxx was the first player to win this award three times. In late October the

Foxx on deck waiting to hit, ca. 1938 (courtesy Sudlersville Memorial Library).

Philadelphia chapter of the Baseball Writers Association of America sponsored a dinner which was attended by more than 1,000 persons. The honored guests at this affair were Dizzy Dean and Jimmie Foxx. Dean was recognized as "the most courageous athlete of 1938" and Foxx as the "outstanding athlete of 1938." Each was presented a silver plaque, appropriately inscribed.[47] In November Foxx was the guest of honor at a banquet in Atlantic City. Sportsmen, city officials, and some of the town's prominent citizens honored Jimmie at a dinner held at the Hotel Traymore. On December 31, the New York chapter of the Baseball Writers Association of America selected Foxx as the "1938 Player of the Year" and announced that he would be honored and presented a plaque at a banquet scheduled for February 5, 1939. On January 7, 1939, the Boston chapter named Foxx the outstanding player of 1938 and announced that he would be honored at a banquet on February 2, to be held at the Copley Plaza Hotel. Before the end of the year, the Baseball Writers Association of America selected Foxx as their choice for first base on the Major League All-Star team. Jimmie received 146 votes to 84 for Greenberg. Other members chosen for this team included Cronin, Bill Dickey, Mel Ott, Johnny Vander Meer, Joe DiMaggio, and others.[48]

In early October, after the baseball season ended, Foxx returned to his family in the Philadelphia area. Jimmie, Jr., was nine years old and was attending boarding school; the past summer he spent at camp in Bridgeton, Maine, and was visited on several occasions by his father. Kenneth, only two years old, lived with his mother. Shortly after Jimmie's return to Philadelphia he and some buddies went on a hunting trip to eastern Maryland. When they returned in early November, Jimmie received word that *The Sporting News* was going to present to the Most Valuable Player in each league a special trophy—a Browning Arms Company "over and under shotgun," valued at $200.00. This gift was presented to Jimmie at a ceremony in Fenway Park on April 23, 1939.[49]

After a brief respite Jimmie was off with some friends on a deer hunting trip in northeastern Pennsylvania. In between his hunting and being honored, Jimmie was the principal speaker at a banquet on October 18, at Clinton, New Jersey. This affair was sponsored by the Tri-County League to honor local athletes and to recognize their accomplishments during the past year. Also at this time, and reflecting his magnificent 1938 season, Jimmie, for the first time in several years, was featured in newspaper advertisements for Hillerich and Bradsby, makers of Louisville Slugger baseball bats.[50]

Although 1938 was a memorable year in Foxx's career, it was also the year that he abandoned any interest in returning to the farm. Ten years earlier Jimmie had made a down payment on a farm near Sudlersville and he was quoted as saying this was an investment for the future and that he hoped to retire to the farm after his playing days. It appears that Foxx's parents lived on the farm until around 1938, when they moved into a house in the village of Sudlersville which they had purchased in 1925 and formerly rented out. Jimmie's farm, in 1938, had a mortgage of $7,000.00 which he had not paid off. In this year the mortgage was paid and the property was transferred to J.C. Jones on June 8, 1938.[51]

After the Christmas holiday season Jimmie began workouts at a local Philadelphia health club. He wanted to get in "fine physical condition" and was going to "cut down on his smoking."[52] On one occasion during these weeks he was the subject of an interview by Frank Yeutter, a sports columnist for the *Philadelphia Evening Bulletin*. Yeutter had known Foxx and had followed his career since he came to Philadelphia in the summer of 1924. He recalled that in 1924 Jimmie was a large, strong, rosy-cheeked country boy who was a "bear with the bat." The transformation over the years was reflected in Yeutter's description of Jimmie as "suave and polished, an entertaining after-dinner speaker, a well-informed commentator on baseball, and the leader of American League batsmen." Although Jimmie was no longer the bashful farm boy, Yeutter noted that he retained his infectious smile, was always gracious, tolerant, modest, and unassuming, and was a gentleman at all times. Yeutter explained that Foxx was now an urban man, one who wore "well-fitted double breasted suits, camel hair coats, and rakish felt hats." Although the changes from boy to man were obvious to Yeutter and his readers, he noted that the one constant and unchanging feature about Jimmie was his enthusiasm for baseball; it was as strong in 1939 as it had been in 1924. Yeutter concluded his story by reporting that Jimmie was never more confident of his game.[53]

After a month of vigorous physical conditioning in Philadelphia, Jimmie hit the banquet circuit during the first ten days of February—and probably most of his weight loss was regained. During these early days of February one observer reported that Foxx probably "lived in his tuxedo." Between February 1 and 9 he was the honored guest at banquets in New York City, Boston, Cleveland, and Philadelphia. The sponsors of these affairs were the local chapters of the Baseball Writers Association of America, and on each occasion Jimmie was presented an award which had been announced the previous autumn. At each of these affairs Foxx entertained the audience with stories of his baseball experiences and about baseball tours to Japan and Mexico.[54]

When he concluded the tour of the banquet circuit, Jimmie, Grove, and Cronin went to Hot Springs, Arkansas, for a couple of weeks at "the baths." Doubtless, his stay at this resort helped him report for camp at his normal playing weight. Foxx and his teammates returned from Arkansas and reported to camp at Sarasota on March 1. Cronin predicted "another great year for Jimmie," noting that he had taken good care of himself over the winter, that he was mentally and physically well, and that he was anxious to get off to a good start.[55] At the Red Sox camp that spring was a twenty-year-old rookie from San Diego, whom the Red Sox had brought up from Minneapolis. This outfielder was Theodore "Ted" Samuel Williams. Williams had been a longtime fan of Foxx, and the veteran and the "kid" established a harmonious relationship from the beginning. In his book, *My Turn At Bat*, Williams relates how that spring Foxx would talk with him about the various pitchers in the league and offer him tips about them. Both of these men would later claim that the other was the greatest hitter he had ever seen.[56]

Although Foxx hit a 450-foot home run in the first exhibition game, he did not make a spectacular showing in the Grapefruit League; he hit only

.294 in fourteen games.[57] Nevertheless, and reflecting his great 1938 season, Jimmie was featured once again this spring in advertisements for Louisville Slugger bats and for Camel cigarettes; the Camel one occupied one-fourth of a newspaper page.[58] When the regular season began, Foxx's hitting improved, and by mid–May he was hitting over .400. However, in the third week of May he suffered a recurrence of sinus infection. On May 15, Dr. James Conway, Red Sox team physician, entered Foxx in St. Elizabeth's Hospital in Boston. Jimmie was suffering severe headaches and had a temperature of 103 degrees. After four days his temperature returned to normal, and Jimmie was released from the hospital.[59] He returned to the lineup, and by the time of the All-Star game on July 11, he was hitting .352. Jimmie was chosen for the All-Star squad but saw no action in the game, which was played at Yankee Stadium before 62,892 fans. The American League won this contest 3-1, and Charles "Red" Ruffing of the Yankees was the winning pitcher.[60] Perhaps the reason Foxx did not appear in the game was that he was recovering from a stomach ailment that had kept him out of action for four games about a week earlier. When the Red Sox were in Washington for a series the last week in June, Foxx became ill, ran a temperature of 102 degrees, and was confined by the team trainer to his hotel room. When the team returned to Boston on June 29, Jimmie became so ill that he was placed on a stretcher and taken from the train by ambulance to St. Elizabeth's Hospital. Dr. Edmund O'Brien examined him and stated that Jimmie would probably be unable to play for about a week.[61] It was later declared that on this occasion Foxx had suffered an appendicitis attack; a short while later a similar attack required an operation.

The 1939 season was less than a month old when one of the most remarkable careers in baseball history came to an end. On May 2, 1939, Lou Gehrig, captain of the New York Yankees, removed himself from the lineup after appearing in 2,130 consecutive games. Gehrig was ill, the victim of amyotrophic lateral sclerosis, and he declared, "I'm not doing the club any good." On July 4 there was a farewell ceremony for him at Yankee Stadium, and his number was retired. Two years later, and less than three weeks before his thirty-eighth birthday, the "Iron Horse" died.[62]

In the summer of 1939 American League President Will Harridge and Commissioner Landis issued certain specifications and rules concerning the size of baseball gloves and mitts which would be permitted in the major leagues. Baseball equipment was undergoing change in the late twenties and thirties. The small gloves and mitts were being replaced by larger and more sophisticated equipment, some of it featuring deep-pockets and long snare-type webbings which would assist in the fielding of ground balls and catching of outfield flies. One of the largest gloves used in the thirties was the first baseman's mitt used by Hank Greenberg of the Tigers. It featured a wide netting above the thumb and the palm area, making it a "virtual scoop or shovel." The players were supportive of this new equipment, but some baseball supporters questioned its use since it could give an advantage to an average or below average player. Baseball officials approved the larger, deep-pocket catcher's mitt in June, 1939. The first baseman's mitt was to be "no more than twelve inches from top to bottom and not more than eight inches across the palm." The lacing between the thumb and the palm was to be "not more than four inches." These regulations outlawed Greenberg's "scoop." All other players were to use gloves weighing no more than ten ounces and no larger than fourteen inches around the palm area. Baseball officials were seeking to maintain the integrity of the game by not allowing too much equipment assistance for the players.[63]

Foxx went on a hitting tear the last week of July; in four days he hit six home runs and moved ahead of Greenberg for leadership in this area. On two different occasions Foxx put together hitting streaks of twelve and thirteen games and sportswriters were confident that he would soon surpass Gehrig's home run total of 493, which was second to Ruth's 714.[64] On August 6, in a game against the Detroit Tigers, Jimmie was given the opportunity to demonstrate his all-around ability as a baseball player. For eight innings the Tigers had pounded Red Sox pitchers Dennis Galehouse, Woody Rich, and Jake Wade for seventeen hits and had a 10-1 lead. In the ninth inning Cronin permitted Foxx to pitch; 35,000 fans rocked Fenway when he walked to the mound. He faced only three batters—he fanned former teammate Pinky Higgins, induced Pete Fox to pop up a weak foul, and retired catcher "Birdie" Tebbets on an infield grounder.[65] Also in August, the Red Sox installed added bleachers in right field, which brought in the fence. This allowed more spectators, but the modification of the right field fence was essentially to create a better target for the Sox's sensational rookie, Ted Williams. Nevertheless, the first home run hit over this revised structure was by Foxx.[66]

On an off day in the latter part of August, Jimmie and Ted Williams, accompanied by Helen Foxx and her brother, joined two of Jimmie's former Athletics' teammates, Bob Johnson and Frank Hayes, for a tuna fishing expedition at Brielle, New Jersey. It was reported that this group "brought in nineteen fish, totaling more than a ton in weight." Helen, it was claimed, brought in two of the catch.[67]

By the first of September Foxx was hitting .360 and had thirty-five home runs. This was his record for the 1939 season since his playing ended on September 9, when he entered St. Joseph's Hospital in Philadelphia. The stomach ailment which had affected Jimmie several times flared up again and was diagnosed by his physician, Dr. Patrick S. Pasquarillo, as appendicitis. He recommended an operation to remove the infected appendix. Assisted by Dr. G.V. Burden, Pasquarilo performed the operation the following day. Jimmie had a normal recovery and on September 22 was released from the hospital.[68] The Red Sox finished the season in second place for the second consecutive year, seventeen games behind the Yankees. The rookie outfielder and admirer

Foxx with young fan, 1939 (courtesy Temple University Libraries).

of Foxx, Ted Williams, hit .327, had thirty-one home runs and batted in 142 runs.[69] Each Red Sox regular would receive more than one thousand dollars from the World Series revenue.

In the 1939 season several reporters sought the opinion of one of baseball's premier hitters concerning American League pitchers. Jimmie diplomatically replied that all of them were "tough," but he found right-handers "more troublesome than southpaws." He told a reporter for the *Philadelphia*

Evening Bulletin that current pitchers were not as "terrifying" as those of the twenties, when Walter Johnson was active and Lefty Grove was in his prime. It was his opinion that Grove was the "hardest man to hit against day in and day out," and Jimmie remarked that he was glad he did not have to bat against him. Jimmie also expressed the opinion that his former teammate, George Earnshaw, was perhaps "the best money pitcher" he had seen. The secret of Earnshaw's success, he explained, was "great control"; he could put the ball wherever he wanted to on any pitch. Foxx admitted that Oral Hilderbrand of the Browns "gave him a lot of trouble." He explained that Hilderbrand had a "jerky motion" that upset a batter's balance and timing. Later Foxx would confess that Buck Newsome gave him much trouble until he "caught on to him." At another time Jimmie replied that Carl Hubbel "was the toughest pitcher I ever faced," but the toughest pitcher he faced in the American League was Johnny Allen, the Tar Heel right-hander who spent most of his career with the Yankees and Indians.[70]

Although Jimmie never boasted about or advertised who his favorite pitchers were, or the ones who gave him the least trouble, it was no secret that his favorite "cousin" was probably his friend, the Yankee southpaw ace Vernon "Lefty" Gomez. On one occasion Jimmie hit three home runs off Gomez in a single game. At another time he hit a rising line drive off Lefty into the upper seats of center field at Yankee Stadium. After the game it was discovered that this blast, which traveled more than 450 feet, had sufficient force to break the back of the seat that it hit in the stands. Among the Foxx/Gomez stories is one concerning Lefty's reluctance to throw any pitch his catcher called for. In one hard-fought contest with the Red Sox, the Sox had two runners on base in the eighth inning when Foxx came to bat. Bill Dickey flashed the sign to Gomez and Lefty shook him off. He did this three successive times and Dickey went to the mound to inquire just what Gomez wished to throw. His reply was, "I don't want to throw that guy anything." On another occasion, Gomez declared he thought Jimmie could hit him blindfolded.

In 1937 Foxx hit one of his longest home runs off Gomez into the upper reaches of Yankee Stadium. Lefty said, "It would take an hour to carry the ball from home plate to where Foxx hit it." Despite the fact that Gomez once declared in a bantering manner that he had "a deep-rooted hatred for Foxx," the two men were friends, and often when the Athletics or Red Sox were in New York or the Yankees were in Philadelphia or Boston, Foxx and Gomez would eat and socialize together. At dinner one day they were talking about the hard luck that Tommy Bridges recently experienced when he lost a no-hitter in the ninth inning as the result of a pinch hitter's single. Both agreed that this was a lousy break for Bridges and that the pinch hitting culprit should be boiled in oil. The next day Gomez pitched a one-hitter against the Athletics, and guess who spoiled his no-hitter—his dinner companion of the previous evening, Jimmie Foxx. Gomez's battery mate, Bill Dickey, was also a friend of Foxx and later was quoted as saying, "I think Foxx would have been the greatest catcher in the history of baseball if he had stuck to it." He also declared that if he were blindfolded in the park he would always know when Foxx hit the ball because "Foxx hit the ball harder than anyone else."[71]

In the closing weeks of the season *The Sporting News* conducted a poll "among fifteen experts" to choose the "leading all-around players in the majors." The experts were to take into consideration ten qualities: ability, dependability, application, team value, popularity, initiative, aggressiveness, courage, fellowship, and deportment. The three top choices of the experts were "Bucky" Walters, a pitcher for the Reds; Joe DiMaggio; and Foxx. The Baseball Writers Association of America named Jimmie to the major league All-Star team for 1939; he received 160 votes for first base, his nearest competitor being Johnny Mize of the Cardinals with forty-eight votes.[72] Foxx was one player featured in a forty-five-minute film, prepared in 1939 by the American League and co-sponsored by the W.K. Kellogg Company, titled "Touching All Bases." This was a four-reel sound film and was available for use by schools and civic and sport organizations throughout the country. Among Foxx's peers featured in this film were DiMaggio, Grove, Cronin, Williams, and Tommy Bridges.[73]

Unlike most seasons, there would be no controversy about the next season's contract for several of the Red Sox regulars. By the close of the 1939 season it was announced that Foxx, Cronin, and Williams had already signed their 1940 contracts. Although terms were not announced, it was assumed that Foxx would receive the same salary as he had in 1939, around $32,000.[74]

Before he could relax and go hunting, Foxx had to honor an invitation he had accepted to be the guest speaker at the ninth annual banquet of the Niagara Falls Baseball Association, which was held on November 1, in Niagara Falls, Ontario. More than twelve hundred baseball fans and supporters were present for this occasion, and the press reported that Foxx "kept the crowd in good humor by outlining many of his diamond experiences" and with accounts of barnstorming trips to Japan and Mexico. A short time after the Niagara Falls affair, Foxx, Helen, and their youngest son left home to spend the winter season in St. Petersburg, Florida, where he was to serve as an official greeter at a golf course and club.[75]

It cannot be ascertained when Foxx began to drink alcoholic beverages; however, it was probably not until the end of prohibition in 1933. From that time forward, beer and ale were available in grocery stores, taverns, restaurants, and elsewhere, and the sale of whiskey was permitted almost as freely; beer was sold in baseball parks. When Foxx was barnstorming in the fall of 1933, there is a reference by the Negro League pitcher, Chet Brewer, to the fact that at one game Foxx was "filled with Canadian beer." On another occasion before Foxx was sold to the Red Sox in 1935, there was a game in which Jimmie went zero for five. This concerned Connie Mack, who asked, "Foxxie, have you been drinking again?" Ted Williams records in *My Turn At Bat* that during his rookie year (1939), he and Foxx would often eat and socialize together. He claims that Jimmie had a "love for Scotch whiskey" and could "drink fifteen of those little bottles of Scotch, miniature bottles and not be affected."[76] By the end of the 1939 season it was known that Foxx was drinking more than previously. There has been some speculation that Foxx's increase in alcohol consumption was related to his frequent sinus trouble. The alcohol probably helped, or seemed to help, relieve him of pain. As we will see, consumption of alcohol would become more of a problem for Foxx.

The year 1939 was perhaps the most memorable one in the history of baseball. This was the year organized baseball and the nation celebrated the one-hundredth birthday of America's national game. Nineteen thirty-nine was the culmination of many years of planning and publicity by various people interested in baseball. One of the earliest to be associated with the history of the game was the former player, team owner, and later sporting goods manufacturer, Albert G. Spalding. Spalding was convinced that baseball was a uniquely American creation and had no connection with the English games of cricket or rounders. To bolster this contention, Spalding suggested that a committee be appointed to study and report on the history of baseball. This suggestion received a favorable response from baseball owners and league officials, and in 1905 a committee, chaired by A.G. Mills, former president of the National League, was created to investigate the issue. Two years later the Mills Committee report was completed, and it declared that baseball was created by Abner Doubleday at Cooperstown, New York, in 1839. The claims of the Mills report were accepted by baseball supporters and sportswriters throughout the country. Some years later (1934), an old, torn and battered baseball, which had belonged to a contemporary of Doubleday's, was discovered in an attic trunk on a farm near Cooperstown. This ball was acquired and put on display in the Cooperstown Village Club.[77]

By the time the battered baseball was found and put on display many people had become interested in baseball and its Cooperstown origins and were thinking about what should be done to mark or memorialize this uniquely American game. Among those concerned and active in this enterprise were the town government of Cooperstown; the Cooperstown Chamber of Commerce; the Otsego, New York, County Historical Society; baseball commissioner Landis; the presidents of the American and National Leagues; numerous baseball sports writers; sporting goods manufacturers; *The Sporting News*; and others. As early as 1917, Stephen Crane, a sportswriter, suggested that a baseball memorial should be established in Cooperstown, the birthplace of the game. Other sportswriters, including Ford Frick, also espoused the idea of a memorial at Cooperstown. Another influential advocate of the establishment of a memorial to baseball was Stephen Clark. The Clark family were natives of Cooperstown, and an earlier member of the family was a partner of Isaac

Singer, the sewing machine manufacturer. The family was affluent and civic minded. They had established the Clark Foundation and had supported the financing of a hospital and recreation center in Cooperstown, as well as providing college scholarships for local high school graduates. By the early 1930s Stephen Clark and the family foundation had become interested in a baseball memorial. Interest of the various groups in the establishment of a memorial were coupled with what should be the appropriate way to observe and celebrate the centennial anniversary of baseball in 1939.[78]

In 1934 the town government succeeded in obtaining from the federal government WPA support to renovate and expand the local baseball playing ground, which had been officially proclaimed Doubleday Field. By this time Clark, baseball authorities, local boosters, and leading sportswriters were supporting the construction of a baseball museum in Cooperstown to house artifacts. This museum would preserve and also explain the origin, development, and growth of the game. The aim was to create a museum and have it open to the public by 1939. Following the decision to construct a museum the sponsors issued an invitation for artifacts to be placed there. One of the early respondents to this invitation was Cy Young, who donated his large collection of baseball memorabilia for the museum. Others would follow his example.[79]

From 1934 to 1939, with the construction of Doubleday Field and the decision to establish a museum, there was increasing publicity and planning for the anniversary year, 1939. *The Sporting News* suggested that a part of the celebration be a "memorial game" at Doubleday Field. In 1934 the former sportswriter and early exponent of a baseball memorial, Ford Frick, became president of the National League. Frick envisioned more than baseball artifacts for the proposed museum. He suggested a plan whereby "the superstars of the game could be enshrined in a Hall of Fame that would be a part of the museum." His concept of a Hall of Fame was based on the Hall of Fame for Great Americans that had been initiated by New York University in 1901.[80] Frick's suggestion was embraced by major league baseball and museum supporters, and it was agreed that those selected for inclusion in the Hall of Fame would be chosen by the Baseball Writers Association of America, an organization founded early in the century and consisting of baseball writers from every major newspaper in the nation. It was determined that the first members of the Hall of Fame would be chosen in 1936.

Prior to the election of the first members of the Hall of Fame, the baseball writers nominated a number of candidates—all were to represent the game since 1900. From this list the writers were to vote for those to be inducted into the Hall and, to be elected, one was required to receive seventy-five percent of the votes. Later it was decided to also select for the Hall some players who performed prior to 1900. It was also agreed that current players were ineligible for election until five years after their careers ended. However, the Baseball Writers Association of America reserved the right to modify this practice if they considered it appropriate. The first players elected to the Hall of Fame were announced in the fall of 1936: Babe Ruth, Honus Wagner, Christy Mathewson, Walter Johnson, Ty Cobb, Cy Young, Napoleon Lajoie, Tris Speaker, George Sisler, Grover C. Alexander, Eddie Collins, and Connie Mack.[81]

By midyear 1938 the $100,000.00 baseball museum was completed; the Clark family foundation had provided most of the resources for this project.[82] As the centennial year drew closer, plans for the observance of baseball's birthday were formulated and others, including the federal government, became involved in the celebration. In January, 1939, a congressman from Connecticut introduced a measure, which Congress approved, designating June 12 as "National Baseball Day." On February 2, Postmaster James Farley, at a banquet sponsored by the New York chapter, Baseball Writers Association of America, announced that a postage stamp would soon be issued commemorating the beginning of baseball in 1839. One method adopted by baseball owners for calling attention to the game's anniversary was to have sewn on the shirt sleeve of all major league uniforms a small patch or emblem commemorating the centennial.[83]

Those in charge of the Cooperstown celebration decided that the museum would be dedicated on June 12, National Baseball Day. The Hall of Fame would officially be opened on this date, and an "old timers" game would be played at Doubleday Field. When June 12 arrived there were more than 10,000 visitors in the village of Cooperstown, including Commissioner Landis; Postmaster Farley; major league club officials and owners; and a number of retired and current players, among whom were Ruth, Grove, Gehringer, Medwick, Ott, Dizzy Dean, Greenberg, and Lloyd Waner. The old timers game featured a contest between players managed by Honus Wagner and Eddie Collins. The Wagner team won this inaugural contest 4-3.[84]

A month later the first major league team to appear at Doubleday Field was the Philadelphia Athletics. They participated in a game honoring their seventy-six-year-old manager, Connie Mack. This contest was a part of the anniversary celebration. Governor Arthur H. Jones of Pennsylvania threw out the first pitch, and over 3,000 fans saw the Athletics defeat the Pennsylvania Athletic Club 12-6.[85] The centennial year was a major success for baseball; an institution and a practice were established which would continue and contribute to the appreciation of the game. Although the story of Abner Doubleday inventing baseball in 1839 remains a popular one, baseball historians and archivists at the Baseball Museum and Library in Cooperstown and elsewhere recognize it as a myth. Recently, newspaper accounts have been found which reveal that "bass ball" games were not uncommon in some places in upstate New York in the 1820s.

Baseball's centennial year was also the year that major league baseball experienced its first relationship with the new media, television. Technicians had experimented with television for some years, but public awareness of it was limited until 1939, when it was one of the feature exhibits at the New York World's Fair. In connection with the Fair and demonstrations of twentieth-century technological advancement, the National Broadcasting Company televised two baseball games in 1939. The first one was a college contest, played in May at Baker Field in New York City between teams from Columbia and Princeton Universities. The first televised broadcast of major league baseball occurred on August 26, when the National Broadcasting Company televised from Ebbetts Field a doubleheader between the Dodgers and the Cincinnati Reds. Attendance for that day was 33,535 as the teams split the doubleheader. The *New York Times* reported that "television set owners as far away as fifty miles viewed the action and heard the roar of the crowd."[86]

In the fall and winter of 1939–40 Foxx became involved in what became a disastrous golfing venture in St. Petersburg, Florida. The press reported in November that Foxx was "wintering in St. Petersburg" and that he had "a greeter's job at a golf course." Foxx's involvement, however, was much more than "a greeter." In late December, sports columnist Frederick Lieb informed his readers that Jimmie had entered into a partnership with Harold Paddock, "a golfing architect," who in 1912 had appeared in forty-five games for the Yankees. In the next couple of months Foxx and Paddock acquired leases on two golf courses in the St. Petersburg area—the Jungle Club Course and the Shores Acres Course. On January 21, Jimmie and Paddock were the co-hosts of a pro-amateur tournament at their Jungle Club course. Among the participants were such major league stars as Paul Waner, Paul Derringer, and Wes Ferrell. In February it was announced that the annual Florida State Baseball Players Championship for 1941 would be held at Foxx's Jungle Club. Jimmie was named chairman of this event and other committee members included Joe Medwick, Al Lopez, and Lloyd Waner.[87]

The partnership between Foxx and Paddock was brief. Before the end of February (1940) Foxx filed a petition in circuit court "for the dissolution" of the partnership with Paddock in the operation of two golf courses in St. Petersburg. Foxx asked that a receiver be appointed and that an accounting of the assets and liabilities be provided. He also requested an order "enjoining Paddock from interfering with the finances of the partnership." Foxx's petition claimed that he and Paddock entered into their partnership on October 17, 1939, for the operation of the two courses. Under terms of the agreement each was to put $5,000.00 into the business. Foxx claimed that he invested $5,000.00, but Paddock failed to do so. It was noted that extensive and expensive changes were made at the two courses. Foxx, in requesting that the partnership be dissolved, promised that he would honor the leases and operate the courses alone.[88] The court honored Foxx's petition, and he assumed responsibility for the operation of the golf courses.

When the Red Sox camp opened in March, 1940, Foxx reported and declared that he was fully recovered from the appendectomy of last September. He was in good physical condition and expressed his belief that the Red Sox would be in the thick of the fight for the American League pennant. Eddie Collins was pleased to note that Jimmie had "worked hard in the off season," that golfing and exercise had kept his weight down, and that Jimmie was "as hard as nails and ready to go." Indication of Foxx's readiness to play came in an early exhibition game against the Giants, when he hit a home run which traveled more than 480 feet.[89]

Although the United States had not become involved in the European war that had erupted in September, 1939, there was considerable concern regarding this conflict. Perhaps no nation elicited more sympathy from the American public at this time than Finland. This small Baltic state had become the victim of Soviet aggression and had lost a portion of its territory, falling under the domination of that nation. Relief operations to help the Finns were conducted by various groups in the U. S. On March 17, major league baseball sponsored an All-Star game in Tampa for the benefit of the Finnish Relief Fund. Thirteen thousand spectators witnessed this game between a collection of American and National league players. Both Foxx and Williams participated, and the American Leaguers won 2-1. More than $23,000.00 was raised for Finnish relief.[90]

Before the opening of the season the Red Sox reappointed Foxx team captain. In so doing, Cronin and Collins acknowledged his great value to the team as a performer and his help and assistance to young players. Indicative of Foxx's assistance to youngsters is the comment by Dominic DiMaggio. DiMaggio was a Red Sox rookie in 1940 and for a while shared an apartment in Boston with Jimmie. In his book, *Real Grass, Real Heroes*, DiMaggio recalled that "no one was ever nicer to a rookie than Foxx." Jimmie treated him as an equal, as a peer; and, as he notes, "Jimmie was like that to everyone." He never "high-hatted" anyone. No "star ball player of the modern era," DiMaggio declared, "was ever so modest and unassuming."[91]

The Red Sox were an enthusiastic team in the spring of 1940 and *The Sporting News* picked them to finish second in the American League, one place behind the Yankees. In their opening game, forty-year old Lefty Grove shut out the Senators on two hits as the Red Sox won 1-0. After the first month of the season Foxx had nine home runs and was batting .310.[92] When the Red Sox were in Philadelphia for a series during the last week of April, Jimmie was the speaker and guest of honor at a student assembly at Philadelphia's Northeast High School. On this occasion the students presented Foxx "a silver loving cup" with the following engraved on it: "Awarded to Jimmie Foxx, superstar of baseball, in recognition of the fine qualities he has shown the youth of our nation during his brilliant career—clean living, faithful service, and good sportsmanship."[93]

In mid–May Foxx went on a hitting spree. In one game against the White

Sox and for the forty-fourth time in his career he hit two home runs. One was over the left field roof and out of the park, the longest ball many of those present had ever seen hit. A week later in games against the Tigers, Foxx hit bases-loaded home runs on two consecutive days, and ten days afterwards, in contests with the White Sox, he hit six home runs in three games.[94] On June 13 the Red Sox and the Chicago Cubs played an exhibition game at Doubleday Field in Cooperstown to usher in the second century of baseball in America. This game, which the Cubs won 10-9, was witnessed by 3,500 fans; the receipts of more than $3,500.00 were to help "maintain the game's shrine at Cooperstown." Jimmie was selected for the All-Star game, which was played in St. Louis on July 10. The National League stars recorded their third win in this series by defeating the American Leaguers 4-0. Foxx was at first base for the American League, and he did not have any of the three hits the American League stars managed to accumulate off National League pitching. Foxx was 0 for 3 and he struck out once.[95]

A few days after the All-Star game (July 23), in a contest against the Browns at Boston, Foxx had a collision with John Berardino and suffered a sprained knee. He was forced to leave the game in the fourth inning. He returned a week later but had to leave and was not able to resume play until August 8.[96] When he was able to return to active play the Red Sox catcher, Gene Desautles, was hitting only .225 and the Red Sox were faltering. Foxx suggested to Cronin that he assume catching duties and let Lou Finney continue to fill in at first base, since Finney was hitting over .300. Cronin agreed to Jimmie's suggestion, and on August 8 he returned to the Sox lineup as catcher. This was the first time Foxx had been behind the plate in five years, and certain of his leg and back muscles experienced soreness "as bad as a toothache" until they became adjusted to catching. Although Foxx experienced some muscular discomfort with catching, it did not adversely affect his hitting; within a week he hit five home runs, and the Red Sox won eight of the first twelve games that he caught.[97]

Sore muscles resulting from playing a new position was only one distraction which Foxx had to cope with in August of 1940. At this same time Jimmie developed an abscess at the root of a molar. He had the tooth extracted, and although it was painful and contributed to a throbbing headache, Foxx donned the pads, mask, and mitt and was behind the plate three hours after he left the dentist's office. He caught the entire game against the Yankees. All the while Foxx was hitting over .300, and on August 17 he passed Lou Gehrig's home run total of 493 to become second to Babe Ruth in this category. On August 30, Jimmie suffered his first catching injury—a foul tip struck him on the instep of his left foot. He had to leave the game and although x-rays revealed no broken bones, the injury was painful and caused swelling, Foxx was out for several days, and when he resumed play on September 12, it was at first base. Foxx's performance in the summer of 1940 prompted the editor of *The*

Sporting News to declare that "Jimmie is the most versatile player the American League has ever had." Later that fall the Red Sox acquired veteran catcher Frank Pytlak from the Indians, an indication that management was not going to risk further injury to Foxx.[98]

In addition to suffering various aches and pains in his leg and back muscles, the troublesome effects of an infected jaw tooth and a painful bruise on his instep, Foxx experienced a serious batting slump in September. Around mid–September the seemingly annual recurrence of chronic sinus trouble returned to torture Jimmie. He told one reporter that for three weeks he was "a victim of blinding headaches." During these weeks he wore glasses for practice to try to improve his eyesight, and he put them on immediately after the game was over. However, he refused to wear them during the game—probably the result of an ego problem. Had he consented to wear them, maybe his average would have remained above .300; as it was, his average slipped in September, and he ended the season hitting .297, with thirty-six home runs and 119 runs batted in. The Red Sox, picked for second, wound up in fourth place. This marked the twelfth consecutive season that Jimmie had thirty or more home runs and more than 100 runs batted in.[99] A significant milestone in Foxx's career came on September 23 in a game against the Philadelphia Athletics at Shibe Park. In the first game of a doubleheader Jimmie hit home run number 500; it was off the knuckle ball pitcher, George Caster, and was a drive "to the highest point of the center field bleachers," missing the roof about a foot.[100] The Athletics' outfielder, Sam Chapman, later retrieved the ball and gave it to Foxx. It became one of two baseballs that Jimmie prized, the other being the ball which he hit for his first major league home run. Both were hit at Shibe Park.[101] Also during the 1940 season, Foxx played in his first night games; all were road games, since the Red Sox would not install lights in Fenway Park until 1947. In four night contests Jimmie hit .700.[102]

Shortly after the close of the baseball season Jimmie went to St. Petersburg and his golfing business. Invitations were soon issued to all major league players to come and compete in the baseball players tournament which he was hosting in February. In December there was a pro-amateur tournament at his Shore Acres course. At the close of this affair Jimmie and a few others went on a hunting trip to Tom Yawkey's estate near Georgetown, South Carolina. In the meantime, Lew Fonseca, a former major leaguer and in recent years a director for sporting movies, prepared the seventh in a series of American League movies. This was entitled "Batting Around the American League." These films were made available to schools and civic organizations and for instructional purposes. The current one featured Foxx, Williams, Joe DiMaggio, Hank Greenberg, Luke Appling and others. These men demonstrated what was publicized as "models of all that is perfect in hitting technique."[103]

The 1940 season also featured a new product endorsement by Foxx. Since 1933 General Mills, the producers of the breakfast cereal "Wheaties," had sponsored the broadcast of Minneapolis Millers games and also featured various prominent athletes to endorse their "breakfast of champions." In 1933 Babe Ruth was the first major league player to endorse this cereal. In the spring of 1940 a picture of Foxx and Jimmie, Jr., was featured on the back panel of Wheaties boxes. Jimmie and the boy were sitting at the breakfast table enjoying the cereal. For this endorsement Foxx probably received less than one hundred dollars.[104]

After Foxx returned from the hunting trip in South Carolina, he brought his family to St. Petersburg. Jimmie was busy preparing for the golf tournament to be held in February; however, he also played golf, went swimming and fishing, and tried to keep in good physical condition. The baseball players tournament, was held at his Jungle Club course, February 6–9, and Jimmie was assisted by members of the local Chamber of Commerce. There were more than fifty entries for the tournament and *The Sporting News* provided a trophy which was presented to the winner. Among the baseball dignitaries at the tournament, but who did not compete, were Commissioner Landis and Senators owner, Clark Griffith. The tournament concluded with a banquet at the Suwanee Hotel in St. Petersburg. At this time the winner was announced and presented a trophy. Marvin Shea, a coach for the Detroit Tigers, was the winner of the baseball players 1941 golf tournament.[105] This was Jimmie's last involvement with the golf course business. Travel restrictions minimized tourist activities in Florida, and later in the year the federal government took over the golf course property for naval use. This terminated Foxx's golf venture; by this time estimates concerning the amount of money Foxx had lost in the golfing venture ranged from $40,000.00 to $100,000.00.[106]

The week following the end of the golf tournament the Foxx family experienced a serious fright. Their four-year-old son, William Kenneth, fell out of a moving automobile when a door accidentally opened. He was rushed to a hospital where it was discovered that he suffered shock and bruises, but no broken bones.[107] During this time Foxx was negotiating with Eddie Collins concerning his 1941 contract. It was rumored that the Red Sox wanted to reduce his salary, but *The Sporting News* urged Collins and the Red Sox to remember Jimmie's contribution as a team man, as one who in the past season caught, played first base, filled in at third, hit thirty-six home runs and drove in more than a hundred runs. Although Jimmie signed his contract before the end of February, no terms of the contract were revealed, but it was assumed that it was for less than the $32,000.00 which he was paid in 1940, probably around $22,000.00 since the 1941 contract contained no bonus clause as his previous one had.[108]

Since the Red Sox had not been able to win a pennant with established players whom they had purchased from other clubs, it seems that by 1939 they were moving toward acquiring young players who would shortly replace the veterans. This trend was manifested in the recent acquisitions of minor leaguers

Ted Williams and Dominic DiMaggio. At the Red Sox camp in 1941 were
three minor league first baseman who had been invited there so that Cronin,
Collins, and others could evaluate them for possible future signing. These
players were Paul Campbell from Louisville, Tony Lupien from Little Rock
and Al Flair from Scranton—all AAA players. It was reported that Foxx arrived
in camp "in great shape" but that he would take it easy in the exhibition
games and permit the youngsters to have more playing time.[109] The Red Sox
closed out the Grapefruit League season with a series of contests against the
Cincinnati Reds. Three of these games were played in Havana, Cuba, on
March 28, 29, and 30. Baseball was popular in Cuba, perhaps more so than
anywhere in Latin America. The game had been introduced there before the
end of the nineteenth century by barnstormers from the United States and by
Cuban students who had acquired knowledge of the game while spending
time in the United States. The Cuban fans knew and appreciated the game,
and they gave their loudest and most prolonged applause to Foxx. Jimmie was
at first base for each of the games played in Havana, and although he hit no
home runs, he had a triple and a double, as the Reds won two of the three
games.[110]

Foxx hit his first exhibition game home run in Birmingham, Alabama, in
a game against the Reds on April 5, a drive over the left field fence. The series
with the Reds was concluded in Cincinnati several days before the opening of
the regular season. In a game on April 9, Jimmie hit "the longest ball ever seen"
at Crosley Field. This blast "hit the top of a beer sign on a laundry building
across the street" from the park, "then bounded on the roof of another building before going out of sight."[111] Doubtless, the young men aspiring to replace
Foxx at first base were impressed by his performance.

This spring the Red Sox management was also concerned about Foxx's
status with his local draft board. On September 16, 1940, Congress passed the
Selective Service Act, which required the registration of all men between the
ages of twenty-one and thirty-five. These men were liable for one year of military training and the first registration was on October 19. Foxx registered on
this date at the draft board near his home in Jenkintown, Pennsylvania. On
April 24, 1941, shortly after the baseball season opened, Foxx received a ques-
tionnaire from his draft board. The information he provided would determine
his classification. Although Jimmie reportedly said, "I'm ready if Uncle Sam
wants me," he doubted he would be called up because he was married and the
father of two young sons. In a few weeks Jimmie received a 3-A classification,
the one generally given to men with dependents. This assured Foxx and the
Red Sox management that his baseball career would not be interrupted at this
time.[112]

The Red Sox got off to a weak start, winning nine and losing eight of their
first games; Foxx was hitting .308. In early May there was a flareup of his sinus
trouble, and he was aggravated by an attack of diarrhea. In mid–May third

baseman Jim Tabor was injured and Foxx went to third base while Lou Finney filled in at first.[113] Dan Daniel, a prominent sports columnist, wrote that Foxx was having "a harrowing campaign" with sinus trouble, stomach ailment, and impaired eyesight, and rumors circulated that Jimmie was going "to call it quits." Illness kept him out of the lineup for several games in late May and again during the last week of June.[114] Despite the fact that Jimmie was experiencing a horrible year, he was hitting .300 by the time of the All-Star game. He was selected a member of the All-Star squad for the ninth consecutive year, the only American League player accorded this distinction. The game this year was played in Detroit on July 8, and the Americans won the contest 7–5. Foxx entered the game in the seventh inning, went to bat one time, and was struck out by Claude Passeau of the Cubs, the same pitcher whom Ted Williams hit for a home run in the ninth inning to win the game.[115]

The week following the All-Star game Jimmie "enjoyed his best day of the season." In a doubleheader with the Tigers he had three hits in each game: two were home runs, his thirteenth and fourteenth; two were doubles and two were singles. On this day he scored five runs and batted in five others. At the same time Foxx was enjoying his best day of the season, the spectacular record of another player came to an end. Joe DiMaggio's feat of hitting safely in fifty-six consecutive games was ended on July 17 in a game at Cleveland. He had established a major league record which many commentators doubted would ever be matched.[116]

The 1941 season also witnessed the end of the playing careers of two of baseball's most famous pitchers—a southpaw and a right-hander, one from the American League and the other a National Leaguer. Robert M. "Lefty" Grove of the Red Sox and Foxx were teammates for eight years with the Athletics, including the 1931 season when Grove led all major league pitchers with thirty-one victories and four losses. Foxx followed Grove to Boston in 1935, and the two Marylanders were teammates again. Grove developed arm trouble in Boston and was never as effective as when he was pitching for Connie Mack. Nevertheless, he continued to win and gradually approached his goal of winning 300 games. In a home game on July 25 against the Indians, Lefty finally won his three hundredth game. Foxx gave considerable help to his teammate when, in the eighth inning, he hit a triple with two men on base and he scored on an overthrow to third. This gave the Red Sox enough runs to assure Grove the victory. At that time Grove was the twelfth pitcher, and second southpaw, to attain this many wins. This was Grove's final victory and he retired at the end of the season.[117] The career of another thirty-game winner also closed in 1941 when Dizzy Dean ended the season with the Chicago Cubs. Dean was one of the most colorful personalities in major league baseball during the thirties and, before he injured himself in the 1937 All-Star contest, was one of the game's greatest pitchers. His best season was in 1934 when he won thirty and lost seven for the St. Louis Cardinals.

Throughout the last half of the 1941 season Jimmie continued to hit around .300; however, in August he was out of the lineup for several days because of a back ailment and the recurrence of sinus trouble. One physician informed Jimmie that he was smoking too much and that smoking, together with unhealthy sinuses, adversely affected his eyesight. Jimmie told the doctor that he had not touched tobacco in three months and despite not being well, he continued to play.[118] The fact that Foxx was having "a miserable year" is shown in his statistics: he was hitting only .300, his home run output experienced a marked decline, and, for the first time in thirteen years, he would have less than thirty home runs for the season. Throughout the campaign, actually beginning before spring training, there was some speculation by the press that 1941 would be Jimmie's last year with the Red Sox. Such rumors appeared frequently in newspapers during the last half of the season. One was that Foxx was going to the Browns; another had him returning to the Athletics. There was also speculation that he would be sold or traded to the Tigers or Indians. A degree of credence was given to the rumor that Jimmie would return to the Athletics when the press reported that on a visit home he had a conference with his old boss, Connie Mack.[119]

Both Cronin and Collins denied all rumors and speculation that Foxx was going to leave Boston. In late November Collins declared that Foxx would be offered a contract for 1942, and he expressed confidence that Jimmie would sign.[120] At the same time as the rumors that Foxx would leave Boston, some speculated that he would be offered a manager's job in major league baseball. John Lardner, sports columnist for the *Philadelphia Evening Bulletin*, and others thought that Jimmie was well qualified "as a leader and strategist" and that he would make a fine manager. It would be claimed later that in the fall of 1941 Red Sox officials attempted to get Foxx the managerial position with both the Browns and the Indians but were unsuccessful.[121]

The 1941 season ended as the speculation concerning Foxx increased. The Red Sox finished in second place, seventeen games behind the Yankees. This would assure each Red Sox regular a one thousand dollar supplement as the team's share of World Series revenue. Foxx finished the season hitting an even .300, about where he had been all year long. And, although his home run total dropped to nineteen, 1941 marked the thirteenth consecutive year he batted in more than one hundred runs—his 1941 total was 104. His teammate Ted Williams hit a spectacular .406 to become the first major leaguer to hit .400 since Bill Terry of the Giants hit .401 in 1930. Williams also led the American League in home runs with thirty-seven and he batted in 120 runs.[122]

While the press and others were speculating about his future, Foxx and Ted Williams flew to California at the end of the season to play in several exhibition games for $250.00 an appearance. These games were arranged by Joe Pironne, a West Coast promoter. Jimmie and Ted joined a group of Pacific Coast League players and participated in games at Los Angeles, San Francisco, and Oakland. In addition to playing games involving Coast League stars, Pirrone had also scheduled several contests with the Eastern Colored Giants of the Negro League, a team that was barnstorming in the West. The game in Los Angeles was against the Colored Giants and the minor-major All-Stars won 9-6. The feature of this contest was the exhibition of the versatility of Foxx. Each inning he played a different position, pitching in the ninth inning. This exhibition venture ended in San Francisco; here Foxx played with one group of Pacific Coast All-Stars and Williams with the other. Although the promoter obtained Foxx and Williams for these games, the games were an economic failure. The attendance in San Francisco was less than 2,000, and Williams later told Eddie Doherty, director of Red Sox public relations, that the exhibition venture was "a financial flop."[123]

After the California experiment was over, Jimmie headed for sun and golf in St. Petersburg, although he no longer was affiliated with any golf course there. In mid–November he made a visit to his native Eastern Shore of Maryland. Foxx and Bill Nicholson, another native of the area and outfielder for the Cubs, were invited as honored guests at the second annual banquet of the Eastern Shore Sports Writers Association. This affair was held at the Easton, Maryland, fire house on November 18. More than 300 baseball fans were present to pay tribute to these two major leaguers and natives. Among those present were Frank "Home Run" Baker, Max Bishop, Rube Walberg, and George Case of the Senators.[124]

In early December the Red Sox asked waivers on Foxx, and there was a flurry of speculation that he would wind up with the Giants. When Foxx was questioned about the waiver his response was that he would go wherever he was sent. Collins sought to play down the rumors, saying, "it is customary to ask waivers on a lot of players in the off season" and affirmed that Jimmie would be sent a contract for 1942. About a week later, and after the waivers were recalled, Cronin explained to a Philadelphia reporter that the Red Sox were not planning for either Foxx or himself to be regulars in 1942. It was envisioned that Tony Lupien would become the regular first baseman and that Johnny Pesky, up from Louisville, would replace Cronin as short stop.[125] In the meantime Foxx was in Florida, working to keep in good physical condition and looking forward to participating in the baseball players golf tournament in February. A St. Petersburg sportswriter decried the idea that Jimmie was about finished and that the Red Sox were not counting on his being a regular in 1942. He wrote that Jimmie was only thirty-four years old and that "in action and condition" he seemed much younger. He noted that Foxx was still one of the fastest men in the American League and was a man who "stays in shape twelve months of the year and never dissipates." He thought it was ridiculous for anyone to say Foxx had a bad season since he hit .300 and had a fielding percentage of .992.[126]

Foxx and his family spent most of the winter in St. Petersburg. Their youngest son was not old enough to enter school and Jimmie, Jr., was in boarding school. Foxx played golf, fished, and kept in good condition. He had decided that if any of the young prospects for first base wanted his position, they would have to win it; he was not ready to abdicate.[127] In the meantime he had begun contract talks with Collins and Cronin, and on February 26 it was announced that he had agreed to terms and signed his 1942 contract. Although terms were not revealed, it was speculated that he had signed for about one-half of what he was paid in 1941, approximately ten or twelve thousand dollars.[128]

Spring practice was a dismal experience for Jimmie because he fell, and broke a toe on his left foot before the Grapefruit League exhibition games started. In March he tripped over a bench in the Red Sox dressing room when he was heading for the shower, fell, and broke the bone.[129] This accident relegated Jimmie to the bench for several weeks. In the interim, Tony Lupien played first base. By the first week in April, after a wait of three weeks, Foxx returned to first base. His hitting and fielding were not impaired, but his running was still "not up to par."[130] Jimmie started the season at first base, and through the first week of May was hitting .326. However, shortly afterwards he went into a slight slump and his average fell below .300. A recurring sinus infection affected his eyesight and, although he wore glasses during practice, he refused to wear them during the game. One reporter declared that ballplayers knew Foxx was having "eye problems" and were critical of his refusal to wear glasses. It was the opinion of some players that Jimmie was "too vain" to wear glasses and that he was risking shortening his career by such behavior.[131]

Misfortune continued to plague Jimmie. On one occasion in mid–May he was on the mound pitching batting practice when Tony Lupine hit a line drive which struck Jimmie in the side, fracturing a rib and causing a painful bruise. This accident required bandaging of his torso and made it almost impossible for him to swing the bat. Nevertheless, he continued to try to play. His batting average slipped to .270. At the same time, infected teeth required that Jimmie have three extracted, an operation that forced him to miss several games.[132]

Although the Red Sox had asked waivers on Foxx in the fall of 1941 and he was passed on by all of the American League teams, the waiver was withdrawn. At this time and since it seemed obvious that the Red Sox were trying to move Jimmie, some, including Foxx, felt that the Red Sox should give him his release so that he would be free to make an arrangement with a club on his own. The Red Sox refused to release Jimmie; instead, they signed him to a new contract. However, the Red Sox continued to try to dispose of Foxx even after the 1942 season started. In May waivers were again asked on Foxx and when all American League teams passed, the Cubs and Phillies expressed interest in Jimmie. Now officials for the Red Sox negotiated a deal in which they were able to sell Foxx to the Cubs for more than the $7,500.00 waiver price—probably $10,000.00. The sale was announced on June 1, and news of the sale was a surprise to Jimmie, who had no previous knowledge of the negotiations or what was happening. On this date Foxx was not in Boston. He had been called to his home in Jenkinton, Pennsylvania, because of the illness of his son, Kenneth. His son became suddenly ill, was taken to the hospital for observation, and, the next morning, was operated on for appendicitis. After the operation and a good prognosis for his son, Foxx took the train for Boston. He was accompanied by his oldest son, Jimmie, Jr., who was going to Boston for a brief visit with his father. The announcement of his sale to the Cubs came at the same time he and his son were journeying to Boston, and Foxx did not know of his sale until after he reached his apartment and was given the news by Dom DiMaggio.[133]

Although news of his sale to the Cubs came as a surprise and shock to him, Foxx's response to the situation was a most diplomatic one. He told a reporter, "I hate to leave Boston. ... I have enjoyed my stay here. ... I think it is the greatest town in baseball. ... I have been very happy here." He admitted that he "didn't know much about the National League" but that he knew "Chicago was a great city" and that "he looked forward to playing for his old friend Jimmy Wilson," who was the manager of the Cubs.[134] Jimmie's teammates—Williams, DiMaggio, Cronin, and others—praised him as "one of the nicest guys they had ever known." Williams declared, "He's the greatest guy I've ever known. ... I never expect to meet a star with as fine a disposition as Jimmie. ... He was a fine friend to me." Cronin stated that Jimmie "was one of the greatest guys I was ever associated with, and I regret he will no longer be with the Sox. We all wish him well."[135]

Cronin's remarks were public relations comments. Players were aware that there were tensions between Cronin and such old Athletics as Grove, Foxx, and others. There was some speculation that Cronin was suspicious and jealous of Foxx, especially of his friendship with Red Sox owner Tom Yawkey. Cronin feared Foxx might use this friendship in an attempt to take his job as manager. The *Philadelphia Inquirer*, in a story on June 2, was probably reporting the situation in Boston more accurately when it declared that the sale of Foxx to the Cubs "ended one of the bitterest internal feuds in baseball." For the past six years, this paper affirmed, the Red Sox house had been a divided one—Cronin on one side and Grove, Foxx, Cramer, and the former Athletics on the other.[136]

Sportswriters, fans and even umpires were disappointed that Foxx was leaving Boston. For example, the day after Foxx departed, 2,727 fans "crowded" Fenway for a game with the Indians. During the contest some fans began chanting, "We want Foxx," and they booed and jeered Cronin when he came to bat. Umpires Bill McGowan, Cal Hubbard, and Eddie Rommel expressed regrets that Jimmie was going to the National League. They acknowledged that Foxx was not only popular with the fans and his peers, but that he was equally popular with the umpires. He made "umpiring a pleasant profession.

He never alibied his mistakes. ... [H]e never blamed an umpire or complained if an umpire made a mistake," declared Rommel. They all agreed, "It's too bad there aren't more like Foxx in baseball." Rommel noted that he had known Jimmie throughout his career and that Foxx had never done anything to embarrass a teammate, an opponent, or an umpire. "I hate to see him leave the American League and I wish him well in Chicago."[137] Foxx's sense of decency and fair play and his rapport with umpires and others would accompany him to the National League. Jimmie's career would remain free of altercations with umpires, and he would eventually conclude his career without ever having being tossed out of a game by an umpire.

Before departing Boston, Jimmie told a reporter that he had talked over the telephone with both manager Jimmy Wilson and Cubs general manager James Gallagher. He informed them that he would report later in the week but that he would not be able to play for a while because of his cracked rib.[138]

Notes

1. *Philadelphia Inquirer*, December 10, 1935; James Charlton, ed., *The Baseball Chronology* (New York: Macmillan, 1991), p. 282.

2. *The Sporting News*, January 2, 11, 1936; *Philadelphia Evening Bulletin*, January 11, 24, 1936.

3. *The Sporting News*, January 2, 1936; assorted clippings, January 30, 1936, in Max Bishop scrapbook, Babe Ruth Museum, Baltimore, Maryland.

4. *Philadelphia Evening Bulletin*, February 6, 1936; *The Sporting News*, January 16, 1936.

5. *The Sporting News*, March 19, 1936; *Boston Globe*, March 26, 1936.

6. For example, see *The Sporting News*, April 9, 1936; *Philadelphia Evening Bulletin*, April 15, 1936.

7. *The Sporting News*, April 23, 1936; *Boston Herald*, January 30, 1943; Mark Stang and Linda Harkness, *Rosters* (Smyrna, Ga., n.p., c. 1991).

8. *The Sporting News*, May 14, July 2, 1936; *New York Herald Tribune*, July 24, 1951.

9. *Philadelphia Evening Bulletin*, May 26, 1936.

10. *The Sporting News*, May 14, June 18, 1936.

11. *Ibid.*, February 6, 1936, May 8, 1941.

12. *Ibid.*, July 9, 1936.

13. *Ibid.*, July 23, 30, August 27, September 23, 1936.

14. *Ibid.*, August 6, 1936.

15. *Ibid.*, September 10, 1936; Rick Wolff, editorial director, *The Baseball Encyclopedia*, eighth edition (New York: Macmillan, 1990), p. 849.

16. For example, see *The Sporting News*, September 17, 24, October 1, 1936.

17. *The Sporting News*, December 17, 1936.

18. *Boston Herald*, June 2, 1942; interview with Kenneth Foxx, January 11, 1992.

19. *Baltimore Sun Magazine,* June 20, 1976; *Philadelphia Inquirer,* January 31, 1937.

20. Assorted clippings, September 24, 1936.

21. *The Sporting News,* January 7, 1937; *Philadelphia Inquirer,* January 31, 1937.

22. *Philadelphia Evening Bulletin,* January 23, 1930; *The Sporting News,* January 14, March 25, 1937.

23. *Philadelphia Inquirer,* March 4, 1937.

24. Robert Gregory, *Diz: Dizzy Dean and Baseball During the Great Depression* (New York: Viking, 1992), p. 246.

25. *The Sporting News,* March 25, 1937.

26. *Ibid.,* December 29, 1938; April 15, May 13, 1937; *Philadelphia Evening Bulletin,* April 17, 1937; assorted clippings, April 16, 1937, in Foxx files, Baseball Library, Cooperstown, New York.

27. Assorted clippings, March, 1939, in Foxx items, Nanci Canaday collection.

28. *The Sporting News,* May 6, June 3, July 8, 15, 1937.

29. Charlton, ed., *Baseball Chronology,* p. 295; Wolff, ed., *Baseball Encyclopedia,* p. 1923.

30. *The Sporting News,* June 3, July 1, 1937.

31. *Ibid.,* June 3, 1937.

32. *Ibid.,* December 13, 1941, June 27, 1940; Dan Warfield, *The Roaring Redhead, Larry MacPhail—Baseball's Great Innovator* (South Bend, Ind.: Diamond Communications, Inc., 1987), pp. 98–99.

33. Marc Okkonen, *Baseball Uniforms of the Twentieth Century* (New York: Sterling Publishing Company, 1991), p. 8; Bob Broeg and William J. Miller, *Baseball from a Different Angle* (South Bend, Ind.: Diamond Communications, 1988), p. 253; Charlton, ed., *Baseball Chronology,* pp. 316, 423.

34. *The Sporting News,* October 14, December 16, 1937.

35. *Philadelphia Evening Bulletin,* September 23, 1937; assorted clippings, June 6, 1940, in Foxx files, Baseball Library, Cooperstown, New York.

36. *The Sporting News,* December 9, 1937; *Philadelphia Evening Bulletin,* December 28, 1938; *Philadelphia Inquirer,* October 9, 1937; *Boston Herald,* June 3, 1940.

37. *The Sporting News,* September 30, 1937; *Philadelphia Evening Ledger,* November 17, 1937; *Boston Herald,* November 23, 1937.

38. *The Sporting News,* January 27, December 18, 1938.

39. *Ibid.,* February 3, 1938, January 12, 1939; *Philadelphia Inquirer,* January 26, 1939.

40. *The Sporting News,* March 10, 17, 1938.

41. *Ibid.,* May 19, 26, June 16, 23, 1938.

42. *Ibid.,* June 23, December 8, 1938; Thomas Meany, *Baseball's Greatest Players* (New York: Grosset and Dunlap, 1953), p. 91.

43. *The Sporting News,* July 14, 28, 1938.

44. Charlton, ed., *Baseball Chronology,* p. 302; *Philadelphia Evening Bulletin,* December 28, 1938; *The Sporting News,* June 16, August 11, 1938.

45. *The Sporting News,* August 18, 1938.

46. *Boston Globe*, October 2, 1938; Wolff, ed., *Baseball Encyclopedia*, p. 913.

47. *Boston Globe*, November 2, 1938; *Philadelphia Evening Bulletin*, November 2, 1938.

48. Assorted clippings, November 14, 1938, in Foxx files, Baseball Library, Cooperstown, New York; *Philadelphia Inquirer*, December 31, 1938; *Boston Globe*, January 7, 1939; *The Sporting News*, January 12, 1939.

49. *Philadelphia Inquirer*, November 3, 1938; *The Sporting News*, November 3, 1938, April 27, 1939.

50. The Sporting News, October 13, 20, December 8, 1938.

51. See copy of title search in Sudlersville Memorial Library, copy prepared by J. and M. Clements, September 9, 1990; also, see *Washington Post*, October 24, 1987.

52. *The Sporting News*, December 29, 1938.

53. *Philadelphia Evening Bulletin*, January 19, 1939.

54. *The Sporting News*, February 2, 9, 16, 1939; *Philadelphia Evening Bulletin*, February 6, 1939.

55. *The Sporting News*, February 23, March 16, 1939.

56. Ted Williams, *My Turn at Bat: The Story of My Life* (New York: Simon and Schuster, 1969), p. 60; *Miami Herald*, March 6, 1956.

57. *The Sporting News*, March 23, April 13, 1939.

58. *Ibid.*, March 30, April 20, 1939.

59. *Ibid.*, May 11, 25, 1939; *Philadelphia Evening Bulletin*, May 16, 17, 1939; *Philadelphia Inquirer*, May 17, 1939.

60. *The Sporting News*, July 6, 13, 1939.

61. *Philadelphia Evening Bulletin*, June 29, 1939.

62. *The Sporting News*, May 4, 1939; Frank Graham, *Lou Gehrig, a Quiet Hero* (New York: G.P. Putnam's Sons, 1942), p. 208.

63. *The Sporting News*, June 22, 1939, August 10, 1955.

64. *Ibid.*, August 10, 1939.

65. *Ibid.*, August 10, 1939.

66. *Ibid.*, August 24, 1939; *Boston Globe*, July 23, 1967.

67. *The Sporting News*, August 24, 1939.

68. *Philadelphia Evening Bulletin*, September 9, 11, 22, 1939.

69. *The Sporting News*, October 12, 19, December 28, 1939.

70. *The Sporting News*, January 19, 1939, February 22, August 30, 1945, February 25, 1928; *Philadelphia Evening Bulletin*, January 19, 1939; *Boston Herald*, January 18, 1958.

71. *Philadelphia Inquirer*, May 10, 1954; *Boston Globe*, January 29, 1951; for examples of Gomez/Foxx stories, see *The Sporting News*, September 27, 1932, June 10, 1937; Charles Einstein, editor, *The Second Fireside Book of Baseball* (New York: Simon and Schuster, 1958), p. 216; Arthur Daley, *All The Home Run Kings* (New York: G.P. Putman, 1972), pp. 44-45; John Holway, *The Sluggers* (Alexandria, Virginia: Redefinition, 1989), p. 152; John F. Steadman, "Foxx's Unbelievable Power," in *Baseball Digest* (December, 1962), p. 78; Tom Meany, "The Beast, They Called Him," in *Baseball Digest* (September, 1967), pp. 78-79; *Philadelphia Evening Bulletin*, January 28, 1951.

72. *The Sporting News*, October 12, 1939, January 11, 1940.

73. *Ibid.*, October 26, 1939.
74. *Ibid.*, October 5, 1939.
75. *Ibid.*, November 9, 16, 1939.
76. *Philadelphia Evening Bulletin*, January 23, 1958; Williams, *My Turn At Bat*, p. 60.
77. Dan Guttman, *Baseball Babylon, from the Black Sox to Pete Rose, The Real Stories Behind the Scandals That Rocked the Game* (New York: Penguin Books, 1992), pp. 328, 331.
78. James A. Vlasich, *A Legend for the Legendary: The Origin of the Baseball Hall of Fame* (Bowling Green, Ohio: Bowling Green State University Popular Press, c. 1990), pp. 29, 36.
79. *Ibid.*, p. 30ff.; *The Sporting News*, January 13, 1938.
80. *The Sporting News*, May 31, 1934; Vlasich, *A Legend for the Legendary ...*, pp. 37-38.
81. Vlasich, *A Legend for the Legendary*, p. 42; *The Sporting News*, December 24, 1936; Charles C. Alexander, *Our Game, An American Baseball History* (New York: Henry Holt and Company, 1991), p. 172. Exceptions for the five-year period have been Lou Gehrig and Roberto Clemente.
82. *The Sporting News*, January 13, 1938.
83. *Ibid.*, February 9, 1939; Okkonen, *Baseball Uniforms*, p. 5.
84. *The Sporting News*, June 15, 1939.
85. *Ibid.*, July 27, 1939.
86. *New York Times*, August 27, 1939; Warfield, *The Roaring Redhead*, p. 90.
87. *The Sporting News*, November 16, December 21, 1939, January 11, February 29, 1940.
88. *Ibid.*, February 29, 1940.
89. *Ibid.*, March 21, 1940.
90. *Ibid.*
91. Dom DiMaggio with Bill Gilbert, *Real Grass, Real Heroes: Baseball's Historic 1941 Season* (New York: Kensington Publishing Corp., 1990), pp. 37-38; *Boston Herald*, June 2, 1942; *The Sporting News*, April 11, 1940.
92. *The Sporting News*, April 25, May 23, 1940.
93. *Ibid.*, May 2, 1940.
94. *Ibid.*, May 23, 30, June 6, 1940.
95. *Ibid.*, June 20, July 4, 18, 1940.
96. *Ibid.*, July 25, August 1, 8, 1940.
97. *Ibid.*, August 8, 15, 1940.
98. *Ibid.*, August 15, September 5, 12, 26, December 19, 1940; *Philadelphia Evening Bulletin*, August 17, 1940.
99. *The Sporting News*, September 26, October 10, December 19, 1940.
100. *Philadelphia Inquirer*, September 24, 1940.
101. *Philadelphia Evening Bulletin*, January 28, 1951.
102. *The Sporting News*, December 19, 1940.
103. *Ibid.*, November 7, December 26, 1940.
104. Assorted items, 1940, in Dell Foxx scrapbook #1; *Sports Illustrated* (April 5, 1982), pp. 72-74.
105. *The Sporting News*, February 6, 13, 1941.

106. *Ibid.*, August 5, 1967; *Philadelphia Evening Bulletin*, June 2, 1943; Bob Broeg, *Super Stars of Baseball* (St. Louis: The Sporting News, 1971), p. 85.

107. Assorted clippings, February 15, 1941, in Foxx files, Baseball Library, Cooperstown, New York.

108. *The Sporting News*, January 30, February 4, 1941; *Philadelphia Evening Bulletin*, August 15, 1941.

109. *The Sporting News*, February 27, March 6, 1941.

110. *Ibid.*, April 3, 1941.

111. *Ibid.*, April 17, 1941.

112. *Philadelphia Evening Bulletin*, April 24, May 14, 1941.

113. *The Sporting News*, May 8, 22, 29, 1941.

114. Assorted clippings, June 4, 1941, in Foxx files, Baseball Library, Cooperstown New York; *The Sporting News*, June 5, July 3, 1941.

115. *The Sporting News*, July 3, 17, 1941.

116. *Ibid.*, July 17, 1941; Charlton, ed., *Baseball Chronology*, p. 316.

117. Bruce Kuklick, *To Every Thing A Season: Shibe Park and Urban Philadelphia, 1909–1926* (Princeton: Princeton University Press, 1991), p. 96.

118. *The Sporting News*, August 7, 1941; assorted clippings, August 23, 1941, in Foxx files, Baseball Library, Cooperstown.

119. *Philadelphia Evening Bulletin*, August 15, 1941; *The Sporting News*, August 21, September 11, October 16, November 13, 27, 1941; *Boston Globe*, October 4, 1941.

120. *Boston Globe*, October 4, 1941; assorted clippings, November 29, 1941, in Foxx files, Baseball Library, Cooperstown.

121. *Philadelphia Evening Bulletin*, September 18, 1941; *The Sporting News*, August 21, 1941; *Boston Herald*, June 2, 4, 1941.

122. Wolff, ed., *Baseball Encyclopedia*, p. 1600.

123. *Los Angeles Times*, October 1, 8, 9, 1941; *The Sporting News*, October 9, 16, 23, 1941.

124. *The Sporting News*, October 23, November 27, 1941; *Philadelphia Evening Bulletin*, November 18, 1941.

125. *Boston Globe*, November 29, 1941; *The Sporting News*, December 4, 18, 1941; *Philadelphia Evening Bulletin*, December 11, 1941.

126. *The Sporting News*, December 25, 1941.

127. *Ibid.*, February 12, 1942.

128. *Philadelphia Inquirer*, June 1, 2, 1942; *Boston Herald*, June 4, 1942.

129. The Sporting News, March 19, 26, 1942.

130. Ibid., April 16, 1942.

131. *Philadelphia Inquirer*, March 23, June 1, 1942; *Boston Herald*, June 2, 1942.

132. *Boston Herald*, June 2, 1942; *The Sporting News*, June 4, 1942; *Philadelphia Evening Bulletin*, June 1, 2, 1942.

133. *Philadelphia Evening Bulletin*, June 1, 1942; *Boston Herald*, June 1, 2, 1942.

134. *Boston Herald*, June 1, 3, 4, 1942; *Boston Globe*, June 2, 1942.

135. *Boston Herald*, June 1, 4, 1942.

136. *Philadelphia Inquirer*, June 2, 1942; Peter Golenbock, *Fenway: An*

Unexpurgated History of the Boston Red Sox (New York: G.P. Putnam's Sons, 1992), pp. 96, 136, 143.

137. *Chicago Tribune*, June, 1942; *Boston Herald*, June 3, 1942; *Philadelphia Evening Bulletin*, August 13, 1941; *The Sporting News*, July 17, 1941.

138. *Boston Herald*, June 2, 1942; *Chicago Tribune*, June 4, 1942.

Six
The War Years, 1941–1945

The war that began in Europe in September, 1939, was of great concern to the United States government and to the people of the country. After the fall of France and Norway to the Germans, Soviet aggression in the Baltic area, and the expansion of the Japanese in South East Asia, the United States Congress instituted conscription as a preparedness measure in the fall of 1940. The first major league baseball player to be drafted into military service was Hugh Mulcahy, a pitcher for the Philadelphia Phillies; he entered the army in March, 1941.[1] Few other major leaguers, however, were drafted in 1941. Later that year the war took a drastic turn; on December 7, 1941, the Japanese attacked the United States naval installation at Pearl Harbor in the Hawaiian Islands. This brought the United States into a war which by now had grown to worldwide proportions. The response of major league baseball to this national crisis was to pledge total dedication to the war effort. At the winter meeting of major league owners and officials in Chicago a few days after Pearl Harbor, Ford Frick, president of the National League, wired President Franklin D. Roosevelt that major league baseball has pledged "complete cooperation and assistance in this time of national crisis." He concluded with the statement that "we are yours to command." *The Sporting News*, in its first issue after Pearl Harbor, declared that "baseball was ready to close down if asked to do so by President Roosevelt."[2]

Baseball officials were concerned to show their complete support of the war effort and at the same time did not wish to elicit any criticism that some might view as using manpower and materials in nonessential or perhaps frivolous ways.[3] In an attempt to seek guidance or advice as to whether baseball should cease trying to do business as usual, Commissioner Landis wrote to President Roosevelt in early January, eliciting his opinion as to what course baseball should follow. Two days later, on January 15, 1942, the President replied to Landis. He recommended that baseball proceed with its programs and schedule. Baseball, he noted, should be given no special status or concessions in draft deferments or travel allocations, but he advised that baseball continue as best it could. He declared, "I honestly feel that it would be best for the country to keep baseball going." He noted that more people would be working longer hours and that they needed recreation to take their minds off work. He concluded his letter to Landis with the suggestion that the teams play more night games since this would permit day-shift war workers to attend games occasionally.[4]

Baseball owners responded to the President's suggestion by increasing the number of night games permitted to a team from seven to fourteen for all clubs except the Senators; they were allowed to play twenty-one games at night. The one place where night baseball was banned during 1942 and 1943 was New York City. This was done because the lights from the city made it easier for enemy submarines to detect and prey on coastal shipping. In the first six months of 1942 about 300 ships, of one type or another, were sunk along the east coast of the country. Since city lights provided silhouettes of ships in the area, New York City experienced brown-outs and minimized the use of lights in the area until the submarine menace was removed, which was by the end of 1943. Night baseball resumed in the New York area in the spring of 1944.[5]

A Gallup poll taken in the spring of 1942 indicated that more than two-thirds of the American public supported the opinion of their president and approved the continued operation of major league baseball. A poll of servicemen, taken about the same time, revealed that over 80 percent of them believed that major league baseball should continue to operate during war time.[6]

Baseball executives termed the President's letter to Landis a "green light" for baseball to continue its normal course, or as near normal as possible with the means and resources available. Among the means of demonstrating the patriotic ardor of organized ball, all major league owners began to have the National Anthem played prior to every game and to admit men in uniform to games without charge. In November, 1942, the Selective Service Act was modified by Congress to permit the drafting of men from ages eighteen to thirty-eight, and deferments were limited to men working in war industries or agriculture and certain hardship cases. Within a year, two hundred nineteen major league players were inducted into the armed forces. By the time hostilities ceased in 1945 more than a thousand major league players were in the military forces.[7]

Although baseball continued during the war, some minor leagues suspended play. For example, the Texas League officials decided to suspend operations for the duration of the war. The major leagues, however, continued to operate, but the quality of play was not what it had been in the pre-war years. Major league rosters in the war years included a diversity of players: from fifteen-year-old Joe Nuxhall of the Reds to forty-one-year-old Al Simmons, whom the Red Sox enticed out of retirement, and the one-armed outfielder, Pete Gray, who played for the St. Louis Browns in 1944. Some general managers such as William O. DeWitt of the Browns used a few part-time players, men engaged in essential war work who occasionally "moonlighted" as major league baseball players.[8] Perhaps most of the regular players were men classified 4-F, by their draft boards. These were men who were unable to pass the induction physical examination. In 1944 there were over 260 major league players classified 4-F and these men constituted the majority of players on some clubs. For example, in 1944 the Browns' roster included eighteen players who were classified 4-F.[9]

During the war some baseball men such as Clark Griffith, owner of the Washington Senators, sought to help alleviate the player shortage by recruiting players from Latin America. Although some Latin Americans had been on major league rosters since the early twentieth century, there was no significant attempt by any club to sign them until after 1940. Griffith appointed a Latin American friend and baseball enthusiast, Joe Cambria, as a scout for the Senators. His aim was to find and sign promising young Latin players for the Washington club. The efforts of Cambria and others resulted in more than fifty Cuban baseball players being signed by the Senators and a few other teams during the war years. The Senators, however, were more active in recruiting Latin players than any other club. They had, for example, eighteen Latin players at spring training in 1944. Although most of the Latin players recruited were Cubans, a few players from Mexico, Puerto Rico, and Venezuela were also given a chance to play major league baseball in the early 1940s.[10]

While Griffith and others sought to help replenish the player ranks with Latin baseball players, there were some who advocated that the major leagues should remove the color line and sign black players. Since the 1920s there had been two Negro baseball major leagues, and in the off seasons, from the late 1920s through the thirties, black and white major league stars often engaged in barnstorm games against each other. Although some of the black players won the praise and respect of their white opponents, there was no attempt by any American or National League club to sign black players prior to the war years. However, during the thirties some sports writers such as Heywood Broun, Shirley Povich, and Dan Parker suggested that major league baseball should permit the signing of black players.[11]

In 1942 Leo Durocher, manager of the Brooklyn Dodgers, said that he "would hire colored players if he were not barred by the owners" and if the commissioner would permit him to do so.[12] This prompted a rejoinder from Landis who shortly thereafter issued a statement declaring, "Negroes are not barred from organized baseball by the commissioner and never have been during the twenty years I have served as commissioner." Landis denied that there was any rule or agreement among baseball authorities which barred Negroes from major league baseball. At the same time Ford Frick, president of the National League, said he "would welcome a Negro player in the National League." Despite such statements, the baseball status quo prevailed throughout 1942 and 1943.

However, there were several publicized "try outs" for black players involving the Pirates, Phillies, Red Sox, Indians, and others, but there were no signings.[13]

At the winter meeting of major league owners and officials in December, 1943, the black actor and activist, Paul Robeson, made a plea to the baseball establishment that Negro players be allowed to enter organized ball.[14] However, baseball owners took no action to sign blacks. It was not until the fall of 1945, two months after the end of hostilities in World War II, that the first black player was signed by a major league club. In October of that year Branch Rickey, president of the Brooklyn Dodgers, signed Negro League star Jackie Robinson to a contract with the Montreal Royals of the International League, a triple-A farm club of the Dodgers.[15] There was no negative reaction to this signing by baseball owners; however, there was opposition to major league baseball breaking the color line. Within a week of Robinson's signing, J.B. Martin, president of the Negro American League, and T. Wilson, president of the Negro National League, sent a protest to the new baseball commissioner, A.B. Chandler. They offered a vigorous protest to Rickey's signing of Robinson, and they accused the Dodger president of breach of contract. They claimed that Robinson earlier had agreed, orally, to play the following season for the Kansas City Monarchs.[16] Despite the protest of Negro League officials, Robinson's contract with the Dodgers was honored, and he was with Montreal in 1946. In another area the color line was also abolished during the war. Segregated seating of spectators in major league baseball parks had ended in all major league parks except at Sportsman's Park in St. Louis. In the spring of 1944 this practice ended, when it was announced that Negroes would no longer be confined to seats in the screened-in right field pavilion at the park.[17]

The war not only affected the quality of play in the major leagues, it also affected the quality of the baseball used by the leagues. Since 1920 the baseball used by both the American and National League had a cork and rubber center. During the winter of 1941–42 the Japanese army overran the principal rubber-producing regions of the world in southeast Asia. This resulted in termination of the rubber supply for the western nations. The federal government almost immediately banned the use of crude or scrap rubber for nonessential items, including baseballs. This prompted the major manufacturers of baseballs, A.G. Spalding and the Reach Company, to experiment with producing a satisfactory replacement ball. By 1943, company personnel and baseball authorities had approved a substitute known as the blata ball. This ball was no different in appearance from the ball used prior to the war. However, its center consisted of ground cork bound together with blata, which was a nonessential material obtained from processing the milky-white juice obtained from blata trees in the West Indies. Blata was also used in the manufacture of golf balls and telephone cable.[18]

The blata ball was not a popular substitute; in comparison with the prewar ball it was dead. Frank McCormick, the first baseman of the Cincinnati

Reds, declared that hitting the blata ball "was like hitting a piece of concrete." The manufacturers admitted that it was twenty-five percent less resilient than its predecessor. In the meantime, scientists in the United States discovered how to make synthetic rubber. Beginning in 1944, the manufacturers of baseballs were allowed to use synthetic rubber to replace blata. The era of the dead ball was only one season.[19]

During the last three years of the war (1943–1945) the training and travel schedules of the major league clubs were modified to meet certain suggested travel specifications of the federal government. In December, 1942, the Director of the Office of Defense Transportation requested that Commissioner Landis and the baseball owners arrange a schedule to "eliminate waste in mileage traveled" and to lessen the burden on railroad capacity, which was being heavily taxed by the military.[20] In the first week of January, 1943, baseball executives met with Landis in Chicago to devise plans to curtail travel. By the end of the month major league baseball had agreed on the following items: (1) the 1943 schedule was revised so that no team would visit another league city more than three times a season and (2) the season would open a week later than usual. It was claimed that the revised schedule would save "five million man miles in travel."[21]

The baseball owners also adopted a new format for spring training. Before the end of January, Landis directed all sixteen of the major league teams to conduct their spring training north of the Mason-Dixon Line and the Ohio River. The only exceptions were the St. Louis teams; they were permitted to train at any place within the state of Missouri. The beginning of spring training was set for March 15, and among the sites where the teams would train were: Red Sox at Tufts College in Medford, Massachusetts; Philadelphia Athletics at Frederick, Maryland; Yankees at Atlantic City; Senators at College Park, Maryland; Cubs and White Sox at French Lick, Indiana; the Phillies at Wilmington, Delaware; and the Tigers at Evansville, Indiana.[22]

Major league baseball devoted considerable attention to charity and relief activities during the course of the war. Such activities actually preceded the nation's involvement in the war. The initial activity in this area was the spring All-Star game in Tampa, Florida, played in March, 1940, to aid the Finnish Relief Fund, which was directed by former President Herbert Hoover. This game resulted in more than $23,000.00 for the fund. Major league officials also agreed that the proceeds from the 1941 summer All-Star game would be donated to the United Service Organization to provide sports equipment for the armed services. Major league baseball donated $53,000.00 to the USO, the first time in the history of the All-Star game that the proceeds were not directed to a fund to aid needy ball players. Also in the summer of 1941, some clubs began the practice of admitting men in uniform to games without charge.[23] At a joint meeting of American and National League owners and executives and Commissioner Landis in January, 1942, it was decided that in the coming season there would be two All-Star games and that the proceeds from both would go to aid the Army-Navy Ball and Bat Fund. This practice was continued in 1943 and 1944, years when there were two All-Star games each season. It was also agreed at this January meeting that a portion of the World Series receipts would be donated to relief funds for servicemen.[24] In addition to the decision to devote the proceeds from the All-Star games to armed forces recreational purposes, each of the sixteen major league clubs agreed to play at least one exhibition game during the season and donate the proceeds to the Army-Navy Fund for athletic equipment or to the American Red Cross. One estimate is that major league baseball contributed more than $2.9 million to war charities and causes in the years 1940–45.[25]

At the January, 1942, meeting of baseball owners and executives they decided that at least 10 percent of their salaries would be used to purchase United States Savings Bonds or "war bonds," and they urged that the players follow their example.[26] Individual clubs also sponsored special sales or auctions to promote the sale of war bonds. For example, in the fall of 1942 the glove of Cardinal outfielder Terry Moore was auctioned by a St. Louis radio station and was "sold" for the purchase of a $5,000.00 war bond. On another occasion an autographed baseball was auctioned for a $7,500.00 bond, and a portrait of Connie Mack was auctioned by the Philadelphia Sports Writers Association for $16,000.00 in war bonds. Baseball clubs sold war bonds and stamps at their admission gates, and they urged all employees to participate in club plans for the purchase of bonds with each pay check. One baseball historian estimates that the National League alone was responsible for the sale of over $1 billion in war bonds.[27] The government urged citizens to conserve paper, kitchen fats, tinfoil, and other items and to contribute such to centers designated in towns and cities. These items, it was claimed, were essential to the war effort, and they would be recycled for additional use or, as kitchen fats, would be used to manufacture explosives. Baseball owners participated in this conservation effort by offering, on certain designated days, free admission to the game for persons bringing to the park depository certain quantities of bundled newspapers or pounds of kitchen grease.[28]

Major league baseball contributed to the national war effort by promoting the sale of war bonds, participating in conservation projects, alerting the public to the constant need of blood by the Red Cross and urging the public to participate in the blood donation program of this agency. For example, in Brooklyn, Red Barber, who broadcast the Dodger games, made daily appeals for the public to contribute blood at their local Red Cross donation center.[29] In local areas players and team officials often set examples for others by making appointments with donor centers and contributing blood. On one occasion in the fall of 1942, when Foxx was visiting in Boston, he went to a Red Cross blood donor center and donated a pint of blood. He was quoted in the press as saying, "It gave me more satisfaction than hitting a home run in

Fenway Park." He declared, "It was a real thrill knowing my blood will be used to save the life of an American fighting man."[30]

Baseball owners and President Roosevelt were acutely aware of the positive influence baseball had on the morale of the public as well as that of the men and women in uniform.[31] Among the activities of major league baseball during the war to enhance and boost morale was arranging to broadcast a number of regular season games and the World Series over the Armed Forces Radio Service. Before the end of the war this project "encompassed twenty short wave stations along the East and West coasts"; these stations beamed play-by-play coverage to 166 outlets around the world. During the off season, copies of the World Series films were shipped abroad to be shown to the armed forces stationed throughout the world.[32]

There were no barnstorming tours for major league players in the off season during the war years. However, a number of major league players did travel, some of them extensively, during the war. In the fall-winter of 1944–45 major league baseball sent five contingents of players, managers, and umpires overseas to visit troops in the various war theaters. This was a joint project of major league baseball and the United Service Organization. It was a project designed to help maintain morale among servicemen by permitting them to see and talk with various baseball stars. Among the players who participated in this program were Mel Ott, Frank Frisch, Carl Hubbell, Leo Durocher, Joe Medwick and Paul Waner.[33]

In the summer of 1942 the Cubs acquired Jimmie Foxx, hoping that his bat would add power to their lineup and supplement the long-ball hitting of Bill Nicholson, a native of Chestertown, Maryland. The sports section of the *Chicago Tribune*, June 2, 1942, headlined the announcement that Foxx would arrive in the city within a couple of days. Both general manager James Gallagher and field manager Jimmie Wilson stated that they had talked with Foxx and that the veteran first baseman was pleased that he was coming to Chicago. "We need his wallop," Gallagher declared, "and he looks like a good bet to supply it. ... He is still dangerous." Two days later, when Foxx appeared at Wrigley Field in a Cubs uniform, he was besieged by fans who gave him a hearty welcome and sought to make him "feel at home."[34]

When Jimmie reported to manager Wilson, it was decided that he would not enter the lineup immediately. Foxx was still in pain from the broken rib and bruises suffered two weeks earlier when a batted ball struck him in the side. After Foxx checked in with the Cubs he was given a physical examination by the club physician, Dr. John F. Davis, who advised that Jimmie should rest a few days before attempting to play.[35] However, despite the pain and impeded movement of arms and torso, Foxx was given little rest. The Cubs were in the doldrums and Wilson needed help. Foxx, always the team player, felt that for the best interests of the team, he should try to ignore his pain and help the club. Wilson did not insert him into the lineup immediately, but he did ask him to pinch hit. His first game appearance was two days after he came to Chicago. In a game with the Giants he pinch hit for third baseman Stan Hack in the eighth inning and lifted a long fly to right field. Two days later, on June 6, he was at first base and for the next six weeks he played this position rather regularly. Although Foxx was in the lineup, his "wallop," which the Cubs eagerly expected, did not materialize.[36] His rib was slow to heal and the painful bruise lingered, all of which had a significant effect on Foxx's swinging at the pitch and on his batting average. In mid–June Jimmie also suffered a muscle injury in one of his legs and had to leave the game. This injury kept him out of the lineup for several games.[37]

In late June Jimmie had one of his better days; in a game against the Dodgers he hit a triple off his old nemesis, Johnny Allen, as the Cubs won 6–0. Foxx's hitting, however, remained anemic and reflected his physical condition. At the end of June his batting average was .171 and he had only twelve hits for seventy times at bat. One of his hits was a home run and one was a bunt. Some observers, including the sports editor of the *Chicago Tribune*, Arch Ward, implied that perhaps Foxx's hitting would improve if he wore his glasses while at bat. Jimmie ignored this suggestion, but when his hitting remained below .200 entering the second half of the season, Manager Wilson replaced him at first base with Glenn Russell.[38]

Throughout the second half of the season Foxx was used sparingly—often as a pinch hitter. On other occasions he would alternate with Russell and Phil Cavarretta at first base. In one game in late September when Wilson needed to relieve his catcher, Jimmie agreed to catch the second game of a double header with the Reds. Foxx's hitting did not improve and on occasions the fans would boo him. Jimmie's teammates were aware that his injuries hampered his performance. Lou Novikoff, a Cub outfielder, and others were aware that Foxx's swing was "out of sync" and that he was not swinging the bat as formerly.[39] Eventually, and at the suggestion of Cubs' management, he had his eyes examined to see if his sight was impaired. The physician's report, as noted in *The Sporting News*, was that "there was nothing wrong with Foxx's eyes." Jimmie's chronic sinus affliction was also bothering him this summer and it probably affected his sight.[40]

In an interview with a sports reporter, Foxx implied that part of the explanation for his poor hitting performance was the difference between the National League and the American League umpires' conception of the strike zone for hitters. He explained that in the National League "everything from the shoulders down to the bottom of your pants is a strike," whereas in the American League "the strike zone is from the letters on your shirt to just above the knees." This, he concluded, made the National League a "pitcher's paradise."[41]

Other factors affected Foxx's performance in Chicago. Although his bruised and broken ribs healed and his leg muscle improved, Foxx's routine was greatly upset by the "irregular hours" associated with the Cubs' schedule. On one occasion he noted that the night schedule of many road games, the twilight games and regular day games, often following in succession, upset one's eating and sleeping schedule. The modified schedule, he explained, helped to account for his losing twenty-eight pounds the first two months he was in Chicago.[42]

In no way, perhaps, was the National League more different for Jimmie than in the type or design of uniforms used by the Cubs. Uniforms worn by all major league players prior to 1940 were made from light flannel fabric and they were constructed to allow for a "maximum of bagginess consistent with the idea that baseball clothing ought to allow for a maximum of movement within the garment."[43] Baseball uniforms were loose fitting and might carry the name of the team in letters across the front of the shirt and the player's number on the back. In 1940 the Cubs changed the design and the fabric used in making the team uniform. The new uniforms were made from "a knitwear substance" that was supposed to be cooler than flannel. Instead of being baggy, the new uniforms were tight-fitting or "more revealing" and, it was claimed, allowed the player greater freedom of movement.[44] When Foxx arrived he was given one of these new style uniforms and a new number—not #3 which he had worn at Philadelphia and Boston, but #16. The change of number did not faze Jimmie, but he did not like the uniform, which he dubbed "a monkey suit." He said wearing it made one feel like a "skinned rat" and that the material would not absorb perspiration. He stated that the "uniform was tight where it should be loose" and did not present a "dignified appearance."[45] The sports columnist Dan Daniels wrote that the Cub uniform made the players look like visitors from Mars, and that many of the players "felt demeaned" wearing it. Daniels termed the new uniforms "bush league," claimed they made the players a "laughing stock," and were more appropriate for the circus than for baseball players. *The Sporting News* echoed these sentiments and claimed that the uniforms gave the players an inferiority complex which adversely affected their playing.[46] After a three-year experiment, the Cubs management abandoned the use of this new style uniform and returned to the use of the traditional uniform.[47]

Foxx was keenly aware that his performance was a big disappointment to the Cubs fans—as it was to himself. He was somewhat frustrated by his play and by the seeming utility role he was fulfilling for the Cubs. On one occasion he told a reporter from the *Philadelphia Inquirer* that when the time came in his career that he could no longer play as a regular he would quit the game, that he would not become a "bench warmer."[48] Foxx and the Cubs finally finished a long, miserable season; the team finished in sixth place in National League standings and Foxx with a batting average unlike any he had ever known, .205. In the "city series" between the Cubs and White Sox, which was a tradition in Chicago and was played after the end of the regular season, the

White Sox won four games to two. Foxx's only appearance in this series was as a pinch hitter in the third game and he struck out. The series provided a salary supplement of $218.38 to Jimmie's salary of approximately $10,000.00.[49]

Shortly after the close of the season the Cubs acquired first baseman Heinz Becker from Milwaukee, and speculation began concerning the future of Foxx. *The Sporting News* reported that Foxx would become manager of the Los Angeles Angels, the Cubs affiliate in the Pacific Coast League. It was common knowledge that Foxx wanted to manage, and he had, on occasion, stated that he would like to manage when his playing days were over and that his aim was eventually to manage in the majors. There were rumors in the fall of 1942 that Jimmie was going to Los Angeles, where he was to be groomed to take over as manager of the Cubs if he did well with the Angels.[50] Such rumors all proved to be groundless. Foxx remained on the Cubs' list of players and he was expected to report for spring camp at French Lick, Indiana, in March, 1943.

During the fall and winter months of 1942–43 Foxx was employed as a salesman for the New York-based oil firm, E.F. Houghton Company. This position paid Foxx $800.00 a month and his territory was New England. He operated from a Boston residence.[51] Foxx knew that he was still on the Cubs' roster and was expected to report to the team in mid–March. However, throughout the off season months he debated with himself as to whether he should leave baseball. He was very disappointed with his 1942 performance, but he never communicated to the Cubs that he was contemplating leaving the game. It appears that by late February he had arrived at a decision concerning his baseball career. He told a sportswriter from the *Philadelphia Inquirer* that he had a good job and "this looks like a good time to quit. ... I'm almost at the end of my career anyhow." He continued by declaring, "I want to get out of baseball before I have another bad season. ... I don't want people to remember me like that." One week later, on March 9, 1943, Foxx announced that he was retiring from baseball, that his career was over.[52] This announcement was news to James Gallagher and the Cubs, who acknowledged that although Foxx had not "figured largely" in Cubs plans for 1943 they were sorry to lose him. The general manager emphasized that the decision to quit was Foxx's alone and that the Cubs were not involved in his decision to retire. *The Sporting News* featured a lengthy editorial on Foxx's retirement, declaring that he was leaving the game "with a resplendent record." The editorial asserted that it took "a lot of courage to do what Foxx is doing—quitting the game after seventeen years" and concluded by noting that "courage is something Jimmie never lacked" and wished him good luck in his retirement.[53]

The decision to retire from an activity to which he had devoted a lifetime was undoubtedly a traumatic one, even though it was arrived at after several months of serious thought. During these same months there were also other things on Foxx's mind. On January 27, 1943, Helen Foxx filed suit for divorce in the Court of Common Pleas of Montgomery County, Pennsylvania. She charged Jimmie with "cruel and barbarous treatment" and declared that she had suffered such "indignities" as to render her life "intolerable" and "burdensome."[54]

When Jimmie went to the Red Sox in 1936 the family did not change its residence from Jenkintown to Boston. Helen and Jimmie, Jr., who was seven years old, remained at home and in the spring of 1936, Helen gave birth to their second son, Kenneth. Jimmie had an apartment in Boston and he would be with the family when the Red Sox came to Philadelphia to play the Athletics, but throughout the spring training and baseball season the family was separated for most of the time. In the off season Foxx often went hunting and barnstorming. From the time Jimmie, Jr. was eight or nine years old he was placed in boarding school—first in the Germantown Academy near Philadelphia and later at the Riverside Military Academy in Georgia.[55] Helen cared for Kenneth and she seemed to be more of a "homebody" than Jimmie, although she did accompany him to Japan in 1934. Foxx was a person who always seemed to be on the go, whether in or out of baseball season.

The separation which the family experienced from 1936 on doubtless contributed to the weakening of family ties. Also, during these years (1936–43) Jimmie's health began to decline. The chronic sinus trouble and its accompanying pain had an adverse effect on his eyesight and very probably contributed to his increasing use of alcohol, which seemingly affected his inability to manage his finances. Foxx's St. Petersburg, Florida, golf course venture, to which Helen was not privy and which resulted in the loss of at least $40,000.00 for Foxx, put further strain on the marriage. This financial disaster, following shortly after Jimmie had been forced to dispose of his Maryland farm and coupled with the large mortgage on the family home in Jenkintown, exacerbated family tensions. The final strain on the marriage and doubtless the one which prompted Helen to file for divorce was the friendship Jimmie developed with a New England woman, Dorothy Anderson Yard.

The divorce proceedings which Helen initiated on January 27, 1943, were concluded on June 1 of that year when the Court of Common Pleas of Montgomery County, Pennsylvania, granted her a divorce from Jimmie on grounds of "indignities."[56] At this time Jimmie's address was given as the Sheraton Hotel, New York City. He did not contest the divorce, and Helen was granted custody of the couple's two sons and given the home in Jenkintown. The *Philadelphia Recorder* covered the divorce proceedings more extensively than any other newspaper. It reported Mrs. Foxx charged that Jimmie "drank in excess, was abusive when drinking," and that he was more concerned with baseball than he was with his family. She charged that Jimmie was "lacking in consideration and responsibility" and that he was like a "selfish boy who never grew up." She claimed that their home in Jenkintown, which they had purchased in 1936 for $18,000.00, still was only half paid for and that it carried a mortgage of $9,000.00. She asserted that Jimmie squandered $42,000.00 in golf course ventures in Florida and also loaned large sums of money to his irresponsible brother, which were never repaid. She charged that Jimmie never had time to play with the children but found time to become interested in a woman named "Dottie."[57] There is no record that Jimmie made any response to the court's action. However, nearly twenty years later in a general autobiographical interview with Austen Lake of the *Boston Herald*, Foxx recalled his life with Helen, telling the writer that "he marveled that she had put up with him as long as she did."[58]

A short while after the divorce Helen sold her home—probably forced to do so because of the mortgage—and moved to Ocean City, New Jersey. Some years later she married Richard Mayer and they continued to reside in Ocean City. She and Mayer had no children, and she died in that city at age 65 on September 30, 1973, a victim of cancer.[59]

Helen's divorce from Jimmie was granted on June 1, 1943; two and one-half weeks later, Jimmie married the woman named in Helen's petition for divorce. The Dottie whom she had mentioned was a twenty-five-year-old divorcee from Auburn, Maine, who was the mother of two small children—a two-year-old son, John, and a one-year-old daughter, Nancy. Mrs. Dorothy Anderson Yard had divorced her husband, H. Nabor Yard, in January, 1942. How long Jimmie and Dorothy had known each other is unclear. In her divorce petition, Helen alludes to a "Dottie" whom Jimmie met in St. Petersburg in 1942.[60] The *Boston Globe* noted that on occasions in the past Foxx had been a frequent visitor in Auburn, Maine, and that several times he had appeared as a guest speaker before different local civic groups.[61] It appears that Dorothy and Jimmie had known each other for some time. They were married on June 18, 1943, at the home of friends in Short Hills, New Jersey.[62]

One other event in 1943 made that year a significant one in the life of Jimmie Foxx. In addition to declaring his retirement from baseball, a divorce and remarriage, this was also the year that his mother died. Mrs. Martha Smith Foxx, a lifelong member of the Methodist Episcopal Church and one of the founding members of the Sudlersville Community Betterment Club, died on August 26, 1943, at the Kent and Queen Anne's Hospital in Chestertown, Maryland. She was in the hospital convalescing from a broken hip when she suffered a heart attack and expired. She was sixty-five years old and was survived by her husband, S. Dell Foxx and two sons, Jimmie and S. Dell, Jr., a staff sergeant in the United States Army.[63]

After his marriage to Dorothy Yard, the couple and her two children made their home in Short Hills, New Jersey. Throughout 1943 and into 1944 Foxx continued his employment as an oil salesman for E.F. Houghton Company. By the winter of 1943–44 the Selective Service Administration was beginning to reclassify some men in the 3-A category—men with dependents—and induct them into the army. During the first week of January, 1944,

Foxx received notice from his draft board to report for a physical examination on January 17. Jimmie had originally registered with Selective Service in the Philadelphia area. However, he was permitted to report for the examination to the induction station in Newark, New Jersey, which was near his home. He reported on January 25, was given a preliminary examination and instructed to return the next day for a final examination. At the examination on January 26, Foxx was rejected for military service and given a 4-F classification. Although no reason was reported as to why he was classified as physically unqualified for military service, the press speculated that it was because of his sinus condition or because of his poor eyesight.[64]

Foxx's 4-F classification practically coincided with the report that several Cubs players, including first baseman Phil Cavarretta and one of their backup catchers, were scheduled to be called into military service. The prospect of losing players to the draft prompted Cubs vice-president James Gallagher to contact Foxx and persuade him to return to the Cubs for the 1944 season. His return, Gallagher emphasized, would help to keep baseball active during the war, and this, he explained, would be good for public morale. About this same time President Roosevelt once again acknowledged the salutary effect that major league baseball had on national morale and he urged that baseball continue. Therefore, in February Foxx quit his job with the oil firm; Commissioner Landis transferred his status from voluntary retirement to active; and he agreed to report to the Cubs spring camp in mid–March.[65]

The Cubs were scheduled to begin spring training on March 19 at their wartime training site in French Lick, Indiana. Two days after the first arrivals it snowed and spring practice was delayed for several days. Foxx and one or two others did not arrive until April 2. A *Chicago Tribune* reporter who was covering the Cubs reported that Foxx looked well and that he had gained about ten pounds since he last donned a Cubs uniform. He noted that the Cubs would proceed slowly with Jimmie and that he would "have to toughen up his long idle muscles."[66] One week after his arrival in camp, Foxx was in the lineup for an exhibition game with the Reds. Manager Jimmy Wilson had talked with him about the possibility of helping the Cubs with catching chores. Jimmie agreed to help the club as best he could, although both men acknowledged that he was not primarily a catcher. In the game with the Reds it was observed that Foxx handled the catching chores "without a hitch during his four-inning stint." In this game he was one for three at bat and when running out a hit it was noted that "nothing seemed to be wrong with his legs."[67]

Before the season opened Foxx moved his family from New Jersey to Chicago. Any expectations the Cubs or Foxx might have entertained for a good year were offset by a miserable showing on behalf of the team. Very early in the season the Cubs fell to last place in the National league, and in the midst of a thirteen-game losing streak, manager Jimmy Wilson was replaced by Charley Grimm, formerly manager of the Milwaukee Brewers.[68] As the season

Bill Nicholson and Foxx, 1944 (courtesy Sudlersville Memorial Library).

progressed the Cubs gradually improved and they ended the season in fourth place. However, Jimmie's effort to "get back in shape" was hampered by a batting practice accident which fractured a couple of his ribs. The result of this injury was that he would spend most of his time on the bench and pinch hitting.[69] From mid–April until July 5, Foxx appeared in only fifteen games, eleven as a pinch hitter. He caught one game and was at third base for several games. During this time he went to bat twenty times; had one hit, a double; and he struck out five times. As a pinch hitter he was 0 for 11 and when he was removed from the active player roster on July 5 to become a coach, he had a batting average of .050.[70] When Foxx was in the game he fielded flawlessly; however, his "batting eye" failed him.[71] A reporter for the *Philadelphia Inquirer*, after observing Jimmie at bat, wrote that "his batting eye is dim. ... He cannot follow the curve ball any more." *The Sporting News* declared that Foxx was no longer able to "get his eye on the ball or coordinate his swing."[72]

Jimmie served as a coach for the Cubs until late August when he was optioned to the Portsmouth, Virginia, Cubs of the Class B Piedmont League. Portsmouth's catcher and manager, Bill Steinecke, was purchased by the Yankees after Rollie Hemsley, one of their catchers, entered the Navy.[73] On August 26 James Gallagher announced that Foxx was being sent to Portsmouth to manage a Cubs affiliate in the Piedmont League for the remainder of the season. It was also noted that Foxx would be a playing manager and that he might take over one of several positions—first base, third base, catcher, or outfield.[74] Gallagher and other executives were aware of Jimmie's desire to "try his hand" at managing, and they thought that Portsmouth would provide an opportunity for him to test his ability as a manager. Foxx arrived in Portsmouth on August 28 and met with club owner Frank D. Lawrence and the players. He later told reporters, "We will be out there hustling. ... We're going to try ... for the pennant." Jimmie also had high praise for the ball park at Portsmouth.[75]

When Foxx arrived in Portsmouth the team was in second place in the Piedmont League standings and was engaged in a struggle with the Lynchburg Cardinals for the pennant. There were eleven games remaining before the season ended; however, the championship playoffs would continue until the last week of September. Foxx's debut as a manager came on August 28 in a game at Newport News. He did not participate in this game as a player, but he did act as a coach along the third base line. He explained that he was reluctant to make any lineup changes since the team was "going well," having won their last five games. Jimmie's first appearance as a player was in a game against Roanoke, a game the Cubs were losing 3-1. Late in the game Foxx hit for the pitcher and struck out.[76]

The Cubs first home game under the leadership of Foxx was on September 2. There had been considerable publicity in Portsmouth and adjoining areas concerning the appearance of the veteran American League slugger, and there were more than 3,500 fans present for the game with the Norfolk Tars. The Cubs were victorious 2-1, and Jimmie did not insert himself into the game. In the remaining games of the season Foxx's participation was mainly as a pinch hitter—sometimes with devastating results. For example, on one occasion in a game with Norfolk he hit into a triple play. His most effective effort as a player came on September 5 when he started the game against Newport News as a pitcher. Whether he planned it or not, Foxx pitched the entire nine innings, giving up six hits—only one an extra base double—and striking out eight batters in a game the Cubs won 3-1. It was reported that in this game Foxx displayed a "smooth delivery and mixed his pitches up well."[77]

In addition to his managerial duties Foxx also participated in public relations activities arranged by Frank Lawrence. For example, one day he was accompanied by Lawrence to a program at the Portsmouth Community Boys Club, where he was introduced to a group of 150 youngsters. Jimmie told them stories about his career and experiences in baseball and later autographed baseballs for them.[78]

When the Piedmont League season ended on September 10, the Cubs were in the same place in the standings they had occupied when Foxx arrived—second place.[79] The championship playoffs involved Lynchburg, Portsmouth, Norfolk, and Richmond. Prior to the close of the regular season the question was raised of Foxx's eligibility for the playoffs. To be eligible for the playoffs a player was generally required to be in the league for thirty days prior to the beginning of the playoffs. This practice might be altered if all of the participating clubs approved of a team using a player who did not meet the thirty-day rule. Lawrence and the sports editor of the Norfolk newspaper supported the inclusion of Foxx as a player and waiver of the thirty-day rule for him. They argued that he would be a big draw, that his appearance would be "good for baseball" and also for league revenues. Despite the pleas of Lawrence and others, the Lynchburg Cardinals refused to waive the thirty-day rule, and Foxx was not allowed to appear in any of the playoff games as a player.[80]

In the first round of the playoffs Portsmouth defeated Norfolk four games to three and Lynchburg eliminated the Richmond Colts. The championship series was between Lynchburg and Portsmouth. This series went seven games and was concluded on September 30; Foxx and the Cubs lost four games to three.[81]

Although the Cubs did not win the Piedmont League championship, mid–September was a time of celebration for Jimmie. When he came to Portsmouth in late August his family did not accompany him—they remained at their home in Chicago. At this time Dorothy was expecting the birth of their first child, and she was forbidden by her physician to travel. On September 14 Foxx received word from Chicago that he was the father of a son, and that both son and mother were doing well.[82] For several days thereafter Foxx was the recipient of congratulations and well-wishes, as he celebrated the event by passing out cigars to friends and others. Jimmie and his wife named this son James Emory Foxx, Jr., II.[83]

When the playoffs ended, Foxx returned to his family in Chicago to see what, if anything, baseball might have for his future. He was still under contract with the Chicago Cubs. When Lawrence was asked about the possibility of Foxx returning to Portsmouth in 1945, he replied that he did not expect that Chicago would "let him have Jimmie next year."[84] Early in November there was some press speculation that Foxx was the leading candidate for the managerial post with the Hollywood Stars of the Pacific Coast League. Another rumor was that he would be retained by the Cubs as a "roving coach for their farm clubs." Nothing materialized from these rumors. Jimmie assumed that he would remain as a coach with the Cubs since they had not informed him otherwise. However, later in the fall when he was in Buffalo attending the winter meeting of baseball executives and officials, Charlie Grimm, the Cubs manager, told him on the last day of the gathering, "I'm sorry Jimmie, but we can't use you any longer." Without explanation or forewarning, Jimmie was without a job for the coming season. Shortly afterwards it was announced that Cubs outfielder Ival Goodman would manage Portsmouth in 1945.[85]

Foxx and his family remained in Chicago throughout the winter of 1944–45. He was hoping "to land a job as manager," while also waiting to see what the government might do with men classified 4-F in the draft.[86] In December the director of the Office of War Mobilization and Reconversion, James F. Byrnes, suggested to General Lewis B. Hershey, director of Selective Service, that all athletes classified 4-F be re-examined. Byrnes and others were of the opinion that if athletes in this classification could participate in various contests, they could fight, or at least contribute their energies to "war work." In his State of the Union Address on January 6, 1945, President Roosevelt seemed to echo these sentiments when he suggested national legislation requiring that the nation's 4-Fs be used "in whatever capacity is best for the war effort." Shortly thereafter, Congressman Andrew J. May of Kentucky introduced a measure known as the "work or fight bill," which would require 4-Fs to enter the military service or engage in essential war work. Baseball men believed that if this measure became law it would mean the end of baseball for the duration of the war. It was another Kentucky politician who helped to kill the May bill and "save baseball." Senator Albert B. "Happy" Chandler declared that "baseball should have the right to use rejects if it would mean keeping the game going." He maintained that baseball was a valuable morale factor for the American public and that it "was worth continuing in war time" and declared that he would work to kill the "work or fight" measure when it came to the Senate.[87] A week later, J. Edgar Hoover, director of the Federal Bureau of Investigation, let it be known that he also supported baseball, noting that it was a powerful influence on morale and said that 4-Fs should be permitted to play baseball. In early March President Roosevelt's response to a reporter's question was that he considered baseball "a very good thing for the population during the war." A week later Paul McNutt of the War Manpower Commission ruled that 4-F baseball players could continue to play baseball. By April the "work or fight" sentiment in the Congress subsided and the May bill was killed in the Senate.[88]

In the meantime Foxx had been released by the Cubs, and no one had offered him employment in baseball. His 4-F status remained unchanged, and he was still living in Chicago. However, during the winter of 1944–45 ownership changes in major league baseball occurred in Philadelphia which would bring Jimmie back to the place where his major league career began twenty years earlier. In 1942, because of economic problems, Gerry Nugent was forced to sell the Phillies. The new owner, William Cox, operated the team for only one year before Commissioner Landis banished him from baseball for betting on the team. Ownership of the Phillies was acquired by Robert M. Carpenter, Sr., a millionaire manufacturer and a DuPont heir. Carpenter's son Robert M. Carpenter, Jr., a twenty-eight-year-old baseball enthusiast, was installed as president of the club.[89] Soon after taking control of the club Carpenter hired Herb Pennock as general manager. Pennock was a former American League pitcher and farm director for the Red Sox. Carpenter and Pennock hoped to rejuvenate the Phillies and build a winning team for a city that had not had a winner in over ten years.

At this time no club in recent National League history had a more pathetic record than the Phillies; their image was one of futility. Carpenter and Pennock not only hoped to present the fans an improved team, they also sought to change the image of the club, to give the team a new name or identity. They believed that this would help to stimulate interest in and revitalize baseball in the Quaker City. To achieve this, the Phillies' management announced in January, 1945, that they were conducting a contest to determine a new name for the club. From January 25 through February 27 fans and members of the public were invited to suggest a new name and insignia for the Phillies. Each entry was to be accompanied by a letter of not more than 100 words explaining the writer's suggestion. At the same time that the contest was announced, Carpenter explained that he was not dissatisfied with "Phillies" but that he wanted a new cognomen which indicated "a new spirit of the team." Entries would be judged by a panel consisting of Philadelphia sportswriters, radio commentators and club officials. Three prizes would be awarded: those who offered the three best suggestions would be given season tickets to home games. The entry judged the best would also receive a $100.00 war bond. The contest drew more than 5,000 letters. The winning entry, "Blue Jays," was submitted by Mrs. John L. Crooks of Philadelphia.[90] Carpenter and the judges agreed with the explanation that "Blue Jays" represents a colorful "personality" and reflects "a new team spirit." It seems that the only reported opposition to the new name was a statement from the student council of the Johns Hopkins University. They explained that "Blue Jays" had been the nickname of that university's teams for eighty-six years and they were not pleased that it was being usurped by the "hapless Phillies." The name "Blue Jays" was never wholly accepted by the fans or the press in Philadelphia and in 1949 the club discarded it and reverted to "Phillies."[91]

At the same time that management was seeking a new name for the Phillies, Pennock was busy trying to find a sufficient number of players to open the season. When he and Phillies manager Fred Fitzsimmons heard that Foxx had been released by the Cubs and that Jimmie was still hoping to remain in baseball, Pennock contacted him about the possibility of returning to Philadelphia. He and Fitzsimmons knew that Foxx was thirty-seven years old, but he was also 4-F and could "help out" a team at almost any position and as a pinch hitter. He would be a valuable utility player in a time of stringent player shortage and players with uncertain tenure.[92]

At this time Foxx was employed by the oil company he previously worked for and he was living in Short Hills, New Jersey, although his family had not yet moved from Chicago. On February 11, the *Philadelphia Inquirer* reported that Foxx had signed a one-year contract with the Phillies, terms undisclosed, and that he was in the process of moving his family from Chicago. It appears that the family was unable to obtain suitable housing in the Philadelphia area due to the wartime housing shortage. Instead, they located in Lewes, Delaware, over 100 miles from the city. Jimmie told reporters, "I'm not through. ... My legs are as good as ever," and he informed them that he would report to the Phillies' spring camp at Wilmington, Delaware, on March 14.[93] *The Sporting News* account of Foxx's signing with the Phillies noted that physically Jimmie seemed in good condition although he was about ten pounds over his normal playing weight of 185 pounds. It was noted that "his eyes did not focus with the same speed as they did twenty years ago," and as a result he could not "whip the bat around as quickly as formerly." To correct this condition Foxx was "going to choke up on the bat a bit." He and Pennock thought this would help his hitting.[94]

When the Phillies/Blue Jays camp opened at Wilmington seventeen players were present, including a couple of teenage Hamner brothers from Richmond, Virginia; Foxx; and two other veterans who were trying to make a comeback, Gus Mancuso and Chuck Klein. Foxx was assigned uniform number 24, and he eagerly entered into training.[95] Early in the training period Jimmie demonstrated his hitting power by blasting several long hits out of the Wilmington park. However, his spring playing was hampered when he developed bursitis in one of his ankles and was forced to begin the season sitting on the bench. He pinch hit in several early games and after a week was inserted in the lineup at third base. However, in May he was out of the lineup for a number of games. Once he was called home because of the illness of his eight-month-old son; later he developed a severe cold, ran a temperature of 102 degrees, and was administered sulfa drugs by his physician, who feared Foxx's condition might develop into pneumonia. He confined Jimmie to his home and to bed for about a week.[96] When he was able to resume playing, Jimmie was sent to first base and he remained at this position for most of the time thereafter. At the end of May he was hitting .309 and one of his hits, on May 18, was a pinch hit grand slam home run off Ken Burkhart of the Cardinals.[97]

During the spring of 1945, after an interim of five months, major league owners chose the second commissioner of baseball. Judge Kenesaw M. Landis, the first commissioner, died of a heart attack at his home in Chicago on November 25, 1944, at age seventy-eight. During the winter the owners had appointed a committee to seek a successor, to screen applicants and to suggest

Foxx in his last season, with Phillies, 1945 (Temple University Libraries photograph).

a person for the position. Throughout the spring training period the press speculated on possible successors to "the Judge." Among those mentioned were James A. Farley, Carl Vinson, Larry McPhail, and others. On April 24, at a meeting of major league baseball owners, it was announced that the new commissioner was Albert B. "Happy" Chandler, who was currently a United States Senator from Kentucky.[98]

During June, Foxx's batting average slipped from .309 to .260, and the Phillies or Blue Jays (fans and press used the terms interchangeably), despite a name change, fell to last place in National League standings. Reflecting a common practice when a team is not doing well or failing to fulfill expectations, Carpenter and Pennock fired the manager. Fred Fitzsimmons was replaced by Ben Chapman, a former major league outfielder and Red Sox teammate of Foxx's, who had managed Richmond in the Piedmont League in 1944.[99] Chapman was named manager at about the same time the major league All-Star game was usually played. This game for 1945 was originally scheduled to be played in Boston; however, it was canceled and there was no All-Star game in 1945. The reason given for cancellation of the game was that transportation facilities were being heavily taxed by demobilization of troops following the surrender of Germany in May. Instead of playing an All-Star game, baseball owners agreed that each club would play an exhibition game and donate the proceeds to a war charity.[100]

One of Chapman's experiments was to allow Foxx greater opportunity to pitch. In the exhibition game against the Athletics on July 10, played for charity in lieu of the All-Star game, Foxx made his debut as a Phillie pitcher. He worked three and one-third innings, and the Phillies won 7-6. Chapman said that Foxx's best chance to "stay active in the big leagues was as a pitcher," and he wanted to give Jimmie a chance to pitch.[101] From mid–July to the end of August Foxx appeared in nine games as a pitcher, often in relief. At other times he was used mainly as a pinch hitter. His most memorable game as a pitcher came on August 19 in a home game against the Cincinnati Reds. Chapman was "desperate for pitchers" and he asked Jimmie if he would start the second game of a doubleheader. He told Foxx to "hang in there ... [and] ... if by a miracle you last five innings I'll take you out." At the end of five innings Foxx had struck out six, walked four, and allowed not a single hit in a game the Phillies were winning 5-0. Although Jimmie's fast ball, change of pace, sinking screw ball, and an occasional knuckler were performing spectacularly, his arm was "dead tired." Nevertheless, Chapman decided to leave him in the game. In the sixth inning with two out, Jimmie gave up a hit and walked a batter and Chapman took him out of the game. Anton Karl, the relief pitcher, preserved Jimmie's victory and his major league record as a pitcher would remain one win and no losses, for a winning percentage of .1000.[102]

In late August and into September Foxx occasionally appeared as a relief pitcher or pinch hitter. In early September he played several games at first base and on September 9, in a game against the Pirates, Foxx was four for five. One hit was a double and one was home run number 534, his last major league homer.[103] Foxx's batting average did not improve, remaining around .260. He closed the season with an average of .268.[104] It appears that by mid-season Foxx had come to the conclusion that his days as a major league performer were over. In late June he told Arthur Daley of the *New York Times*, "When the war is over, I'm through. If I were to quit today I guess I'd have played enough."[105]

In late August Jimmie was one of a group of Phillie players who visited the veteran's hospital at Valley Forge. He was a big hit with the veterans and he spent some time going from room to room, shaking hands and talking with the men. It was also about this time that Foxx had a long interview with J.G. Taylor Spink of *The Sporting News*. In this encounter Foxx summarized much of his philosophy of baseball as well as revealing his encompassing knowledge of the game. When Spink commented on Foxx's versatility and how he could perform well at most any position, Jimmie indicated that this had been a hindrance to his career. The advice he offered to youngsters was to select one position and "stick with it." "When a fellow tries to play more than one position," he declared, "it shortens his career." Shifting from first to third to catching, he explained, requires the use of different muscles and the changing "takes something from the muscles." Changing positions and the effect it has on one's coordination and reaction, he asserted, also "hurts your timing at bat." He claimed that in swinging the bat, certain muscles become attuned to a pattern of movement. However, that rhythm can be broken or abused by playing different positions and it will "throw your hitting out of gear."[106]

Foxx also answered Spink's queries concerning the playing of certain positions. The first base position, he said, was a combination of action and freedom of movement. One had to learn to shift feet properly and quickly and how to make cut-off plays and field drag bunts. One also had to make quick decisions. The principal requirement, he noted, for a third baseman is a strong arm and the ability to "come in fast on bunts." If one has a strong arm and can field bunts, he maintained, one can knock down grounders with his chest or glove and throw the runner out at first. Shortstop was described by Foxx as the toughest position in the infield. It was necessary for one to have quick reflexes so that he could break to left or right in a moment. A good arm and strong wrist were essential. Catching, Foxx asserted, was the most demanding position in baseball. The catcher must have a strong arm and a good mind. It was essential that he know and remember the weaknesses and strengths of opposition hitters. It was also essential that the catcher know his pitchers— the days they have "their stuff" and the days they do not, and to be diplomatic in discussing this with one's pitcher. He claimed that a catcher must know his pitchers better than a psychiatrist does his patients. The catcher, he declared, was the brains of the game. Jimmie felt that fewer problems were involved in playing the outfield. However, one must always be aware of where the fences are located and know the proper base to throw to when returning the ball to the infield.[107]

On September 16 Foxx made a brief appearance in a game the Phillies lost to St. Louis 10-3. This was his last performance as a pitcher. For the season he made nine appearances on the mound in which he pitched twenty-three innings; his record was one win, no losses, with an earned run average of 1.59. He gave up thirteen hits, walked fourteen and struck out ten. His last appearance was in a game against the Dodgers in Brooklyn on September 23. He played first base and was one for three, a double, and the Phillies won 4-3. He ended the season hitting .268, having appeared in 89 games. He hit seven home runs to bring his total to 534, more than any right-handed batter in the history of the game at that time and second on the all-time home run list behind Babe Ruth.[108]

Prior to Foxx's last game he had announced that he was leaving baseball and had accepted a sales promotion position with Hathaway Bakeries, Inc., of Cambridge, Massachusetts. He would begin work there on September 30. This position had been developing during the summer and Foxx had agreed to accept it and begin work at the end of the baseball season. He had bought a house in Needham, Massachusetts, and moved his family there before announcing his departure from baseball on September 21.[109] Jimmie concluded the season with the Phillies, was given his unconditional release, and departed for Boston. When he left the Phillies, manager Ben Chapman said, "Jimmie leaves with the best wishes of the Phillies management," and general manager Pennock declared, "Jimmie has done everything we have asked of him—and more." At this time a sportswriter for the *New York Sun* declared, "There was never a nicer, more even tempered guy" in the game than Jimmie Foxx.[110]

Foxx's job with Hathaway Bakeries included working with local people to form baseball leagues for youngsters, frequent visits to schools and playgrounds in the Boston area, and presenting brief talks on sports and giving demonstrations on playing baseball. His position also included a fifteen-minute weekly radio program on Sunday from 1:45 to 2:00 P.M. on youth and sports. One of his earliest public relations appearances in the Boston area was as a speaker at the Arlington Junior High School rally celebrating the students' sale of over $100,000.00 in war bonds and stamps since Pearl Harbor. On another occasion he was the principal speaker at a victory loan rally at the Simpson Drydock in East Boston.[111] Foxx appears to have been happy to return to the Boston area. Soon after his arrival he told a reporter for the *Boston Globe* that he was pleased to be returning to Boston, that he had "more friends there than anywhere else."[112]

Notes

1. Bill Gilbert, *They Also Served: Baseball and the Home Front, 1941–1945* (New York: Crown Publishers, Inc., 1992), p. 12.

2. Richard Goldstein, *Spartan Seasons, How Baseball Survived the Second World War* (New York: Macmillan, 1980), p. 15; William Mead, *Baseball Goes to War* (Washington, D.C.: Farragut Publishing Company, 1985), p. 35.

3. Goldstein, *Spartan Seasons*, p. 13.

4. *Ibid.*, pp. 19-20; Mead, *Baseball Goes to War*, pp. 35-36; David Q. Voigt, *American Baseball*, 3 volumes (Norman: University of Oklahoma Press, 1966–1983), II, p. 256; *The Sporting News*, January 22, 1942.

5. Mead, *Baseball Goes to War*, p. 38; Goldstein, *Spartan Seasons*, pp. 124-25.

6. Goldstein, *Spartan Seasons*, p. 56.

7. Mead, *Baseball Goes to War*, p. 99; Voigt, II, p. 257; Bruce Kuklick, *To Every Thing a Season: Shibe Park and Urban Philadelphia, 1909–1976* (Princeton: Princeton University Press, 1991), p. 96f.

8. Gilbert, *They Also Served*, p. 141; Mead, *Baseball Goes to War*, pp. 19, 94, 105; Goldstein, *Spartan Seasons*, p. 58.

9. Mead, *Baseball Goes to War*, p. 146.

10. Gilbert, *They Also Served*, p. 117; Peter C. Bjarkman, ed., *Encyclopedia of Major League Baseball Team Histories: American League* (Westport, Conn.: Meckler Publishing Company, 1991), pp. 503-504; Michael M. Oleksak and Mary Adams Oleksak, *Beisbol, Latin Americans and the Grand Old Game* (Grand Rapids, Michigan: Masters Press, 1991), pp. 44-45.

11. Donn Rogosin, *Invisible Men, Life in Baseball's Negro Leagues* (New York: Atheneum, 1985), p. 181.

12. *The Sporting News*, July 23, 1942.

13. *Ibid.*, July 23, 1942, April 19, 1945; *Chicago Daily Tribune*, September 2, 1942; Rogosin, *Invisible Men*, pp. 194-95.

14. *The Sporting News*, December 9, 1943; Rogosin, *Invisible Men*, pp. 194-195.

15. *The Sporting News*, November 1, 1945.

16. *Ibid.*, November 15, 1945.

17. Goldstein, *Spartan Seasons*, p. 263.

18. *Ibid.*, p. 131; Bob Broeg and William J. Miller, Jr., *Baseball from a Different Angle* (South Bend, Ind.: Diamond Communications, Inc., 1988), p. 21; *Chicago Tribune*, March 14, 1943.

19. Goldstein, *Spartan Season*, pp. 130-32; Mead, *Baseball Goes to War*, pp. 78-79.

20. *Chicago Tribune*, December 1, 1942; Mead, *Baseball Goes to War*, p. 73.

21. *Chicago Tribune*, January 21, 1943.

22. *Ibid.*, January 8, 23, 1943.

23. Goldstein, *Spartan Seasons*, pp. 73-74; Mead, *Baseball Goes to War*, p. 224.

24. *The Sporting News*, February 5, 1942; Goldstein, *Spartan Seasons*, p. 65.

25. Mead, *Baseball Goes to War*, p. 6; *Chicago Tribune*, January 9, 1943, June 28, 1944; Gilbert, *They Also Served*, p. 210.

26. Goldstein, *Spartan Seasons*, p. 64.

27. Mead, *Baseball Goes to War*, pp. 6-7.

28. Goldstein, *Spartan Seasons*, pp. 88-89.

29. Red Barber and Robert Creamer, *Rhubarb in the Catbird Seat* (Garden City: Doubleday and Company, 1968), pp. 78-79.

30. *Philadelphia Evening Bulletin*, December 3, 1942; Goldstein, *Spartan Seasons*, p. 87.

31. For example, see *The Sporting News*, January 22, 1942; *Chicago Tribune*, April 16, 1941.

32. Goldstein, *Spartan Seasons*, p. 95.

33. *Ibid.*, p. 83; James Charlton, editor, *The Baseball Chronology* (New York: Macmillan, 1991), p. 334.

34. *Chicago Tribune*, June 2, 4, 1942.

35. *Ibid.*, June 4, 1942.

36. *Ibid.*, June 5, 10, 1942.

37. *Ibid.*, June 15, 1942.

38. *Ibid.*, June 8, 16, 27, 29, July 18, 20, 1942.

39. *Ibid.*, July 30, September 23, 1942; *The Sporting News*, July 30, 1942.

40. *The Sporting News*, August 13, 1942.

41. *Ibid.*, July 30, 1942; *Philadelphia Evening Bulletin*, August 7, 1942.

42. *The Sporting News*, August 27, 1942.

43. Charles C. Alexander, *Our Game, an American Baseball History* (New York: Henry Holt and Company, 1991), p. 184.

44. *The Sporting News*, May 2, 1940, February 11, 1943.

45. *Ibid.*, August 27, 1942; assorted clippings, July 23, 1942, in Foxx files, Baseball Library, Cooperstown, New York.

46. Assorted clippings, July 30, 1942, in Foxx files, Baseball Library, Cooperstown, New York; *The Sporting News*, February 11, 1943.

47. *The Sporting News*, February 11, 1943.

48. *Philadelphia Inquirer*, August 7, 1942.

49. *Chicago Tribune*, June 2, October 3, 7, 1942; *The Sporting News*, October 8, 1942.

50. For example, see *Philadelphia Inquirer*, August 7, 1942; *Boston Globe*, August 7, 1942; *The Sporting News*, November 12, 1942.

51. *Philadelphia Evening Bulletin*, March 3, 1943; *The Sporting News*, March 18, May 6, 1943.

52. *Philadelphia Evening Bulletin*, March 3, 1943; *Philadelphia Inquirer*, March 3, 1943; *The Sporting News*, March 11, 1943; Ed Rumill, "Looking Backward with Jimmie Foxx," in *Baseball Magazine* (November, 1944), p. 422; *Boston Globe*, March 9, 1943.

53. *Boston Herald*, March 9, 1943; *The Sporting News*, March 18, 1943.

54. Petition for Divorce, in Office of Prothonotary, Montgomery County, Pennsylvania, January 27, 1943.

55. *Boston Herald*, June 2, 1942.

56. *Philadelphia Inquirer*, June 3, 1943.

57. *Philadelphia Recorder*, June 3, 1943; *Philadelphia Inquirer*, June 3, 1943.

58. *Boston Herald*, July 5, 1960.

59. Conversation with Kenneth Foxx, January 11, 1992; assorted clippings in Foxx files, Sudlersville Memorial Library, Sudlersville, Maryland.

60. *Philadelphia Recorder*, June 3, 1943. Spelling of the daughter's name was later changed to Nanci; other references to her in this study are spelled Nanci.

61. *Boston Globe*, June 26, 1943.

62. *Philadelphia Inquirer*, June 26, 1943; *The Sporting News*, July 1, 1943; *Boston Globe*, June 26, 1943.

63. *Philadelphia Evening Bulletin*, August 28, 1943; *The Sporting News*, September 2, 1943; *Queen Anne's Record-Observer*, September 2, 1943.

64. *The Sporting News*, January 13, February 3, 1944; *Philadelphia Inquirer*, January 26, 27, 1944; *Chicago Tribune*, January 26, 27, 1944.

65. *Philadelphia Evening Bulletin*, February 25, 26, 1944; *Chicago Tribune*, February 26, 1944; *New York Times*, February 26, 1944.

66. *Chicago Tribune*, March 21, April 4, 1944.

67. *Ibid.*, April 9, 1944.

68. *Ibid.*, May 2, 7, 1944.

69. Assorted, undated items, 1944, in Foxx files, *Philadelphia Inquirer* Archives.

70. *Chicago Tribune*, July 6, 1944.

71. *Ibid.*, April 27, 1944; *The Sporting News*, May 4, 1944.

72. Assorted clippings, 1944, in Foxx files, *Philadelphia Inquirer* Archives; *The Sporting News*, July 13, 1944.

73. *Philadelphia Evening Bulletin*, August 26, 1944.

74. *Chicago Tribune*, August 26, 1944; *Richmond Times-Dispatch*, August 26, 1944; *Portsmouth Star*, August 27, 1944.

75. *Portsmouth Star*, August 28, 1944.

76. *Ibid.*, August 29, 31, 1944; *Richmond Times-Dispatch*, August 29, 1944; *The Sporting News*, August 31, 1944.

77. *Richmond Times-Dispatch*, September 3, 4, 6, 1944; *Portsmouth Star*, September 6, 1944.

78. *Portsmouth Star*, September 6, 1944.

79. *Richmond Times-Dispatch*, September 11, 1944.

80. *The Sporting News*, September 7, 28, 1944.

81. *Portsmouth Star*, October 1, 1944.

82. *Ibid.*, September 15, 1944.

83. *Ibid.*, September 15, 1944; *The Sporting News*, September 21, 1944.

84. Portsmouth *Star*, November 20, 1944.

85. Jimmie Foxx, "I'm Through with Baseball Forever," in *Baseball Monthly* (May, 1962), p. 54; *The Sporting News*, November 16, 29, December 14, 1944; assorted clippings, December 6, 1944, in Foxx files, Baseball Library, Cooperstown, New York; *Portsmouth Star*, December 5, 1944.

86. *The Sporting News*, January 18, 1945.

87. *Ibid.*, February 1, 1945.

88. Goldstein, *Spartan Seasons*, pp. 202-203; Mead, *Baseball Goes to War*, p. 221; *The Sporting News*, March 29, 1945.

89. Bjarkman, ed., *Encyclopedia of Major League ...*, pp. 410-11; Mead, *Baseball Goes to War*, pp. 126-27; Voigt, II, p. 271.

90. *Philadelphia Inquirer*, January 25, 1945; *Chicago Tribune*, March 5, 1945.

91. *The Sporting News*, March 16, 1945; Bjarkman, ed., *Encyclopedia of Major League ...*, p. 411.

92. *Philadelphia Inquirer*, February 8, 1945; *Philadelphia Evening Bulletin*, February 10, 1945.

93. *Philadelphia Inquirer*, January 26, February 11, May 9, 1945; *Philadelphia Evening Bulletin*, February 10, 1945.

94. *The Sporting News*, February 22, March 15, 1945.

95. *Ibid.*, March 22, 1945.

96. *Ibid.*, March 22, April 12, May 10, 17, 1945.

97. *Ibid.*, June 7, 1945; Charlton, *The Baseball Chronology*, p. 336.

98. Charlton, ed., *The Baseball Chronology*, p. 331; *The Sporting News*, May 3, 1945.

99. *The Sporting News*, July 5, 1945.

100. Charlton, ed., *The Baseball Chronology*, p. 336.

101. *The Sporting News*, July 12, 19, 1945.

102. *Ibid.*, August 23, 1945; assorted clippings, August 20, 1945, in Dell Foxx scrapbook #1; assorted clippings, August 17, 1940, in Foxx files, Baseball Library, Cooperstown, New York.

103. Allen Lewis article in *Phillies Report*, February 22, 1990.

104. *The Sporting News*, October 8, 1945.

105. *Ibid.*, June 28, 1945.

106. *Ibid.*, August 30, 1945.

107. *Ibid.*, August 30, 1945.

108. Bjarkman, ed., *Encyclopedia of Major League ...*, pp. 913, 1837; *The Sporting News*, September 17, 20, 1945.

109. *Boston Herald*, September 21, 1945; *Philadelphia Inquirer*, September 21, 1945.

110. *Philadelphia Inquirer*, September 28, 1945; Allison Danzig and Joe Reichler, *The History of Baseball: Its Great Players, Teams and Managers* (Englewood Cliffs, N.J.: Prentice-Hall, 1959), p. 178.

111. *Ibid.*, September 21, 1945; *Boston Herald*, September 21, November 11, 1945.

112. *Boston Herald*, September 24, 1945; assorted clippings, October 11, 1945, in Foxx files, Baseball Library, Cooperstown, New York.

Seven

Post Baseball Career: The Early Years, 1946–1951

During the winter of 1945–46 Foxx was employed by the Hathaway Baking Company in Boston. His duties were mainly in the area of public relations and included work with young people. Although Foxx enjoyed his work for the bakery, his main interest was still baseball and he wanted to maintain his association with the game. In the spring of 1946 he was offered an opportunity to do this when the CBS affiliate in Boston, WEEI, employed him as a sports broadcaster. His duties at WEEI were "to do a sports broadcast from 6:15 to 6:30 six nights a week," beginning on Monday, March 25.[1] In entering the area of sports broadcasting Foxx was following a precedent begun by a number of other major league players. For example, Dizzy Dean began broadcasting Cardinal games for sponsor Falstaff Brewing Company in 1941. Other former major league players in radio announcing/broadcasting at the time included Waite Hoyt, Harry Heilmann, Bump Hadley and Charles "Gabby" Street.[2] Jimmie's sponsor at WEEI was T. Noonan and Sons, makers of "Vest Pak" razors and men's toiletries.[3] Foxx liked this job; it kept him in close contact with baseball and especially the Red Sox, who that season won the American League pennant. And, as Jimmie later stated, the radio job "paid him good money"—one thousand dollars a month.[4]

In addition to conducting his daily radio program, Foxx also engaged in public relations activities. On one occasion during the opening week of the baseball season he visited sick and wounded servicemen in Lowell General Hospital at Fort Devens. He spoke to a large audience of veterans, regaling them with stories about players and incidents of the game. He also predicted that the Red Sox would win the American League pennant that year. In assessing players he had known, he expressed the opinion that his former teammate, Dominic DiMaggio, was a better defensive outfielder than his brother Joe, the star center fielder of the Yankees.[5]

The 1946 season was an interesting and exciting one in Boston. The Red Sox won the American League pennant by twelve games, their first league title since 1918. This season also marked the arrival of night baseball in Boston. The first major league night game in the city was played on Saturday, May 11; the Braves lost to the Giants 5-1. The Red Sox would not have lights installed at Fenway Park until a year later.[6] Joe Cronin, player-manager for the Red Sox, announced his retirement as a player in 1946. Johnny Pesky became the regular shortstop but Cronin remained as manager of the team.[7] Two of Foxx's peers were moved into managerial positions during this season; Bill Dickey replaced Joe McCarthy as manager of the Yankees and Ted Lyons succeeded Jimmy Dykes in Chicago. Foxx viewed these changes with interest and hoped that a position in major league baseball would "open up" for him. In September he revealed to a reporter for the *Philadelphia Inquirer* that although he was enjoying his radio work, he wanted to get back into baseball. "Baseball," he said, "is what I know and what I ought to work at."[8]

Foxx's desire for a position in baseball was echoed by Harold Kaese, sports columnist for the *Boston Globe*. He reported that Jimmie wants to get back in baseball." During the World Series, which was between the Red Sox and the Cardinals, a number of baseball owners and general managers were in Boston. Foxx talked with some of these people and expressed his desire to return to the game. Kaese tried to help Jimmie, writing that "a better fellow never deserved a better break from the game than Foxx." He noted that Foxx's knowledge of the game and his ability to establish an easy rapport with others, whether veterans or rookies, were positive traits for one seeking a position in organized ball. Kaese concluded by expressing the opinion that Foxx would be an excellent coach or manager for a major league club.[9] About this same time *The Sporting News* reported that both Cronin and Red Sox owner Tom Yawkey were inclined to employ Foxx as a coach, but did not do so, because of the opposition of general manager Eddie Collins. The reason for Collins' opposition to Foxx as a coach was not revealed.[10]

Despite the fact that it was public knowledge Foxx wanted a job in major league baseball, nothing materialized for him in 1946. Throughout the season he conducted his radio sports program and probably could have remained at WEEI. He seems to have been an effective radio personality, even though one columnist criticized his efforts as a sports announcer. There is no evidence that either health problems or alcohol hampered Foxx in fulfilling his responsibilities as a broadcaster. However, after the World Series was over, Jimmie went to Florida on vacation and while there he had an opportunity to return to baseball.[11]

In mid–October Foxx left Boston and went to St. Petersburg, Florida. While vacationing in this area, a place where Jimmie was rather well known and respected, he was invited to resume his affiliation with organized baseball. The Florida International League was organized and inaugurated play in 1946. It was a class C league and included the following cities: Tampa, Miami Beach, West Palm Beach, Lakeland, Miami and Havana, Cuba.[12] Throughout

1946, businessmen and baseball enthusiasts in St. Petersburg were busy renovating and enlarging the city stadium, Al Lang Field. They were also active in organizing and planning to secure a league franchise for 1947. W.D. Curd, an electric power company executive, was chosen president of the St. Petersburg Baseball Association and at the fall meeting of league executives, St. Petersburg was admitted to membership in the Florida International League. At this meeting held in Miami, Fort Lauderdale was also admitted to membership in the league.[13]

A short while later, on November 21, 1946, it was announced that Jimmie Foxx had been signed as general manager and field manager of St. Petersburg's entry in the Florida International League.[14] The Foxx family moved to St. Petersburg in the fall of 1946, and Jimmie began to prepare for the upcoming season. During the winter, renovations were completed on the ball park and lights were installed. A contest was sponsored by the club and local newspaper to select a name for the team. "Saints" was submitted by Miss Cathy Camp, and she was awarded a season's box seat ticket for her winning suggestion.[15]

Foxx's major task was to find and sign players, form a team and have it ready for spring training, which was scheduled to begin on March 10. In December Foxx and a club colleague went to Cuba to interview prospective players and invite them to spring camp. They were in Cuba about a week and signed seven players who were to report in March. Two of the seven were pitchers, one was a catcher, three were infielders and one was an outfielder. It was reported that these were among the "most promising youngsters in the Cuban winter league."[16] Among the others signed before the season opened were a former pitcher for the Phillies, Isidore Leon; and Jimmie's old nemesis, Johnny Allen, who he said would be the mainstay of the pitching staff. Jimmie would also participate in some games since he was designated as "playing-manager."[17] At the same time that Foxx was busy assembling a team and preparing for spring training, he was actively soliciting equipment and uniforms for the team from the business community and sporting goods dealers.[18]

Professional baseball returned to St. Petersburg after a twenty-year hiatus on April 9, 1947. The local newspaper reported that Foxx and the club owners had worked hard and had invested more than $40,000.00 to bring organized baseball to the city. Under newly installed lights and before 4,011 fans, Johnny Allen pitched the Saints to a 4-2 victory over the Tampa Smokers.[19] On this occasion a number of prizes donated by local merchants were awarded. Foxx told reporters that plans were also being formulated to observe a "ladies night" and to organize a Knothole Gang for youngsters in the area. Before the end of April a Knothole Gang was formed for youngsters in the St. Petersburg area. Membership was open to black and white children ages eight to fifteen. Local sponsors paid the one-dollar fee for up to 600 members, who were issued membership cards that would admit them to Saints games without charge.[20]

After winning the season's opener, the Saints lost their next two games to Tampa. In the third game Foxx inserted himself into the lineup as a relief pitcher. His initial appearance was an unspectacular one; in three innings he struck out three batters but gave up five hits and five runs. On April 14, Ladies Night, the Saints defeated Fort Lauderdale 3-2 and evened their record at 3-3.[21] Several days later and with the Saints trailing Miami, Foxx made his second appearance as a player. He entered the game as a relief pitcher in the seventh inning and promptly gave up a home run and three other hits in a game that Miami won 10-8. In this contest Foxx got his first hit of the season, a double.[22] During the third week of April the Saints went to Cuba for a four-game series with Havana. The *St. Petersburg Times* reporter who traveled with the team was very impressed with the Havana ball park. He declared it was "on a par with most major league parks in the United States" and noted that it would "seat 30,000 with ease." The manager of the hotel in Havana where the Saints stayed was enthusiastic in his welcome of Foxx and the Saints. He told Jimmie that he was a long-time fan of his and had been present at the 1930 World Series game when Foxx had hit a game-winning home run.[23] The welcome given the Saints by the Cuban team was very inhospitable as the Cubans won four straight, leaving the Saints tied for third place in league standings.[24] The ineptness of the Saints continued after leaving Havana, and before they returned home on April 29 they were last in the league, having won only two games and lost seven on a ten-day road trip.[25]

After their return home the Saints improved, and by May 5 they were in sixth place in league standings, two from the bottom. On May 1 and 3 they defeated the Cubans twice, becoming the first team in the league to perform this feat. In each game they attracted crowds of more than 2,000. However, the Saints suffered a relapse, and a week later they were only a half-game from the cellar.[26] With the May 8 deadline for limiting each team to fifteen players, Foxx announced that he was retiring as a player, "would let the younger guys play," and that he would manage "from the bench." At this time Foxx's stats as a player were six times at bat, one run, one hit, for a batting average of .167.[27]

Foxx continued as manager of the Saints for ten days after announcing his retirement as a player. During this time the Saints continued to lose and fell to last place in an eight-team league. Some of the fans began to boo Foxx, blaming him for the inept performance of the team.[28] Jimmie, however, had some supporters; for example, one fan wrote to the local newspaper to denounce the team owners rather than Foxx for the poor showing of the Saints. He blamed the owners because they had not obtained competent players.[29] With the team floundering, the owners did what owners have done throughout the history of the game. They fired the manager. On May 17 Jimmie was released, and several days later a former teammate, Lou Finney, was named manager of the Saints.[30] At this time the Saints were seventeen games out of first place

Foxx, Santa Claus and children, 1947 (courtesy Temple University Libraries).

and were playing .333 ball.[31] A few days later Jimmie was also replaced as general manager of the Saints by Edward S. Dean. However, as Jimmie explained later, his manager's contract was for a complete season, and although he was replaced, he continued to draw his salary until the end of the season.[32]

Foxx's departure from St. Petersburg prompted an extended and appreciative column from Dan Hall, sports columnist for the *St. Petersburg Times*. He wrote, "It is with regret ... that Jimmie Foxx is no longer ... manager of the Saints." Hall declared that "Jimmie had done his absolute level best at running the Saints. ... He had to start from scratch ... and find players where and when he could get them." The columnist was critical of fickle fans who booed "one of the greatest players of all time." He noted that Jimmie's duties as general manager, his involvement in public relations work and other activities, limited the attention he could devote to the team. It was Hall's impression that the Saints owners were expecting entirely too much from Jimmie, and when the players failed to perform they decided to replace him. Hall concluded by saying, "We are sorry to see Foxx go ... and he carries our sincere wishes for success."[33]

At the time Foxx left St. Petersburg he let it be known that despite his experience with the class C franchise, he was not through with baseball. He told a friend at the *Philadelphia Inquirer* that he would like to return to the majors as a coach or manager. However, no one in major league baseball offered him an opportunity to serve.[34] In an interview several years later, Jimmie was asked about his experience with the Saints. He replied, "The situation there looked like an interesting challenge ... but it turned out to be a bad move."[35]

In the summer of 1947 Foxx and his family left Florida, and for the next four years they lived in various places in New Jersey and in the Philadelphia area. On one occasion the *Philadelphia Inquirer* noted that Foxx was living in Millburn, New Jersey, and later that year the *Philadelphia Evening Bulletin* reported that he was a resident of Hammonton, New Jersey.[36] For a while after his return from Florida, Foxx was associated with a tavern at Hammonton, on the "main highway between Philadelphia and Ocean City." Jimmie was also active in local civic affairs. For example, at a Christmas party held at the Moose Lodge #548 in Philadelphia on December 21, Foxx dressed as Santa Claus and distributed gifts to more than "200 kids." Several days later at a Kiwanis Club party for children in Hammonton, New Jersey, Foxx again played Santa Claus and distributed gifts to more than eighty youngsters.[37]

During the summer of 1947 Foxx earned a few extra dollars playing semi-pro baseball. This was not a new experience for Jimmie; in 1943, the year he was out of baseball, he played for a semipro team near his home in Short Hills, New Jersey; and in 1947 he played for a semipro club sponsored by a Jersey City beverage concern. Jimmie would continue to be associated with local semipro clubs until he moved from the area in 1952.[38]

In 1947 Jimmie Foxx found himself featured in, of all things, a comic book. Issue #41 of *Real Life Comics*, a fifty-page publication which sold for ten cents, included brief excerpts concerning the life and achievements of "the world's greatest heroes." Among those included in this edition were Eleanor Roosevelt and Jimmie Foxx. The section on Foxx portrayed Frank Baker introducing Jimmie to Connie Mack and noted his game-winning home runs in the 1930 World Series. It also included highlights from his 1932 season and listed his Most Valuable Player awards.[39]

In the spring of 1948 Foxx was appointed sales manager for a Philadelphia distributor of Rheingold Beer.[40] This position in sales also involved public relations activities and some traveling. Although Foxx established an easy rapport with people and was pleased to be back in the Philadelphia area, he continued to hope that someone would offer him a job in major league baseball. During the summer of 1948 the Foxx family was residing in Philadelphia, on Hale Street. At this time his oldest son, Jimmie Jr., came to live with his father. Foxx's oldest son was approaching age nineteen and it seems that he had never established a close relationship with his stepfather, Richard Mayer. Jimmie Jr. lived with the family until he joined the army in 1949. He later served in the Korean War, married a woman in California, and continued to live on the West Coast.[41]

Among the public relations appearances made by Foxx in 1948 none had more nostalgic appeal than the two-day celebration sponsored by Robert Carpenter of the Phillies, to honor twenty of baseball's greatest players of the past. The first day was one of welcoming the visiting guests and veterans, and it culminated with a banquet at the Hotel Warwick. The closing event came the following day at Shibe Park when the honored players were introduced prior to a three-inning game between the veterans and the stars of the "Little Bigger League" in Philadelphia. Among the "famed players of the past" honored in this two-day celebration were Jimmie Foxx, Frank Frisch, Mickey Cochrane, Cy Young, Al Simmons, Lefty Grove, and Paul Waner.[42]

Later that summer, near the end of August, Foxx was the guest at an old-timers game in Lynn, Massachusetts. On this occasion Jimmie arrived in Boston by train, borrowed a car from Joe Cronin, and enjoyed visiting friends in the area. He kidded Ted Williams as "going sissy" because Ted had switched to a lighter, thirty-two-ounce bat. It seems that Jimmie enjoyed this interlude in the Boston area before returning to work in Philadelphia. When a Boston reporter asked Foxx to comment on the large salaries current players were receiving, such as Joe DiMaggio's $100,000.00 a year, his comment was, "I was born ten years too soon."[43]

In the fall of 1948 Foxx was the guest and principal speaker at a baseball banquet in Chatsworth, New Jersey. The Chatsworth team won the championship of the Burlington County League in 1948. That fall local sponsors decided to honor the team and show their appreciation with a banquet and a "name speaker." On this occasion Foxx entertained a gathering of more than 160 persons with stories of his experiences in baseball; including his recollections about Babe Ruth and other greats of the game whom he had known and some of his experiences playing baseball in Japan and Mexico.[44]

On another occasion when Foxx was the guest of a civic group in Harrisburg, a reporter asked him a question about the Baseball Museum in Cooperstown, New York. Foxx suggested that it would be a "boost to baseball" if the museum directors would put a number of the artifacts which the museum possessed—gloves, bats, balls, uniforms, etc.—on a railroad car and tour the country with the exhibit. This, he explained, would allow thousands of people to see "the tools of the immortals" and would be "a terrific shot in the arm" for baseball. Although the concept of traveling exhibitions was used by some organizations and agencies, baseball officials at Cooperstown ignored Jimmie's suggestion.[45]

In 1949 the brewing company for which Jimmie worked was subjected to a prolonged strike and during this time he obtained employment as a representative for the Mid-States Freight Lines, a coast-to-coast trucking firm with offices in Philadelphia.[46] A short while after going to work for the freight company, Jimmie had an opportunity to return to baseball. It was understood that this was a temporary position and one which Foxx was interested in only to accommodate an old friend, Walter "Rabbit" Maranville. The Mid-States Freight Lines granted Foxx a leave of absence to be the interim manager of the Bridgeport Bees of the class B Colonial League. On August 1, Ollie Byers was released as manager of the Bees, and it was announced that his replacement would be Walter Maranville. Maranville, however, was obligated to the *New York Journal-American* as director of its baseball school and program and would be unable to assume his duties as manager of the Bees until later in August. Foxx agreed to serve as "temporary manager." He made it clear, however, that he was not interested in a regular baseball job in the lower minor leagues. The long bus trips in the summer and trying to teach youngsters of limited talent, who wanted to hit home runs, was not what Foxx sought in baseball. He told a reporter for *The Sporting News* that he was still interested in a baseball position, but only if he received an offer "from a major league or triple A club." He also indicated that he "was well satisfied with his job at the Mid-States Freight Lines."[47]

Foxx assumed his duties as "emergency manager" of the Bridgeport Bees on August 3, expecting Maranville would be available by August 18 to take over the team. However, when Maranville's duties in New York prevented his going to Bridgeport until after the season closed at the end of the first week in September, Foxx agreed to remain a few days longer. Jimmie had already made an earlier commitment to participate in a ceremony at Yankee Stadium on August 21 honoring Connie Mack. When Foxx went to New York to keep this assignment, Jim Paules, the Bees first baseman, was appointed to direct the team for the remainder of the season.[48] When Foxx took over as interim manager of the Bees on August 3, the team was in third place in the Colonial League standings; when he left three weeks later, the Bees were in a tie with Stamford for second place.[49] A *Philadelphia Inquirer* reporter, seeking to obtain an insider's report on Foxx as a manager, later interviewed some of the Bridgeport players. He found that they liked Foxx, declaring, "He was a great guy to work under. ... He never told us how 'I did it.' He'd pat us on the back and say 'do the best you can.'"[50]

On August 21, 1949, there was an old-timers game at Yankee Stadium held in connection with honoring Connie Mack on his eighty-sixth birthday and his fiftieth year as manager of the Athletics. Among those present were Foxx, Cochrane, Grove, Simmons and Dykes of the Athletics, and Dickey, Gomez, Crosetti, Chapman, Wally Pipp, and George Selkirk of the Yankees. The ceremony honoring Mack was preceded by a two-inning old-timers game which the Yankees won 3-2. In this contest, Foxx was one for one—a double which batted in a run.[51]

After the ceremony at Yankee Stadium Foxx returned to his duties with the Mid-States Freight Lines. Although Jimmie told the press that he was

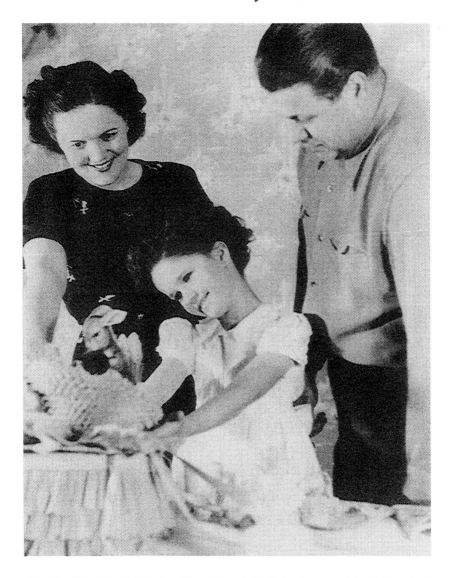

Dorothy, Jimmie and Nanci on Nanci's tenth birthday (courtesy Nanci Canaday).

satisfied with his work, he continued to hope that someone in major league baseball would offer him employment. Earlier in the year, when he was a guest at the Harrisburg Sportwriters and Sportcasters banquet, he had talked with Hank Greenberg about a possible position with the Cleveland Indians, who were owned by William "Bill" Veeck. Foxx assured the sports writers and Greenberg that he was interested in returning to baseball but only as a coach or manager of a major league club. Foxx's conversation with Greenberg prompted press speculation that he might become a member of the Indians' organization.[52] Nothing, however, came from these conversations, and there is no indication that Greenberg ever considered offering Foxx a position with the Indians. Some years later in his autobiography, *Hank Greenberg, The Story of My Life* (1989), Greenberg had the audacity to write that it was "strange" or deplorable that baseball treated its former stars "so shabbily," that owners seemingly "couldn't wait to destroy their dignity" by shunting them aside, and he mentioned the treatment accorded Babe Ruth and Foxx by major league baseball.[53] Greenberg, from 1948 on, was a member of the baseball establishment, first at Cleveland and later with the White Sox. There is no evidence that he ever considered offering Jimmie a job as coach or manager. It appears that he was one of those who participated in the shabby treatment of a great player who was never offered a position in major league baseball after the end of a remarkable career.

Connie and Earl Mack of the Philadelphia Athletics knew of Jimmie's desire for a job in major league baseball, and although Connie often talked of Jimmie as being "like a son," neither he nor the Athletics organization ever offered Foxx a job. In this same year (1949), the Athletics hired two of Foxx's former teammates, Cochrane and Bing Miller, as coaches but they ignored Jimmie.[54] In the spring of 1950 Connie Mack relinquished his duties as manager of the Athletics and Jimmy Dykes was named manager. At the same time Cochrane was appointed general manager. In his book, *You Can't Steal First Base*, Dykes praises Foxx for his ability as a player, his knowledge of the game, and his friendly personality and willingness to help others. However, neither Dykes nor Cochrane ever offered their friend and former teammate a job with the Athletics.[55]

Jimmie continued with his responsibilities at the freight line company and assisted his wife Dorothy in supervising a family of three young children. On January 2, he was the honorary guest of one of the organizations that participated in Philadelphia's annual Mummers Parade. He acknowledged that he was happy to participate in an event that he had watched for many years.[56]

In 1950 Jimmie and the family moved their residence to Maplewood, a new development near Doylestown, a suburb of Philadelphia, and he continued his job with the freight company.[57] This position allowed Jimmie time to participate in old-timer games and to appear before various civic and sports gatherings. For example, in mid–February he was a guest at the annual banquet of the Old-Timers Baseball Association of Reading, Pennsylvania. Among the guests at this affair were Frank "Home Run" Baker, Bill Jurges, Hank Greenberg, and others.[58] Later that summer he was a guest of the Harrisburg Sportwriters and Sportcasters banquet to honor the golden jubilee of Connie Mack's association with the Athletics. Others present to honor their former manager were Lefty Grove, Howard Ehmke, Max Bishop, Frank Baker, Joe

Boley, Jimmy Dykes, and Tris Speaker. Part of this observance was an old-timers game between some Harrisburg old-timers and a collection of veterans who once played for the Athletics. In addition to Foxx, other Athletics who participated in this two-inning affair which preceded Harrisburg's regular Inter-State League contest, were Ehmke, Grove, Cochrane, and Baker.[59]

During the fall and winter, 1950–51, there was speculation in the press and among baseball fans about whom the Baseball Writers Association of America would elect to the Hall of Fame. In the voting a year earlier various sports writers suggested that Mel Ott and Hank Greenberg were qualified for the Hall. Although no one was "campaigning" for Foxx, he was a contender since he had been among the top ten vote-getters the previous year.[60] When the writers' ballots were tabulated and the results announced on January 27, 1951, two men received over seventy-five percent of the votes cast and were thereby elected to the Baseball Hall of Fame. These two were Mel Ott and Jimmie Foxx.[61] The editor of *The Sporting News*, who noted that Foxx had received some votes in every election since the Hall was established, declared that the "ex–Maryland farm boy was one of the mightiest" hitters in baseball and that his election had been too long delayed.[62]

When Foxx received news of his election to the Hall of Fame he told reporters that he was "delighted by such a great honor" and "he thanked all of those who made it possible for his name to be listed along with baseball's greatest." He also declared that "this tops everything that has happened to me; I never expected to be selected from among all the great players."[63] Jimmie's wife was so happy with the news that she broke into tears. Their children and Jimmie's brother Sammy, who was visiting at the time, helped the family celebrate the news.[64]

Arthur Daley of the *New York Times* was not surprised at Foxx's election and several days after the announcement he devoted a column to Jimmie. He noted that no matter how impressive his baseball achievements, Foxx remained "a quiet, amiable and friendly sort of person," never assuming an air of self-importance. However, "this gentle-giant" of a man was a terror on pitchers and made their lives miserable for many years. Daley claimed that Foxx "undoubtedly hit the longest home run ever in Yankee Stadium." It was a blast off Gomez and broke the back rest of a seat two rows from the top of the upper deck in the left field stands. Daley related that when Ralph Kiner, the current Pirate home run hitter, first saw Comiskey Park he gazed in respect at the distant left field stands. He remarked to Daley, "They tell me Foxx hit the left field roof here four times"—a note of awe in his voice. Daley informed him that on one occasion Foxx hit one completely over the left field pavilion, out of the stadium and onto a playground across a street from Comiskey Park—a blast that traveled at least 520 feet.[65]

Foxx and Ott were the fifty-ninth and sixtieth persons to be elected to the Baseball Hall of Fame and, at age forty-three, Jimmie was one of the

Foxx as paint salesman, 1951 (courtesy Temple University Libraries).

youngest to receive this honor.[66] A week after the announcement that Foxx and Ott had been elected to the Hall of Fame they, along with other Hall of Famers, were the honored guests at the twenty-eighth annual dinner of the New York chapter of the Baseball Writers Association, held at the Waldorf-Astoria Hotel in New York City. Baseball commissioner A.B. "Happy" Chandler and approximately 1400 others were present at this affair. Sixteen of the twenty-three living members of baseball's Hall of Fame were present; others in addition to Foxx included Ty Cobb, Tris Speaker, Rogers Hornsby, Cy Young, George Sisler, Eddie Collins, Hugh Duffy, Carl Hubbell, Pie Traynor, Ed Walsh, Mickey Cochrane, and Charlie Gehringer.[67]

A week later Foxx returned to New York along with a number of other Hall of Fame members where they were guests of the National League. League officials sponsored a banquet to celebrate seventy-five years of National League achievement. The affair was held at the Broadway Central Hotel, and 600 people attended the celebration. Foxx and Ott were congratulated on their election to the Hall of Fame.[68] A couple of weeks later, when the Athletics and Phillies went to spring training, a local television station in Philadelphia, WPTZ, sought to utilize some of the publicity recently accorded Foxx. The station arranged for him to appear as a temporary sports commentator along

Family portrait, ca. 1951. Front row: Jimmie Jr. II and Foxx; back row: Dorothy, John and Nancy (courtesy Nanci Canaday).

with one of their regular staff reporters on the program "Sports Pictorial," a weekly program airing on Friday evenings. This did not interfere with Foxx's job at the freight company; it was only a fill-in position at the station because their regular staff person was in Florida with the Phillies and would take over when spring training ended.[69] Throughout 1951 Foxx continued to work for the freight company, and, to help support his family and brother (who seems to have been a frequent guest), Jimmie also took a part-time job at a paint store.[70]

In July Foxx took a brief leave from work, and he and Dorothy traveled to Cooperstown for the ceremonies of induction into the Baseball Hall of Fame. On this occasion a number of baseball dignitaries were present, including Mr. and Mrs. Connie Mack, their son Earl and his wife, and officials from both the American and National leagues. The induction ceremonies were held on July 23 and consisted of speeches on behalf of the new inductees and the dedication of memorial plaques to each man, which were placed in the Hall of Fame where visitors might view them. Foxx was the only new inductee who was present in Cooperstown for the ceremonies. Ott, who was manager of the Portland, Oregon, club in the Pacific Coast League, was unable to be present. Ford Frick, president of the National League, was the principal speaker at the dedication of the Ott plaque. Earl Hilligan, director of the American League

Service Bureau, substituted for William Harridge, president of the American League, who was unable to be present. Hilligan was the principal speaker on behalf of Foxx when his plaque was dedicated and placed in the Hall. He referred to Jimmie's hitting power and described him as "a great all-round guy" who was always "popular with the fans." In brief acceptance remarks Foxx declared that he was "very proud to become a member of the Hall of Fame."[71]

Part of the induction ceremonies included a baseball game at Doubleday Field. Known as the Hall of Fame game and played between an American League and a National League team, this game was an integral part of the induction ceremonies. On this occasion the game featured a contest between the Brooklyn Dodgers and the Philadelphia Athletics. It was played before 9,029 fans, the largest crowd ever to witness this annual affair, who saw the Dodgers win 9-4.[72]

Jimmie participated in one other ceremonial event in the summer of 1951. This was a local celebration confined to Philadelphia. On August 29 the Phillies sponsored an old-timers game as their contribution to celebrating the seventy-fifth anniversary of the National League. This affair took place in Shibe Park before 20,717 fans and featured, among others, Howard Ehmke, Jimmie Foxx, Max Bishop, Lefty Grove, Frank Baker, Cy Perkins, and "Rabbit" Maranville. The game was a two-inning exhibition and preceded the regular contest. The managers of the opposing teams were Phillies old-timers Hans Lobert and Otto Knabe. Foxx was a member of the team directed by Knabe. He played left field, earned a walk, and scored a run in his team's 3-2 victory.[73]

During the last six weeks of the 1951 baseball season Foxx once again served as an interim participant on the Sports Pictorial weekly television program at station WPTZ (channel 3) in Philadelphia. This was a fifteen-minute program which aired on Fridays from 7:00 to 7:15 P.M. It appears that Foxx was associated with this program only from early September until October 12. At this time the station's regular personnel took over the program and Foxx remained with the freight company.[74]

Notes

1. *Boston Globe*, March 20, 1946.

2. *Ibid.*, July 2, 1946; Robert Gregory, *Diz: Dizzy Dean and Baseball During the Great Depression* (New York: Viking, 1992), p. 363.

3. *The Sporting News*, May 2, 1946.

4. Foxx, "I'm Glad I Was a Ballplayer," p. 29; *New York Post*, January 19, 1958.

5. Boston *Globe*, April 19, 1946.

6. *Ibid.*, May 12, 1946.

7. *Ibid.*, June 1, 1946.

8. *Philadelphia Inquirer*, September 23, 1946.
9. *Boston Globe*, September 28, 1946.
10. Assorted clippings, 1946, *The Sporting News* Archives, St. Louis, Missouri.
11. *Boston Globe*, October 14, 1946; Foxx, "I'm Glad I Was a Ballplayer," p. 79; assorted clippings, 1967, in Dell Foxx scrapbook #2.
12. *The Sporting News*, July 17, 1946.
13. *Philadelphia Evening Bulletin*, November 21, 1946; *Philadelphia Inquirer*, November 21, 1946; *St. Petersburg Times*, April 6, 1947.
14. *The Sporting News*, December 4, 1946.
15. *Ibid.*, February 26, 1947.
16. *Philadelphia Evening Bulletin*, December 21, 1946; *The Sporting News*, January 8, 1947.
17. *The Sporting News*, January 8, 1947; *St. Petersburg Times*, April 4, 1947.
18. *St. Petersburg Times*, April 6, 1947.
19. *Ibid.*, April 8, 9, 10, 1947.
20. *Ibid.*, April 8, May 2, 1947.
21. *Ibid.*, April 12, 15, 1947.
22. *Ibid.*, April 18, 1947.
23. *Ibid.*, April 23, 1947.
24. *Ibid.*, April 24, 1947; *The Sporting News*, April 23, 1947.
25. *St. Petersburg Times*, April 29, 1947.
26. *Ibid.*, May 2, 3, 4, 7, 1947.
27. *Ibid.*, May 5, 8, 1947.
28. *Ibid.*, May 17, 24, 1947.
29. *Ibid.*, May 22, 1947.
30. *Ibid.*, May 21, 22, 1947.
31. *Ibid.*, May 17, 1947.
32. Jimmie Foxx, "I'm Through with Baseball Forever," *Baseball Monthly* (May, 1962), p. 54.
33. *St. Petersburg Times*, May 17, 1947.
34. *Philadelphia Inquirer*, May 11, 1947.
35. Foxx, "I'm Glad I Was a Ballplayer," p. 79.
36. *Philadelphia Inquirer*, September 11, 1947; *Philadelphia Evening Bulletin*, December 24, 1947.
37. Assorted clippings, Nanci Canaday collection, 1947; conversation with Kenneth Foxx, January 4, 1992; *Philadelphia Inquirer*, December 22, 1947; *Philadelphia Evening Bulletin*, December 24, 1947.
38. *Philadelphia Evening Bulletin*, January 25, 1944; assorted clippings, Foxx files, Baseball Library, Cooperstown, New York; assorted clippings, *Sporting News* Archives; *Philadelphia Evening Bulletin*, September 14, 1947; *Philadelphia Inquirer*, August 21, 1948, May 7, 1951; *Boston Globe*, January 26, 1951; Bob Gorman, *Double X, The Story of Jimmie Foxx—Baseball's Forgotten Slugger* (Camden, New Jersey: Holy Name Society, Diocese of Camden, New Jersey, 1990), p. 166.
39. See copy of this publication in the Library of Congress.
40. *Philadelphia Evening Bulletin*, May 17, 1948.
41. Conversation with Kenneth Foxx, January 11, 1992.

42. Assorted clippings, August 3, 1948, in Babe Ruth Museum, Baltimore, Maryland.

43. Assorted clippings, January 26, 1951, Foxx files, Baseball Library, Cooperstown, New York; the *Boston Traveler* (Boston, Massachusetts), August 30, 1948.

44. Assorted clippings, Camden, Pennsylvania, newspaper, December 8, 1949, in Foxx files, library of *Philadelphia Inquirer*, Philadelphia, Pennsylvania.

45. *Philadelphia Inquirer*, December 7, 1948.

46. *The Sporting News*, August 17, 1949.

47. *Ibid.*, August 17, 1949; *New York Times*, August 4, 1949.

48. *Philadelphia Evening Bulletin*, August 3, 1949; *The Sporting News*, August 31, 1949.

49. *The Sporting News*, August 24, 1949.

50. *Philadelphia Inquirer*, February 6, 1952.

51. Assorted clippings, August 21, 1949, in Babe Ruth Museum; *The Sporting News*, August 31, 1949.

52. *The Sporting News*, February 9, 1949.

53. Hank Greenberg, *The Story of My Life* (New York: Times Books, 1989), p. 175.

54. *The Sporting News*, August 17, 1949.

55. Jimmy Dykes and C.O. Dexter, *You Can't Steal First Base* (Philadelphia: J.B. Lippincott Company, 1967), pp. 29, 210; James Charlton, editor, *The Baseball Chronology* (New York: Macmillan, 1991), pp. 363, 369.

56. *Philadelphia Evening Bulletin*, December 29, 1949.

57. *Ibid.*, January 28, 1951.

58. *The Sporting News*, February 15, 1950.

59. *Ibid.*, August 16, 1950; assorted clippings, August, 1950, in Babe Ruth Museum.

60. *Philadelphia Evening Bulletin*, January 11, 1951.

61. *The Sporting News*, January 31, 1951.

62. *Ibid.*, February 7, 1951.

63. *Ibid.*, February 7, 14, 1951.

64. *Philadelphia Evening Bulletin*, January 28, 1951.

65. *The New York Times*, January 30, 1951.

66. Assorted clippings, 1959, Dell Foxx scrapbook #2.

67. *New York Times*, February 4, 1951.

68. *The Sporting News*, February 15, 1951.

69. Assorted clippings, March 7, 1951, Foxx files, Baseball Library, Cooperstown, New York.

70. Conversation with Dell Foxx, III, January 18, 1992.

71. *The Sporting News*, August 1, 1951; *Philadelphia Evening Bulletin*, July 23, 1951.

72. *The Sporting News*, August 1, 1951.

73. *Philadelphia Inquirer*, August 30, 1951.

74. *Ibid.*, September 7, 14, 21, 28, October 5, 12, 21, 1951.

Eight
The Daisies, Hurricanes, Marlins and Millers, 1952–1958

In 1952 Jimmie Foxx became associated once again with professional baseball when he accepted an invitation to manage the Fort Wayne, Indiana, Daisies of the All-American Girls Professional Baseball League (AAGPBL). This league was formed in 1943, and its principal sponsor and founder was Philip K. Wrigley, owner of the Chicago Cubs. Wrigley and others were concerned that the war and manpower shortage might bring a temporary end to baseball. Believing that baseball contributed to community unity, exerted a positive influence on public morale, and contributed to family entertainment, Wrigley invested considerable time and over $250,000.00 to the league during its first two years of operations.[1]

Although there had been women's barnstorming baseball clubs since the 1890s and occasionally female athletes such as Mildred "Babe" Didrickson made brief appearances with the male House of David team in the 1930s, the AAGPBL was "America's first, non-barnstorming, professionally established team sport for women."[2] At its inception in 1943 the league was mainly a softball organization. Its transformation to baseball, however, was complete by 1948. In this year pitchers were permitted to throw overhanded, the baseball was practically the same size as a regular baseball, the bases were extended to seventy-two feet apart, and the pitcher's mound to fifty-five feet from home plate. The game which the women played from 1948 on was baseball, but many of the rules and regulations for the players which were formulated earlier were retained. For example, chaperons continued to accompany the team; the uniform of blouse and abbreviated skirt over shorts had not changed; curfew for the players remained the same; and players were expected to behave as ladies at all times, both on and off the playing field.[3]

Teams in the AAGPBL played a 110-game schedule, which extended from May 15 to September 1. Games were nine-inning affairs and were usually

181

Foxx (right) and the Ft. Wayne Daisies, 1952 (courtesy Northern Indiana Histori-cal Society).

played at night. Occasionally there might be a twi-night contest, and double-headers were generally scheduled for Saturday or Sunday. Admission to the games was usually fifty to seventy-five cents. There was a mid-season break in the schedule for an all-star game, and there were play-offs to determine the league champion after the close of the regular season.[4]

An interesting bit of trivia connected with the AAGPBL concerns the first night baseball game played at Wrigley Field. The first major league night game at Wrigley Field was on August 9, 1988, between the Cubs and the Phillies. However, this was not the first night game ever played on the Cubs' home field. On July 1, 1943, two teams of women chosen from the clubs in the AAGPBL played a night game before 7,000 fans at Wrigley Field for the benefit of the Women's Army Air Corps. The lights were temporary and were installed only for this occasion. It would be forty-five years before permanent lights were placed in Wrigley Field—but the women played the first night game at the Cubs' home park.[5]

During the twelve-year history of the AAGPBL, fifteen upper Midwest cities, at one time or another, supported entries in the league. However, only two cities—Rockford, Illinois, and South Bend, Indiana—fielded entries for each year of the league's existence. Fort Wayne, Indiana, and Grand Rapids, Michigan, sponsored teams for ten years and a number of cities for shorter periods of time.[6] From the league's inception, league officials and team owners usually employed retired male baseball players as team managers. Some of these men were ex-major leaguers such as Bill Wambsganss, Josh Billings, Marty McManus, Woody English, and Max Carey.[7]

The Fort Wayne Daisies entered the AAGPBL in 1945, two years after its inception and remained a member of the league until its demise at the close of the 1954 season. At the end of the 1951 season, and after serving for two years as manager of the Daisies, Max Carey resigned. During the winter of 1951–52 team officials contacted the most recent inductee to the Hall of Fame, Jimmie Foxx, and persuaded him to be Carey's successor. Although this position would renew Foxx's association with baseball, it certainly was not with a major league or triple A club. One can only speculate why Foxx was attracted by the Fort Wayne offer. Others who have written about Foxx do not mention his experience with the AAGPBL. Perhaps Jimmie was tired of the freight line and other part-time jobs at which he had worked for several years; maybe the novelty of managing a woman's baseball team attracted his interest; probably any chance to get back in baseball was the principal reason for the decision of a man who loved the game and also missed it very much. Maybe it was the $3,600.00 salary with the possibility of a performance bonus at the end of the season that prompted Jimmie to accept the Fort Wayne offer. Whatever his motivation, the *Philadelphia Evening Bulletin* of February 3, 1952, announced that Foxx had signed to manage the Fort Wayne Daisies for the coming season. In the spring Foxx moved his family from Doylestown to a new residence in Fort Wayne.[8]

Foxx arrived in Fort Wayne a week before the team was to begin spring training on April 20. The *Fort Wayne Journal-Gazette* reported that all six teams in the league were "in good financial position," that the team lineups appeared stronger than ever, and that everyone was anxiously awaiting the opening of the season.[9] During his first few days in Fort Wayne, Foxx met with representatives of the local press and was introduced to the members of the Daisies organization. One day he and the club president went to Kalamazoo where they assisted the local sponsors in forming a fan club for their team. At another time he talked with the business manager Ernie Borg, who had recently completed plans for the team's spring training in Newton, North Carolina. Jimmie also met the Daisies' chaperon, Doris Tetzlaff, who accompanied the team and served as road secretary and business manager. Her duties included seeing that the players "made the trains and buses on time," checking hotel reservations, arranging press interviews, and serving as correspondent for the Fort Wayne newspaper.[10] The *Journal-Gazette* reported that Foxx was an "expansive, friendly type person who was willing to talk" and that he had made many friends during his first few days in the city while he was making preparations for spring training.[11]

On Sunday, April 20, Foxx and a portion of the team departed from Fort Wayne for the spring training facilities. There they would meet the other members of the team who were traveling to the camp from their homes. The first workout was scheduled for April 22. The training site was at the New-ton-Conover ball park, a facility which would seat 6,500 persons. After sev-eral days of calisthenics, running, fielding and batting practice, the first exhi-bition game with the Battle Creek Belles was scheduled for Saturday, April 26. The Belles were also training at Newton and were scheduled to play a series of exhibition games with the Daisies before the opening of the season. The manager of the Belles was the former Cub pitcher, Guy Bush. He and Foxx were on opposing sides of the 1929 World Series. Bush was the winning pitcher in the only game the Cubs won in that series; Foxx was hitless against Bush as the Cubs won 3-1.[12]

The game scheduled with the Belles for Saturday, April 26, was postponed because of rain. On April 29 the teams broke camp and began their exhibi-tion series which continued until a few days prior to the opening of the sea-son. The Daisies and Belles played games in Hickory, Charlotte and Newton, North Carolina before moving north for games in Washington, D.C., and Lynchburg, Roanoke, and Bluefield, Virginia. The final contest before arriv-ing in Fort Wayne was at Charleston, West Virginia. The Fort Wayne press reported that Foxx was generally pleased with the exhibition performances of the team. Rain caused cancellation of five games, and the Daisies won six of the ten games played against the Belles.[13]

In the meanwhile, civic groups and others were busy in Fort Wayne preparing for the May 15 opening game against the Kalamazoo Lassies. Team boosters and local Daisies fan clubs were urging a large turnout for the game. Team officials wanted to win the "President's Trophy" for Fort Wayne. This was an award given annually to the city that had the largest percentage of its population present for the opening game of the season.[14] Fort Wayne did not win this trophy, since their opening game was played on a very "chilly" evening before 2,061 fans. In ceremonies prior to the 8:30 starting time there was a presentation of "the colors" by a local cadet guard and band. The Travelers Pro-tective Association presented manager Foxx a "floral horse shoe" as a symbol for good luck, and the city's mayor threw out the first ball of the season. The Daises provided a happy ending to the ceremonies by defeating the Lassies 8-1. The Daisies' star pitcher, Maxine Kline, who was 18-4 the previous sea-son, allowed only three hits.[15]

After several home games the Daisies departed on a seven-day road trip during which they played .500 ball. At the end of May their record was 5-5 and Foxx expressed concern about the lack of timely hitting by the club. The Daisies improved in June and by June 20 their record was 20 wins and 11 losses, which placed them in second place in the league, two and one-half games out of first. Jo Weaver, the right fielder for the Daisies was leading the league in hitting with a .412 average.[16]

The AAGPBL all-star game was played at South Bend on July 7. The game featured the league-leading South Bend Blue Sox and an all-star contingent chosen by the press and radio sportscasters from the other clubs in the league. Four Daisies were selected for the all-star squad. In a game played before 3,528 fans, the Blue Sox lost 7–6. The star of the game was the Fort Wayne first baseman, Betty Foss, who was two for five in the contest and drove in two runs.[17] The week following the all-star game Foxx took a brief leave and went to Cincinnati. He was an invited guest at the Reds' Hall of Fame night, where he and other members of the Hall of Fame were honored and introduced to the crowd at Crosley Field prior to the regular game. Among those present for this affair besides Foxx were Paul Waner, Connie Mack, Carl Hubbel, Rogers Hornsby, Mickey Cochrane, and Charlie Gehringer. In Jimmie's absence, Doris Tetzlaff, the chaperon and road secretary, served as interim manager of the Daisies.[18]

The Daisies continued to play winning ball throughout July and by the end of the month were only one-half game behind the first-place Blue Sox. Jo Weaver continued to lead the league in hitting, and the Daisies also had the highest team batting average in the league. They also boasted three of the league's top ten pitchers. The season's marathon game occurred on July 29 in a contest between the Daisies and the Grand Rapids Chicks. This was a seventeen-inning affair which lasted for three and one-half hours. Maxine Kline pitched the entire game for the Daisies and was the winning pitcher in a 1–0 game. The hitting star was Betty Foss, whose triple resulted in the winning run.[19]

Throughout the last month of the season the Daisies contested the Blue Sox for the league title. On August 23, with a victory over the Rockford Peaches, the Daisies took over the league leadership.[20] At the same time that the Daisies were emerging at the top of the league, their manager had to miss a game or two because of illness. In his absence Ms. Tetzlaff served as acting manager. Foxx's illness was of brief duration and was probably a recurrence of sinus trouble.[21] The Daisies remained in first place and won their first league title after eight years in the league. In final league standings the Daisies won sixty-seven and lost forty-two for a winning percentage of .615. The team also included the league's leading hitter, best pitcher, and Most Valuable Player. Their home attendance of more than 86,000 was also a record and an increase of six percent over the previous year.[22]

Two days after the close of the season the league play-offs began. Fort Wayne's opponent was the Rockford Peaches; the South Bend Blue Sox's opponent was the Grand Rapids Chicks. The first round in the play-off series was limited to three games. The first round winners then met in a best three-of-five game series to determine the league champion. The Daisies lost in the first round to Rockford, two games to one, and the Blue Sox were the winners in their series. In the final play-offs South Bend defeated Rockford to win the championship.[23]

After the play-offs there was a ceremony in Fort Wayne where the team members were honored with gifts of watches, sweaters, and other items from the team sponsors and friends, and each team member received a bonus check from the club management. The press noted that "most of the Daisies should be back next year" and that league prospects for the future looked good.[24] The *Fort Wayne Journal-Gazette*, however, noted that one question which probably would not be decided for some time was whether Jimmie Foxx would return in 1953 as manager. The sports editor of this paper wrote, "Foxx told us that as of now he would like to come back." However, he also declared that "he doesn't care much for the long bus trips" involved in league play. The editor concluded his comments by emphasizing that "Jimmie had the greatest success of any Daisy manager in the eight years" of their existence. It was rather obvious that the press was hoping Foxx would return.[25]

Jimmie had a very successful year as manager of the Daisies; he was popular with the press and fans. He was also well liked and respected by the players. One researcher who has interviewed a number of the women who were on the 1952 Fort Wayne team declares that not a single one of them would say anything uncomplimentary about Foxx. He was a "fine fellow," was "like a big brother" to them, or was "like a father to us" are typical of the comments of those who played for Jimmie in 1952. Foxx's affable and unpretentious personality was evident whether he was establishing hitting records in the 1930s or managing a woman's baseball team in 1952.[26]

Following the close of the AAGPBL season Foxx and his family returned to the Philadelphia area, and he did not return to Fort Wayne to manage the Daisies in 1953. In Philadelphia he worked at various places; one was, again, as a paint salesman. In the spring of 1953 he served as an instructor and helped to supervise a baseball training school in Newton, North Carolina, where he was assisted by a four-man staff. This school met from early April until the latter part of May and enrolled sixty-nine young men, who came from sixteen different states and Canada.[27] When the training school closed, Foxx returned to Philadelphia and his job as a paint salesman. Later that year he and the family moved to the St. Petersburg area in Florida. His stepdaughter states that Foxx decided to relocate in Florida because he enjoyed the milder winters. He obtained employment as an oil salesman.[28] Jimmie returned to Philadelphia in late January, 1954, as a guest at the fiftieth annual banquet of the Philadelphia Sport Writers Association. On this occasion the writers were honoring the ten "greatest living stars to ever play baseball in Philadelphia." More than one thousand attended the banquet to honor Connie Mack, Ty Cobb, Frank Baker, Mickey Cochrane, Jimmie Foxx, Lefty Grove, Al Simmons, Chuck Klein, Tris Speaker, and Napoleon Lajoie. It was reported that Foxx was "bronze and trimmer than he has been in years" and that he was associated with an oil distributing company in St. Petersburg, Florida.[29]

With the beginning of spring training in 1954, Foxx's desire to return to baseball prompted him to contact Hank Greenberg, general manager of the

Indians, to inquire about the possibility of becoming affiliated with the Cleveland organization. The *Philadelphia Inquirer* reported that Jimmie was eager to return to baseball and had informed Greenberg that he would be interested in returning to the game "in any capacity." Despite Jimmie's efforts no position in major league baseball was offered to him.[30]

During the winter of 1953–54 the Sports Writers Association of Maryland conducted a poll among the sportswriters and broadcasters of the state to select a Maryland all-time, all-star baseball team. The results of this poll were announced in the March 3 edition of *The Sporting News*. This select team consisted of the following men: Babe Ruth, right field; Charlie Keller, center field; Bill Nicholson, left field; Jimmie Foxx, first base; Max Bishop, second base; Frank Baker, third base; Fritz Maisel, shortstop; Babe Phelps, catcher; and Lefty Grove, pitcher.[31]

Later that spring the Boston Sports Lodge B'nai B'rith sponsored a banquet on April 15 at the Sheraton-Plaza Hotel to honor Red Sox owner Tom Yawkey and a selection of Red Sox all-stars from the Yawkey era. Foxx was one of the guests of honor at this dinner, along with Lefty Grove, Bobby Doerr, Ted Williams, Dominic DiMaggio and others. More than seven hundred people were at the banquet to participate in the festivities. Each honoree was presented "a handsome watch, inscribed with a Red Sox seal on a leather covering." Foxx received prolonged applause following his brief comments upon receiving the watch. He told the gathering, "After coming here and talking to so many friends, I sort of feel like I've returned home." He declared, "I spent the happiest years of my baseball life here and Mr. Yawkey was the best boss I ever worked for." He concluded by saying that he would like to return to Boston that coming fall for the World Series.[32]

In mid–August, 1954, Foxx was a guest at an old-timers game in Yankee Stadium. A number of Hall of Fame members were present for this occasion, which was "a special salute" to Bill Terry, a recent inductee to the Hall of Fame. Over 50,000 fans were present for this celebration, including the ninety-one-year-old Connie Mack and former President Herbert Hoover, who threw out the first ball of the game. Among those who participated in the two-inning old-timers game between American and National League squads were Foxx, Al Simmons, Joe Cronin, George Sisler, Bill Terry, Joe DiMaggio, Paul Waner, Rogers Hornsby, and Carl Hubbell. The American League old-timers won 3-2; Foxx played third base, had a single in two at bats, and scored a run.[33]

In the summer of 1954 the Foxx family left St. Petersburg and moved to the Miami area. Foxx was now associated with the Johnny Jones meat packing and distributing company. His position was in sales and public relations.[34] Jimmie was with this firm only a short while before he was given a leave of absence to promote a youth program aimed at combating juvenile delinquency. This program, referred to by the press as the Jimmie Foxx Youth Program, was formed in the summer and early autumn by a group of businessmen who secured Foxx to publicize it.[35] The program was the brain child of Roy Gregory, a businessman in Bridgeport, Connecticut, and Frank Silva, a Boston business executive and former general manager of the Bridgeport Bees. The concept of the program was to recruit major league baseball players and send them out in teams of four to hold baseball clinics for youths and talk to them about baseball, education, and the responsibilities of "good citizenship." The program, as envisioned, would operate for four months during the baseball off season. Once the program was formulated it was necessary to obtain sponsors and to seek approval from baseball commissioner Ford Frick. By mid–October Frick gave baseball's approval to the program and a number of major league players had agreed to participate in its activities. The founders had received pledges of financial support to inaugurate the program from two prominent Pennsylvania businessmen, Ernest Ferranti of Williamsport and Sam Nagelberg of Scranton, and Frank Silva of Boston. A headquarters address was located in New York City at the office of the program's attorney, Louis Kaplan.[36]

The first organization to approve the concept of the Youth Program and agree to cooperate with and help obtain support for it was the Pennsylvania Department of the American Legion. Although the American Legion recommended the program and urged the public to support it, the Legion did not assume any financial obligations connected with the program.[37] The American Legion had been sponsoring youth baseball for more than fifty years and Legion officials in Pennsylvania viewed this program as a supplement to an already successful enterprise.[38]

It was explained that Pennsylvania would be the "testing ground for the program," which would function during the month of January. It was expected that the following year the program would include other states and run for at least four months.[39] Gene Woodling, Yankee outfielder and director of personnel for the Youth Program, had recruited thirty-two major league players to participate. Among them were Joe Coleman, Ralph Houk, Mickey Vernon, Hank Bauer, Gil McDougald, Whitey Ford, Gil Hodges, Curt Simmons, and Del Ennis.[40] They were divided into eight teams, and the aim was for them to hold clinics and conduct programs on sportsmanship and citizenship in each of Pennsylvania's sixty-seven Legion post areas.

Sherman W. Mason, state commissioner of the American Legion in Pennsylvania, was enthusiastic about the program. He told the Legionnaires at their state convention, "We are going to hit the road—baseball bat in one hand and the Bible in the other and the American flag in our teeth. ... We'll knock ourselves out trying to beat juvenile delinquency."[41] It was expected that non-profit civic, religious, and other benevolent organizations in the various counties and cities would help underwrite expenses associated with the program, which were estimated to be approximately $750.00 per clinic. Program directors expected to compensate the players who participated in the program a sum comparable to what they would make on a barnstorming tour.[42] A portion of the sum expected from local sponsors would be used to fund a scholarship proposed by the directors of the Youth Program. They hoped to award one college scholarship each year to the youth who submitted the best essay on the subject "What Baseball Means to Me."[43]

When the Youth Program was announced in the fall of 1954 it received enthusiastic support from the press in New York and Philadelphia, from *The Sporting News* and others. Foxx, who was designated a vice president of the organization, was committed to the program and devoted a great amount of time traveling, promoting, and trying to obtain support for it.[44] He explained to one reporter that the program aimed "to help kids get off on the right foot and keep them out of trouble with the police." He hoped that kids would be persuaded to devote more time to sports than to "gangster movies and books."[45] The enthusiasm expressed for the Youth Program was not reflected in the financial support that it received. The result was that after an initial flurry of activity in the fall and winter of 1954–55, the program was terminated or collapsed because it received inadequate financial support.

Although Foxx was occupied with various business ventures, civic organizations, and the Youth Program he continued to hope that someone would offer him a job in major league baseball. On one occasion when he was in Scranton conferring with officials of the Youth Program, a reporter asked Jimmie why he wasn't "coaching young Red Sox hitters or the potential greats of some other major league organization." Foxx replied, "I'm available for any respectable position," but he emphasized that he was not interested in the lower minor leagues. "Maybe," Jimmie said, "I lack the connections. How else can one think when fellows who never got anywhere have some of the best coaching jobs?"[46]

Throughout the spring and summer of 1955 Foxx continued in sales and public relations with the Jones meat packing company. On April 9 a group of sportsmen and baseball enthusiasts in the Miami/Coral Gables area sponsored a testimonial dinner to honor the baseball Hall of Famer who was now a resident of the area. This dinner was held at Ramon's restaurant in Miami and was attended by 250 fans of Foxx's. On this occasion Miami city commissioner, Randy Christmas, gave Jimmie the key to the city and explained that it "was for both Miami and Coral Gables," where Jimmie's residence was actually located. Foxx was also presented a television set, and telegrams of congratulations and best wishes were read from President Dwight Eisenhower, commissioner Ford Frick, Tom Yawkey, Vice-President Richard Nixon, Florida Governor Leroy Collins, and Florida United States Senator George Smathers. The principal speaker on this occasion was Ted Williams. He described Foxx "as the nicest guy I ever met in baseball. Of all the people I've known in baseball, Foxx is the one I've never heard anyone say an unkind word about."[47] Foxx responded to the tributes paid to him by saying,

"This evening has been a big thrill for me, and I want to thank my friends very much."[48]

Foxx's only connection with baseball in 1955 was to serve as commissioner of the junior baseball program in Coral Gables.[49] However, on several occasions he took leave to attend baseball functions in other areas of the country. For example, in January he was the guest, along with several former teammates, at the twenty-seventh annual dinner of the Old-Timers Baseball Association in Stowe, Pennsylvania. Honored guests on this occasion included members of the 1929–31 infield for the Athletics—Foxx, Bishop, Dykes, and Boley.[50] In early May Foxx returned to Boston as a guest of the Boston Sports Lodge of B'nai B'rith. This organization sponsored a dinner to honor the living members of the Baseball Hall of Fame. Among those present at this affair were Foxx, Bill Dickey, Joe DiMaggio, Carl Hubbell, Joe Cronin, Leo "Gabby" Hartnett, Lefty Grove, and Paul Waner.[51] On two other occasions during the 1955 season Foxx traveled to Kansas City for baseball celebrations. This was the year the Athletics moved from Philadelphia to Kansas City. At the beginning of the season in April there was a party arranged by business and civic dignitaries to honor the men who were bringing major league baseball to the city and to welcome the team to their new home. This affair was held at the Muehlebach Hotel and was hosted by the Joseph Schlitz Brewing Company. Schlitz had agreed to sponsor the broadcast of the Athletics' games for the coming season. Among the honored guests were former Athletics greats Frank Baker and Jimmie Foxx. In his remarks Foxx expressed the opinion that the two best American League baseball teams of all time were the 1927 Yankees and the 1929 Athletics. He also stated that he considered Lefty Grove the "greatest pitcher of all time." He concluded by wishing much success for the Kansas City manager Lou Boudreau and team owner Arnold Johnson.[52]

Foxx's second visit to Kansas City was three months later in mid–July, when the Athletics sponsored their first Hall of Fame celebration to honor those members who had spent most of their careers with the Athletics. Among those present on this occasion were Foxx, Cochrane, Bing Miller, and Connie Mack. The ceremonies included introduction of each Hall of Famer to the crowd prior to the regular season game with the Red Sox.[53] Foxx was also present in New York on July 30 for the Yankee-sponsored old-timers game and a ceremony to honor Hall of Fame members. In ceremonies at Yankee Stadium prior to the regular game, before a crowd of 31,000, each Hall of Famer was introduced and presented a gift by the Yankee management. This gift was an eight-day clock, imported from England. The ceremonies concluded with a two-inning game between former baseball players; in this contest Foxx was one for one, hitting a double off Red Ruffing.[54]

Before the end of the summer of 1955 it appears that Foxx had severed connection with the meat packing firm. A press report on September 27, 1955, noted that Jimmie had successfully "completed the examination and had met the necessary requirements for qualifying" to be an insurance agent. Foxx had been issued a "certificate of qualification, State of Florida," by the office of the state treasurer and insurance commission.[55] In addition to acquiring a license to sell insurance, Foxx was also working as a part-time salesman for the Leo Adeeb Chevrolet Company in Miami Beach.[56] About the same time that Jimmie was licensed to sell insurance and also engaged in selling automobiles, *The Sporting News* announced that he would be returning to baseball in 1956. In the September 21 issue of this sports weekly it was revealed that Perry Moss, who had been coaching both football and baseball at the University of Miami, was going to devote full time to football and that Jimmie Foxx had been employed to coach baseball, beginning in the forthcoming 1956 season.[57]

Spring baseball practice at the University of Miami was scheduled to begin February 9. However, before that date Jimmie had inspected the playing field, conferred with Moss and others about which players were returning and discussed prospects for the Hurricanes' 1956 season. Miami had a nineteen-game schedule that extended from March 27 to April 28 and included contests with Amherst College, the University of Florida, Florida Southern University, Stetson University, Rollins College, and Florida State University.[58] Before spring practice began Foxx was out of town for two engagements. On January 14 he returned to St. Petersburg and participated in an old-timers baseball game played to benefit the March of Dimes. This game featured former American and National League players, was witnessed by more than 3,000 fans, and raised over $3,000.00 for the March of Dimes. Among those who participated in this contest were Foxx, Wes Ferrell, Paul Waner, Dazzy Vance, and Rip Sewell.[59] Several weeks later Foxx was one of the honored guests at a banquet on February 4 at the Emerson Hotel in Baltimore. Maryland sportswriters and members of the "M" Club at the University of Maryland had created the Maryland Athletic Hall of Fame to honor famous sports figures who were born in the state. The initial honorees chosen for the Hall were Babe Ruth, Frank Baker, Jimmie Foxx, and Robert Garrett. It was announced that every year the Hall of Fame committee expected to select three living persons and one deceased for membership in the state Hall of Fame. It was explained that the temporary location of the Hall of Fame was the monogram room at the University of Maryland. At the banquet each honoree was presented a certificate of membership in the Maryland Hall of Fame and informed that a plaque for each would be mounted on the wall of the "M" room. Mrs. Ruth was invited to receive the certificate honoring the Babe.[60]

Several days after Jimmie's induction into the Maryland Hall of Fame, baseball practice began for the Hurricanes. On opening day about fifty hopefuls reported to Coach Foxx at the University of Miami baseball diamond. Although several of those reporting were members of the 1955 team which won 15 and lost 7, the press noted that Foxx needed two "first line outfielders," an infielder, a starting pitcher and reserve strength "all along the line."[61] Foxx's aim was to develop the team slowly, play some inter-squad games, a few contests with class C and D affiliates of major league clubs and then decide which players would comprise the University of Miami roster.

Shortly after Foxx began his duties at the University of Miami he was saddened by the death of one of the major influences on his life. Connie Mack died on February 8 at the age of 93. Jimmie told a reporter that Connie's death was "one of the greatest losses baseball has ever had" and he asserted that there would "never be another like him." Jimmie concluded his comments on Mack by declaring, "He was great to play for."[62] Two weeks later there was a significant announcement in the Miami press concerning Foxx's association with baseball. Jimmie's contract with the University of Miami was only for the three-month college baseball season (February–April) and the salary was $500.00 a month.[63] At this time, being baseball coach was only a part-time position at the University of Miami. In 1955 two associates of Bill Veeck purchased the Syracuse team of the International League and decided to move it to Miami, where it became the Miami Marlins. Veeck agreed to help his friends get established in the city. He arranged a working relationship with the Phillies, and he hired Jimmie Foxx as a coach and to help him with public relations.[64]

There was considerable enthusiasm in the city and area about triple A baseball coming to Miami. On February 11 a number of civic leaders and sports enthusiasts held a dinner for Marlin officials to give them a formal welcome to the city. Foxx was the principal speaker at this dinner.[65] On February 26 the *Miami Herald* announced that Jimmie Foxx had been hired as a coach for the Marlins and that he would assume his duties with them in May, following the close of the Hurricanes' baseball season. It was explained that, in addition to coaching, Foxx would conduct baseball clinics and tryout camps for youngsters in the Miami area and elsewhere in the state. Eddie Stumpf, general manager of the Marlins, explained that "Jimmie would work with players in the area from little leaguers to semipro players."[66]

In the meantime Foxx was trying to prepare the Hurricanes for their opening game with a team from the Key West Recreation Department called the Key West All-Stars. The season's debut was not a pleasant one for either the coach or the team since the Key West contingent won 3-2. On March 15 the Hurricanes went to Hollywood, Florida, for a preseason game with a squad from the Memphis Chicks of the Southern Association League.[67] After a month of inter-squad practice games and several preseason contests, the Hurricanes opened their regular season play against Amherst College on March 27. Miami and Amherst played single games on March 27 and 28 and the visitors won both contests, 9-6 and 6-4. Foxx assessed his team's performance by declaring, "We made a few mental lapses and looked ragged in spots, but I expected it." He said that the team would improve but admitted "we need more pitching."[68] In the first week of April the University of Miami played two

games with the University of Florida Gators of the Southeastern Conference
and although the Hurricanes lost both games, each contest attracted over 500
fans. The press could hardly believe this, since Hurricane baseball games were
usually witnessed by fewer than 100 people.[69]

Before the Hurricanes played their first game of the Florida Intercollegiate Conference, the organization of which they were a member, Coach Foxx
changed his lineup and sought to prepare his team for their contest with
Florida Southern University. He was pleased with his team's performance, as
they won over Florida Southern 4-2 and 12-5. Jimmie complimented his players for their hitting and pitching in these opening conference games.[70] The
Hurricanes were also successful against conference foe Stetson, but were
defeated by Rollins and Florida State. They ended the season with a record
of nine wins and eight losses.[71]

When Foxx assumed his duties with the Marlins in May, the team was
in last place in the International League. Jimmie's immediate task was to work
with the hitters and try to help them become more effective. By mid–May the
Marlins had departed from the cellar and begun a rise in the standings which
would continue. At the end of May they were in sixth place; on June 16 they
were tied for third place; and on August 1 they led the league by one-half
game. Although the Marlins faltered slightly in August they ended the season in third place, five and one-half games behind pennant-winning Toronto
and three and one-half games behind second-place Rochester. Montreal was
in fourth place, one-half game behind the Marlins. The citizens of Miami were
pleased with the Marlins, and the team had a home attendance of 287,385 for
their first season in the International League.[72]

Marlin manager Don Osborn, who allowed Foxx to conduct extra batting sessions with the hitters when he first arrived, gave Jimmie credit for
much of the team's improvement. Sportswriters for the *Miami Herald* and *The
Sporting News* expressed the opinion that "much of the credit" for the Marlins' success should go to the work of Foxx.[73] In the Shaughnessy play-offs after
the end of the season, Miami lost in the first round to Rochester, and Montreal won from Toronto. Rochester won the league championship, defeating
Toronto four games to three.[74]

A very pleasant and proud moment in the life of Jimmie Foxx came about
the same time that he joined the Marlins. In mid–May his eleven-year-old-
son, Jimmie Jr., II, achieved a degree of baseball distinction when he pitched
a no-hit, no-run game in the Coral Gables Police Benevolent Junior Baseball
League. His Coral Gables team defeated a junior league club from Miami
3-0. Jimmie Jr. struck out eight batters and walked three; he also got one of
his team's three hits.[75]

Although Foxx served as a special coach for the Marlins in 1956, much
of his time was spent in public relations activities. He participated in numerous baseball clinics in the state, and he traveled with Veeck to help promote

baseball in Florida. Jimmie later wrote, "Veeck hired me as a coach and public relations man. I made sixty-five appearances in fifty days on speaking tours with him."[76] On one of these public relations occasions, at the Allapattah Optimist Club in Miami, Foxx was the principal dinner speaker. In a talk about baseball records, he predicted that one year someone would break Ruth's record of sixty home runs for the season. He speculated that if Mickey Mantle could remain free from injuries, he might be the one to do it. Jimmie concluded his remarks by declaring that even though some hitter would break Ruth's record, "there will always be only one Ruth." Ruth, he asserted, "had color" as well as exceptional ability. At another time Veeck sent Jimmie to Kansas City when the Athletics sponsored a special ceremony to honor members of Baseball's Hall of Fame.[77]

Although Foxx had a winning season at the University of Miami and the Marlins made the International League play-offs, 1956 had its sad moments for Jimmie. As has been noted, the man who gave him a start in major league baseball and one for whom he had the greatest admiration, Connie Mack, died in February of this year. Three months later his former teammate and roommate, Al Simmons, died from a heart attack at his home in Milwaukee. Foxx told a reporter that "Al, Mickey Cochrane, and I were inseparable when we played with the Athletics." "Al," he declared, "was one of the great hitters." And indeed he was: in twenty-one seasons in the major leagues he achieved a lifetime batting average of .334 and was elected to the Baseball Hall of Fame in 1953. His death came four days after his fifty-fourth birthday.[78]

When the 1956 baseball season ended, Foxx's contract with the Marlins expired. He had agreed to coach the Hurricanes in 1957, but there had been no understanding that he would return to the Marlins. In the meantime he and a sports promoter in Miami arranged to conduct several baseball schools in the area during the off season before Jimmie had to assume his duties at the University of Miami. These schools were held in Miami, Miami Beach, and surrounding areas and they enrolled local students and some from beyond the area. Instruction was given in the fundamentals of playing baseball, and there were also classes in umpiring and in the business management of baseball. The business manager of the Marlins was one of the instructors in the classes on business management. Foxx also worked part-time during the off season as a salesman in a sporting goods store.[79]

In January, 1957, the man who gave Jimmie his first baseball and bat, who taught him how to throw, catch and hit, died suddenly at his home in Sudlersville. Jimmie's father, Samuel Dell Foxx, was eighty years old. When he was a young man, Dell Foxx had been a popular semipro baseball player, and Jimmie later declared that his dad was a better catcher than some he saw in the majors. Jimmie and his brother Samuel Dell Foxx, Jr., who was also living in Miami, attended their father's funeral, which was at the Calvary Asbury United Methodist Church. Interment was at the Sudlersville cemetery.[80]

Several weeks later Jimmie was a guest speaker at a baseball dinner in Manchester, New Hampshire. On this occasion he talked about his work at the University of Miami and said that he "enjoyed coaching college boys" and thought that they would have a good season in 1957. When asked about baseball records he replied that he "wouldn't be surprised" if someone broke Ruth's home run record for one season. However, he added that the longer it takes for one to break the record, the more difficult it would become because of the "constant pressure" on the hitter. He explained that when he hit fifty-eight in 1932, the record was only five years old, that no one paid much attention to it, and he felt no pressure.[81]

It was during the off season, 1956–57, that Foxx knew definitely that he would not be associated with the Marlins in 1957. After the 1956 season ended, the Marlins were sold to new owners and Bill Veeck ended his association with the club. Foxx had been employed by Veeck and not by the Marlin management or manager Don Osborn. Therefore, Veeck's departure from the Marlins also ended the possibility that Jimmie would return to the Marlins as a coach.[82] In February, just prior to the opening of practice for the Hurricanes, Foxx participated in the National Baseball Players golf tournament which was held at Miami Springs. Among those who entered this tournament were Paul Waner, Jackie Robinson, Yogi Berra, Mickey Mantle, Don Drysdale, and Phil Rizzuto. A low medalist score of 75 was turned in by Lou Kretlow and Alvin Dark; Foxx's score was 84. In tournament play Jimmie was defeated three and two by Jack Russell, and the tournament winner was Alvin Dark of the Cardinals.[83]

Spring practice for the University of Miami baseball squad began on February 18, and Foxx told a reporter, "I believe we will be stronger than we were a year ago." Three regulars from last year's team graduated, but Jimmie noted, "We have more material and better pitching." "However," he added, "we need more power and we lack speed."[84] After a couple of weeks of practice and inter-squad games, the team flew to Puerto Rico on March 8 for a two-game series with the Ramsey Air Force team. Although the Hurricanes lost both games 3-2 and 6-0, it was reported that Foxx was not dissatisfied because the team "hit fairly well."[85] The week following the team's return from Puerto Rico they opened the Florida Intercollegiate Baseball Conference season with games at Stetson University in Deland on March 13 and 14. This series was split, each club winning one game. In a three-game series with a visiting team from Yale University the Hurricanes were two and one. The visiting club from Amherst College, however, won two of three from the Hurricanes. A week later Foxx's team rebounded and split a two-game series with visitors from Ramsey Air Force Base.[86] The Hurricanes divided victories against conference foes Florida Southern University and Stetson. They defeated Tampa University and for the first time in several years won from Rollins College. They lost two games to the University of Florida and lost three of four to Florida State, ending the season with eleven wins and twelve losses. Foxx's record as a college baseball coach for two seasons was .500—twenty wins and twenty losses. Perhaps the team's most surprising win was a preseason 2-1 exhibition win over the Marlins.[87]

Foxx's experience with college baseball convinced him that there should be a stronger rapport between major league clubs and college teams. He envisioned major league teams discovering and signing young men to contracts and subsidizing their college education. He explained that in three or four years of college baseball they could develop their skills and be ready for a professional career. During these years they would also obtain an education that would allow them to pursue careers after baseball. Foxx believed that this would be a more practical procedure and less expensive than a club paying a large bonus to a prospective major league youngster. He acknowledged that such a procedure as he suggested would not be possible unless the National Collegiate Athletic Association changed its rules concerning the affiliation of college athletes with professional clubs.[88]

At the close of the 1957 college baseball season, Foxx's association with the University of Miami was concluded. It was reported that the university trustees refused to reemploy him because he did not have a college degree, and shortly thereafter it was announced that the new baseball coach at the University of Miami would be Whitey Campbell.[89] In the summer of 1957 Foxx participated in an old-timers game sponsored by the Marlins and designated the first annual "Stars of Yesterday" game. Others invited to play included Ewell Blackwell, Joe DiMaggio, Ben Chapman, and Johnny Vander Meer. Also, during this summer Foxx went to Philadelphia where he became associated with the sales forces of a "national household cleaning product."[90]

Jimmie's position with the cleaning product firm was of short duration, and by midautumn he had returned to Miami to work for a transfer company. In December he became ill and lost this job. At this time Foxx, his wife, and their three children were living in Miami. They were in straitened economic circumstances, as John, Foxx's eighteen-year-old stepson, was the only member of the family who was working. He was employed as a ticket agent by Eastern Airlines and received a salary of sixty dollars a week. His salary comprised the family's total income, and they had been living off it for some weeks. Foxx was five months behind in rent and was being permitted to occupy his house only because the owner allowed him "the grace to stay there."[91]

The economic plight of Foxx was made known to the nation during January, 1958. The Boston Chapter of the Baseball Writers Association invited Jimmie to be a guest of honor at their annual dinner on January 22, to be held at the Hotel Statler. Foxx had to inform the writers that he was broke, had been ill and out of work for several months, was behind in his rent, and therefore would be unable to come to Boston. In the following days sportswriters and broadcasters throughout the country publicized Foxx's poverty-stricken condition. Jimmie's Boston friend, Jimmy Sillin, mailed him a check for four hundred dollars to pay his rent, a Philadelphia restaurant owner sent him two hundred dollars, and the Boston writers sent him money for a round-trip airline ticket to Boston. Producers of television shows, always on the lookout for human interest stories, and especially those of "celebrities," invited Jimmie and paid his expenses to appear on the NBC "Today" show and CBS's "Ed Sullivan's Toast of the Town" program. Within a week of the news that Foxx was destitute, 252 persons in twenty-two states wrote to him, offering gifts and/or jobs. Foxx's friend Sillin revealed that most of the "small donations" sent to Jimmie were given by him to Boston's "Jimmy Fund," a fund to help finance cancer research for children. Foxx received a dozen or more offers of jobs, most of them in sales or promotional work. Foxx's main desire, however, was to "get back in baseball."[92] Joe Cronin, general manager of the Red Sox, declared that he was "shocked to hear that Foxx was broke" and said he was pleased that the Boston Baseball Writers were bringing Jimmie to Boston. "When he arrives," Cronin told a reporter, "I will see him and we will talk about his situation."[93]

Foxx came to Boston and was honored by the baseball writers at their banquet on January 22. While in Boston Jimmie was the house guest of his friend Jimmy Sillin, and he talked with Cronin and other Red Sox officials. On January 24 it was announced that Foxx had been given a job in baseball. During the 1958 season he would be an "aide to manager Gene Mauch of the Red Sox triple A farm club, the Minneapolis Millers," and his salary would be $8,000.00.[94] It was explained that Foxx's duties would include working with Miller hitters and also visiting other Red Sox farm clubs as batting instructor for their rookies and others who might be experiencing hitting problems. Foxx was happy to be back in baseball. As he said at a press conference, "I'll do whatever I'm asked to do," and "I'll always be grateful to Tom Yawkey and Joe Cronin for giving me this opportunity."[95]

News of Foxx's new position was received with enthusiasm in Minneapolis, and the *Minneapolis Tribune* gave it headline coverage. General manager Tommy Thomas, a former American League pitcher who had often faced Foxx, was pleased that the Red Sox were sending him to the Millers. He announced that Foxx would report to manager Gene Mauch at the Millers' spring camp in Deland, Florida, on March 5. He explained, "It's my understanding that Foxx will work with our hitters in camp and remain with us as a coach the entire season." He called Jimmie "one of the great hitters of all time" and added "If he can teach our batters just a little of what he had as a hitter, then we'll be much more dangerous at the plate."[96]

When Foxx's economic condition was made known, it was revealed that he was not eligible for the players' pension plan which became effective in 1946, one year after Jimmie's major league career ended.[97] The secretary of the Association of Professional Baseball Players of America stated that Foxx was eligible for financial aid from that organization. He said that Foxx had

Foxx and young fan, 1958 (courtesy Nanci Canaday).

been a dues-paying member throughout his major league career, and he implied that if Jimmie had requested assistance it would have been forthcoming.[98] Some sportswriters at this time suggested that all Hall of Fame members should be brought into the pension system, regardless of when their careers ended. They argued that when baseball stars of the past were left out of the system and reduced to poverty, it reflected adversely on major league baseball and was a condition that should be corrected. Others, however, pointed out that Foxx had "squandered money he made during his playing days" and that current players, who were financing the pension plan, were under no obligation to assist former players who "fell on hard times."[99] No modifications were made in the pension plan. Also at this time there were news stories and reports that various persons were negotiating to write a biography of Foxx and to prepare a story of his life to be serialized on television. Another was that a speaking tour was being arranged for Jimmie. Nothing ever materialized from these rumors.[100]

When news of Foxx's economic circumstances became known, Arthur Daley of the *New York Times* wrote that Foxx's plight was indeed a sad one. He noted that during his career Jimmie had earned probably a quarter-million dollars but had been unable to manage his resources. He explained that the good-natured Foxx "was always a quick man with a buck" and was an "inveterate check grabber." He might have been, Daley continued, "everybody's friend," but he "certainly was no businessman." He was a "soft touch" for just about anyone. Daley explained that Foxx had lost a great deal of money in a golf course venture in 1939–41 and that he lost money in the stock market crash of 1929.[101] Foxx probably did lose in excess of $40,000.00 in the golfing venture, but he hardly lost money in 1929. To that time Foxx's salary was minimal, and what he had was invested in the farm in the Sudlersville area. His 1929 World Series check, which constituted the first extra money he had ever known, was not cut and delivered to the Athletics until late October, after the date of the stock market crash.[102]

When it was revealed that Foxx was broke, the sports editor of the *Queen Anne's Record-Observer*, the newspaper for Jimmie's home county and published in Centreville, Maryland, urged that friends of Foxx's send contributions to his office for forwarding to Jimmie. The response to this plea was negligible; not more than fifty dollars was received and the few checks sent to the paper were later returned. The editor commented that "apparently the fifty-year-old native of Sudlersville has few friends left in the county."[103] Foxx had for some years been estranged from the people of his home area. In the late 1920s and into the thirties Foxx was a hero. The home folks were proud of him and eagerly awaited his retirement when he would return to his farm near Sudlersville. However, conditions and sentiments changed after Foxx sold his farm in 1938. He ceased returning in the off season for hunting and visiting; his divorce and hasty remarriage were surprising behavior for one reared in the local Methodist church; and knowledge that Jimmie had a liking for Scotch whiskey also contributed to the estrangement of Foxx from his home area.

Thanks to the generosity of the Boston Baseball Writers Organization, Jimmie was an honored guest at their banquet in January. In his remarks to an audience of 1,000 he expressed his "deep down appreciation" to the people of Boston and declared, "My life is a new book from here on." His experience in recent days, he said, "was more like a dream than reality." "I feel," he continued, "like a guy born again, and it is the most wonderful experience of my life."[104]

While he was in Boston arrangements were made for Jimmie to appear as a guest at the New England Sportsmen's and Boat Show to be held in Boston during the first week of February. This exhibition included boats, hunting and fishing accessories, camping and other outdoor paraphernalia, and it ran for about a week. On this occasion Foxx was one of three sports celebrities who were guests of the show. The others were Ted Williams and the former heavyweight boxing champion, Jack Sharkey. It seems that the principal duty of these men was to walk among the crowd, greet people, make small talk, sign autographs, and have their pictures taken. Ted Williams did give a demonstration for fishermen and revealed his skills at casting. Foxx abstained at this demonstration, explaining that he had not been fishing more than a couple of times in the past ten years. On one occasion during this show Williams introduced Foxx to a visiting group. He said to them, "I want you to meet Jimmie Foxx, one of the greatest of all time. He taught me so much about hitting and playing ball that I can never thank him enough."[105]

After his appearance at the Sportsmen's and Boat Show Foxx returned to his home in Miami. He had received a letter from Gene Mauch, manager of the Millers, welcoming him as a member of the club. Mauch told a Minneapolis reporter that he was "delighted that Foxx was going to be a batting coach" for the team, and he was sure "that he would be able to offer helpful tips and suggestions to the hitters."[106] Jimmie informed Mauch that he was ready to go and would report at Deland on March 5. When the Millers' spring camp opened, Foxx was one of three veterans present to work with the team: Mace Brown, a former Red Sox teammate, was to assist the staff with the pitchers and Bobby Doerr, former Red Sox second baseman, would help instruct the infielders. After a week of practice the Millers engaged in inter-squad games and later began their exhibition schedule. The American Association League opened in mid–April and baseball writers covering the league had named them as their number one pick to win the league pennant.[107]

When the season opened, a sports writer for the *St. Paul Dispatch* interviewed Foxx and wrote a feature article on him. He noted that "Double-X" was a bit heavier than when he was a player, now weighing around 205-210 pounds and that his hair was streaked with silver. But, he observed, even at age fifty, Foxx "still gives one the impression of tremendous physical strength." Although his eyesight was not as keen or clear as formerly, Jimmie could "still do things with the bat," and he mentioned several hits which Jimmie sent out of the park in batting practice. He stated that Jimmie was happy to be back in baseball and that he was not embarrassed by the recent revelation of his poverty-stricken condition. "Jimmie," he wrote, "never felt ashamed. ... He just wanted a job" and was grateful to the Red Sox for giving him a chance.[108]

After the season opened, and Foxx found suitable living quarters, he moved his family to Minneapolis, where they were all hoping for a new start.[109] Although the family and friends of Foxx had high hopes for his future in the spring of 1958, this would be a trying season for him. The summer of 1958 was punctuated by periods of illness as Foxx's health began a rapid decline. In mid–May he suffered an attack of the flu and was confined to bed for several days by his physician. After his seeming recovery he was flown to Boston by the Red Sox to be present for an old-timers game celebrating Yawkey's twenty-five years as owner of the Red Sox.[110] On his return Foxx had a relapse, was ill for most of the month of June, and did not accompany the team for any of its away games. During this time Foxx complained of having dizzy spells, and his physician discovered that his blood pressure was high. The doctor prescribed rest and medication and confined Jimmie to his home for a time. A couple of weeks later Foxx was admitted to Barnadas Hospital in Minneapolis with what the press reported as a "heart attack."[111] Another report was that Foxx had not suffered a heart attack but that he was hospitalized because of "extremely high blood pressure" and was there "for rest and a series of tests." It was expected that as soon as his blood pressure returned to normal he would resume his duties with the Millers. Although Foxx was released from the hospital on July 2, his physician did not permit him to accompany the team on a road trip to Omaha and Denver.[112] By midseason Foxx's condition had improved and he was permitted to rejoin the team. He was with them throughout the remainder of the season.

As the season progressed, the Millers were not fulfilling the preseason expectations of the baseball writers of the league. They were never in the race for the league lead, which was handily won by Charleston, West Virginia. Throughout the season they struggled with Wichita and Denver for a spot in the play-offs. They ended the season in third place, seven and one-half games behind Charleston, one-half game behind Wichita, and two games ahead of fourth-place Denver.[113]

Although Foxx was able to resume his duties as hitting coach for the Millers, his illness seemed to have dampened any hopes he might have held for a job in major league baseball. When one reporter asked him if he would like to return to the majors as a manager, Foxx replied, "I doubt that I'd turn down the opportunity, but at the present I'm not looking for a manager's job." At another time he declared that the challenge of a major league manager's job was for him "more of a dream than a real ambition."[114]

In the league play-offs, the Millers eliminated Wichita four games to two, and Denver defeated the pennant winner, Charleston, four games to three. The Millers then swept Denver in four games. This put the Millers in the "little World Series" against the International League champion, Montreal. Although the experts established the Montreal Royals as the favorite in this series, Foxx told a reporter that he "liked the Millers' chances" and explained, "This club doesn't make many mistakes, it gives very little away." Foxx was correct as the Millers won the series four games to zero. In the play-offs and little World Series, the Millers won eleven consecutive games.[115] Shortly after the close of the season, Foxx and his family moved to Scottsdale, Arizona.

Notes

1. Merrie A. Fidler, "The Development and Decline of the All-American Girls Baseball League, 1943–1954" (M.S. thesis, University of Massachusetts, 1976), p. 75.

2. *Ibid.*, p. 351; *New York Times*, March 26, 30, April 2, 3, 8, 1932.

3. Lois Brown, *Girls of Summer: In Their Own League* (Toronto: Harper Collins, 1992), p. 84. In 1954 the ball used by the AAGPBL was the same as that used in the major leagues; the distance from home plate to the pitcher's mound was the same in the AAGPBL as in the majors. However, the distance between the bases in the AAGPBL was five feet less than in the major leagues. See Fidler, "The Development and Decline ... Girls Baseball League ...," p. 352.

4. *Fort Wayne Journal-Gazette*, March 16, 1952; Brown, *Girls of Summer*, p. 33.

5. Jay Feldman, "The Real History of Night Ball at Wrigley Field," in *The Baseball Research Journal* #21 (1993), pp. 93-94.

6. Fidler, "Development and Decline ... Girls Baseball League ...", p. 33.

7. *Ibid.*, p. 228.

8. *Ibid.*, p. 243; *Philadelphia Evening Bulletin*, February 3, 1952; conversation with Nanci Foxx Canaday, February 15, 1992.

9. *Fort Wayne Journal-Gazette*, March 16, April 16, 1952.

10. *Ibid.*, April 16, 20, 1952.

11. *Ibid.* April 20, 1952.

12. *Ibid.*, April 16, 23, 27, June 15, 1952.

13. *Ibid.* April 30, May 1, 2, 3, 5, 7, 12, 1952.

14. *Ibid.*, May 11, 1952.

15. *Ibid.*, May 15, 16, 1952.

16. *Ibid.*, June 20, 29, 1952.

17. *Ibid.*, June 14, July 3, 8, 1952.

18. *Ibid.*, July 11, 1952.

19. *Ibid.*, July 20, 30, 31, 1952.

20. *Ibid.*, August 24, 1952.

21. *Ibid.*, August 21, 23, 1952.

22. *Ibid.*, August 29, 30, September 1, 2, 1952.

23. *Ibid.*, September 4, 5, 6, 7, 10, 11, 12, 1952.

24. *Ibid.*, September 14, 1952.

25. *Ibid.*, September 14, 1952.

26. Interview with Skip Carpentier of Franklin, New York, June 11, 1991. In 1992 one of Hollywood's most popular releases was the movie *A League of Their Own*. This film focused attention on the AAGPBL and featured a character named Jimmy Dugan. Dugan was a former major league player who was serving as manager of one of the women's teams. It was alleged that the character, Dugan, was based on or patterned after Foxx. Manager Dugan, however, was a crude and vulgar caricature of a manager. A former member of the AAGPBL declares that a manager such as Dugan would not have been tolerated in the league but would have been "drummed out" immediately. See *Richmond Times-Dispatch*, July 20, 1992.

27. Undated item, Foxx files, Sudlersville Memorial Library; *The Sporting News*, April 22, 1953.

28. *Philadelphia Inquirer*, December 2, 1953.

29. *The Sporting News*, January 13, February 3, 1954.

30. *Philadelphia Inquirer*, February 27, 1954.

31. *The Sporting News*, March 3, 1954.

32. *Ibid.*, March 4, April 28, 1954.

33. *Ibid.*, June 2, August 25, 1954.

34. *Ibid.*, October 27, 1954.

35. *New York Times*, October 20, 1954.

36. *Philadelphia Inquirer*, October 11, 20, 1954.

37. *The Sporting News*, December 1, 1954.

38. "50 Years of American Legion Baseball," in *The American Legion Magazine* (July, 1975), pp. 14-17, 39-40; *Philadelphia Evening Bulletin*, November 22, 1954.

39. *The Sporting News*, October 27, 1954.

40. *Philadelphia Inquirer,* November 28, 1954.

41. *Philadelphia Evening Bulletin,* November 22, 1954.

42. *The Sporting News,* November 3, 1954.

43. *Philadelphia Inquirer,* November 28, 1954; *Philadelphia Evening Bulletin,* October 20, 1954.

44. For example, see *The Sporting News,* November 10, December 8, 1954.

45. *Philadelphia Evening Bulletin,* November 23, 1954.

46. *The Sporting News,* October 27, 1954.

47. *Miami Daily News,* April 10, 1955; *The Sporting News,* April 20, 1955.

48. *Miami Daily News,* April 10, 1955.

49. *The Sporting News,* September 21, 1955.

50. *Ibid.,* January 12, 1955.

51. *Ibid.,* May 18, 1955.

52. *Ibid.,* April 13, 1955.

53. *Kansas City Times,* July 20, 1955.

54. *The Sporting News,* August 10, 1955.

55. Xerox copy of certificate, dated September 27, 1955, in possession of author.

56. Assorted clippings, 1955, Nanci Canaday file.

57. *The Sporting News,* September 21, 1955.

58. *Miami Herald,* February 5, 1956.

59. *The Sporting News,* January 25, 1956; *Baltimore Sun,* January 15, 1956.

60. Assorted clippings, January 19, 1956, Dell Foxx scrapbook #1.

61. *Miami Herald,* February 5, 9, March 25, 1956.

62. *Ibid.,* February 9, 10, April 11, 1965; *The Sporting News,* February 15, 1956.

63. *Boston Herald,* January 15, 1958.

64. Bill Veeck, *Veeck—As in Wreck, The Autobiography* (New York: Bantam Books, 1963), p. 325.

65. The International League acquired AAA status in 1946. See Robert Obojski, *Bush League, A History of Minor League Baseball* (New York: Macmillan, 1975), p. 95; *Miami Herald,* February 11, 1956.

66. *Miami Herald,* February 26, 1956.

67. *Ibid.,* March 5, 16, 1956.

68. *Ibid.,* March 28, 29, 1956.

69. *Ibid.,* April 3, 4, 1956.

70. *Ibid.,* April 7, 8, 1956.

71. *1990 University of Miami Hurricane Baseball Yearbook* (Coral Gables: University of Miami, c. 1990), p. 72.

72. *Miami Herald,* May 30, June 16, July 31, September 10, 12, 1956.

73. *Ibid.,* June 22, 1956; *The Sporting News,* June 27, 1956.

74. *Miami Herald,* September 17, 26, 1956.

75. *Ibid.,* May 17, 1956.

76. Jimmie Foxx, "I'm Through With Baseball Forever," in *Baseball Monthly* (May, 1962), p. 55.

77. *Miami Herald,* May 18, June 10, 1956.

78. *Ibid.,* May 27, 1956.

79. *Ibid.,* November 30, 1956.

80. Assorted clippings, January 17, 1957, in Foxx files, Sudlersville Memorial Library; *Philadelphia Inquirer*, January 18, 1957.

81. *Boston Herald*, January 23, 1957.

82. *Ibid.*, January 22, 1957.

83. *Miami Herald*, February 14, 15, 16, 17, 1957.

84. *Ibid.*, February 6, 18, 19, 1957.

85. *Ibid.*, March 8, 12, 1957.

86. *Ibid.*, March 20, 21, 24, 27, 28, 29, April 2, 4, 1957.

87. *Ibid.*, May 31, 1957; *1990 University of Miami Hurricanes Baseball Yearbook*, p.72.

88. Miami Herald, March 26, 1956; February 25, 1957.

89. *Philadelphia Inquirer*, January 18, 1958; *Miami Herald*, July 24, 1957.

90. *Miami Herald*, July 9, 12, 18, 19, 24, 1957; *Philadelphia Evening Bulletin*, October 2, 1957.

91. *Boston Globe*, January 16, February 11, 1958.

92. *Ibid.*, *Philadelphia Evening Bulletin*, January 18, 1958; *Boston Herald*, January 16, 24, February 9, 1958; *New York Times*, January 18, 1958.

93. *Boston Globe*, January 16, 1958.

94. *Miami News*, January 19, 1959; *Boston Herald*, January 13, 1959.

95. *Boston Herald*, January 24, 1958.

96. *Boston Globe*, January 24, 1958; *Minneapolis Tribune*, January 24, 1958.

97. *Philadelphia Evening Bulletin*, January 18, 1958.

98. *Boston Herald*, January 17, 1958; assorted clippings, January 17, 1958, in Foxx files, Baseball Library, Cooperstown, New York.

99. *Boston Globe*, January 17, 19, 23, February 11, 1958; *The Sporting News*, January 29, 1958.

100. *Boston Globe*, January 24, 1958; *Philadelphia Inquirer*, January 24, 1958.

101. *New York Times*, January 20, 1958.

102. William Curran, *Big Sticks: The Batting Revolution of the Twenties* (New York: William Morrow and Company, 1990), p. 254.

103. *Queen Anne's Record-Observer*, January 23, 1958; also see July 3, 1991.

104. *Boston Globe*, January 23, 1958.

105. *Ibid.*, February 1, 2, 3, 7, 1958.

106. *Minneapolis Tribune*, January 28, 1958.

107. *Minneapolis Star*, March 6, April 15, 1958.

108. *St. Paul Dispatch*, April 25, 1958.

109. *Minneapolis Star*, May 9, 1958.

110. *Ibid.*, May 10, 17, 1958.

111. *Boston Herald*, June 21, 1958.

112. *Philadelphia Evening Bulletin*, June 23, 1958; *Minneapolis Star*, July 5, 1958; *The Sporting News*, July 2, 1958.

113. *St. Paul Dispatch*, September 8, 1958.

114. *Boston Herald*, June 18, 1958; *The Sporting News*, August 13, 1958.

115. *Minneapolis Star*, September 24, 1958; *St. Paul Dispatch*, September 30, 1958.

Nine
The Last Years, 1959–1967

In 1958 the Red Sox announced that they were moving their spring training operations from Florida to Scottsdale, Arizona. Foxx, assuming that he would continue as an employee of the Red Sox, moved his family to the Scottsdale area shortly after the close of the baseball season and secured an off-season part-time job as a paint salesman for a local concern.[1] Jimmie's expectation that he would remain a coach with the Red Sox organization vanished when it was revealed in the press on January 12 that he had been fired, that his contract would not be renewed. Joe Cronin, Red Sox general manager, told a reporter, "I feel terrible about it, just awful," but Foxx "had not worked out as a coach." Cronin explained that he had informed Foxx last fall that "Minneapolis was changing its policy regarding coaches," that they were going to use "player-coaches."[2] Foxx expressed shock and surprise at the news that he had been fired. He told a reporter, "The whole thing is a mystery to me." He stated that he had last talked with Cronin during the World Series and that Joe never mentioned to him that he was losing his job. "I'm just puzzled," Foxx said. "I thought I had a future with the Red Sox."[3]

A Miami reporter who was well acquainted with Foxx declared that the real reason Jimmie was let go was a problem that had been plaguing him for twenty years—"his losing battle against alcohol." He asserted that Foxx had experienced drinking problems in 1956 when he was with the Marlins and also when he was baseball coach for the University of Miami. He claimed that it was Foxx's problem with alcohol that cost him jobs with both the Marlins and Hurricanes. He explained that although Foxx had been ill in 1958, he was also "drinking on the job" in Minneapolis.[4] The seriousness of Foxx's drinking problem was repeated by another reporter a short time later. He noted that Jimmie was aware of "rumors" about his drinking but that Foxx "steadfastly denied" such rumors were true and maintained that he had no problem with alcohol.[5]

Foxx remained in Scottsdale for several months after news of his release. He continued to hope that he could "make connections" for a job in baseball, and the press reported that he talked with personnel from the Giants and

Indians but nothing developed for him. In the meantime Jimmie worked at odd jobs and received non-baseball offers from various places around the country. He informed one writer that "I'll work almost anywhere I'm able, ... but doctors have warned me to bypass hard labor."[6] During these months in Arizona, Jimmie's brother, Sammy Dell, was living with the family. Sammy had a job, and Foxx declared that if it wasn't for his help the family would not be eating.[7] Foxx told one reporter that when you "get fifty-one years old nobody wants you." To another he declared, "I would take a job pumping gas at a filling station if anyone would offer it to me." It was reported that an executive of an insurance company in Philadelphia offered to hire Foxx and train him as an insurance underwriter if Jimmie would come to Philadelphia. Another offer was reported to have been made by a chamber of commerce official in Stockton, California.[8] Nothing, however, came from such reports.

Eventually, in mid–May, it was announced that Foxx was moving to Galesburg, Illinois, and would become associated with a restaurant. Three Galesburg men, Tony and Nunck Mangiere and Joe Donato, invited Jimmie to come to Galesburg and serve as a public relations man and greeter for a restaurant they planned to open. The steak house was scheduled to open later in the year and would be named the "Jimmie Foxx Restaurant."[9] Foxx and his family moved from Scottsdale to Galesburg in June; the restaurant was to open about Labor Day. Jimmie made one trip from Galesburg before the restaurant opened. In early August he was a guest of the Kansas City Athletics at a game honoring members of Baseball's Hall of Fame. Present with Foxx for this affair were Lefty Grove, Frank Baker, Rogers Hornsby, and others.[10]

In late August, about a week before the Jimmie Foxx Restaurant was to open, Foxx's wife Dorothy injured a wrist. He accompanied her to the doctor's office for treatment and while waiting for the physician to examine his wife's wrist, Foxx collapsed and was rushed to St. Mary's Hospital. The first report was that he had "fainted"; however, Dr. Howard Graham, the physician who attended Foxx at the hospital, corrected this report by asserting that Jimmie had suffered a heart attack.[11] Dr. Graham confirmed that Foxx also was exhausted, suffered from high blood pressure, and that he would remain in the hospital for seven days or more. Later Graham stated that Foxx had suffered "no serious damage to his heart."[12]

Jimmie's illness postponed the opening of the steak house for several weeks. However, from September, 1959, to June, 1960, Foxx was associated with the restaurant that bore his name. When his contract with the owners expired on June 1, it was not renewed, and Jimmie was unemployed once again. When the press heard of his misfortune and publicized the fact that he had applied for and was receiving $35.00 a week unemployment compensation, several people offered Foxx jobs. One man in Allentown, Pennsylvania, offered him a job as stadium manager.[13] Another offer came from a former major league baseball player who was now the vice president of a large nursery near

John, Jimmie, Dorothy, Nanci, and Jimmie Jr. II, 1959 (courtesy Nanci Canaday).

Cleveland, Ohio. Michael "Mickey" O'Neil, formerly a catcher for the Braves, offered Jimmie a job with the William C. Moore Company, a nursery specializing in plants and shrubs.[14] Foxx accepted O'Neil's offer and agreed to move to the Cleveland area.

Before Foxx was able to leave Galesburg, he suffered two misfortunes. In late June he underwent a hernia operation.[15] After he recuperated, the family began preparing for the move to Ohio. It was while packing and moving items preparatory to leaving that Foxx suffered a serious fall. When moving a box from one room to another, Jimmie tripped and fell down a flight of twelve steps, knocking himself unconscious. He was taken to the hospital where the first report was that his injuries were mild, that his back was not broken and that he had suffered a mild concussion. However, x-rays revealed that he had injured his spine and suffered a fracture of the skull.[16] Foxx remained in the hospital for three weeks before he was permitted to go home. His doctors also advised a rest of six to eight weeks before going to work for the nursery. Although Foxx would be permitted to do "light work," the fall which he suffered resulted in partial paralysis of his left side and required his use of a walking cane.[17]

Shortly after his release from the hospital Foxx was permitted to accompany his family to Lakewood, Ohio, a suburb of Cleveland, where they had rented a house. It was expected that Foxx would be able to resume work by mid-autumn. While he was recuperating, O'Neil assisted him in supporting his family. When Foxx started to work at the nursery, he and O'Neil soon discovered that Jimmie was not able to perform the physical labor the job required, and Jimmie was forced to seek other employment.[18] He soon obtained, through the assistance of a friend, a position as deputy clerk in Cleveland's municipal court. The friend was Francis O. Gallagher, a local umpire and the nephew of Ms. Helen J. Lyons, clerk of Cleveland Municipal Court. He recommended that his aunt employ Foxx and she did; the position of deputy clerk paid a salary of $5,200 a year.[19] This position, however, was later withdrawn from him when civil service officials declared Foxx was unqualified for it. Jimmie next secured employment with the Ohio State Unemployment Office. This position paid a salary of $4,000.00 a year and Foxx worked for this office throughout 1961 and the beginning of 1962.[20]

Foxx's only connection with baseball when he was in the Cleveland area was in the spring of 1961 when he assisted the La Riche Ford team in the Lakewood Inter-City League. He served as hitting coach for this team. His son, Jimmie Jr., II, who was developing into a star athlete at Lakewood High School and would earn letters in football, basketball and baseball before graduating in 1964, probably played in the intercity league.[21]

In August of 1961 Foxx was honored by an organization in his home state. At this time he was inducted into the Maryland Shrine of Immortals. The Shrine of Immortals was created in 1960 by the Maryland Professional Baseball Players Association as a "permanent, living memorial to the game's superstars with a Maryland background."[22] The Baltimore Orioles' authorities were sympathetic to the concept and became supporters of the project. The aim was to select two members each year for the Shrine and to create a Maryland baseball museum at the home of Babe Ruth. Here plaques to Shrine members and baseball artifacts and photographs would be exhibited. The concept was patterned after the Baseball Museum and Hall of Fame at Cooperstown. Also, a part of the plan was to sponsor an old-timers game at the Orioles' stadium to be held in connection with the induction ceremonies. The first two stars selected for induction into the Shrine of Immortals were chosen by the directors of the Maryland Professional Baseball Players Association. Subsequent members were to be elected by the fans, who were given a special ballot at an Orioles game—one which had been publicized as the occasion when fans could vote for membership into the Shrine. The ballot included nine names and the fans were to vote for two by circling the names of their choice.[23]

The first two players inducted into the Shrine of Immortals were Babe Ruth and Frank "Home Run" Baker. Ceremonies for the Shrine of Immortals Day, September 2, 1960, began with a luncheon at the Park Plaza Hotel in Baltimore. Among the guests present were Rogers Hornsby, Lefty Grove, Eddie Rommel, Max Bishop, and Mickey Cochrane. Also present was Mrs. Babe Ruth, who accepted the plaque honoring her late husband, and Frank Baker. Baker responded with brief remarks acknowledging he was very pleased with the honor of being selected for the Shrine.[24] After the luncheon and prior to a regular game between the Orioles and Yankees, there was a two-inning old-timers game. This contest featured players from the 1919–1925 Orioles teams—teams which won seven consecutive International League pennants—and a group of "Maryland All-Stars."[25] The gate receipts from the annual Shrine of Immortals game were to help create and support the Shrine museum.

Ballots were given to fans who attended the first Shrine game. Each ballot contained the names of nine baseball players with "Maryland connections," and fans were asked to vote for two. The first ballot included the names of Grove, Foxx, Rommel, Hornsby, Marquand, George Weiss, Jack Dunn, Sr., Buck Herzog, and Friz Maisel. Fans were to return their ballot to the ticket office or mail it to the Orioles. Their selection would be announced prior to the second Shrine game. When the votes were counted, it was revealed that the fans had selected Lefty Grove and Jimmie Foxx for membership in Maryland's Shrine of Immortals. Induction ceremonies were held at Baltimore on August 12, 1961. Grove was present to receive his award, but Foxx was unable to attend the ceremonies. Joe Cronin, president of the American League, accepted Jimmie's award and spoke briefly, declaring that Foxx was unequaled as a right-handed power hitter. Frank Baker told the story of how, in 1924, he had tried to interest Miller Huggins and the Yankees in Foxx and they laughed at the idea of signing a sixteen-year-old boy. Connie Mack, however, had accepted Baker's judgment of Foxx and agreed to purchase him from Easton.[26] Although Foxx was unable to be present at the time he was inducted into the Shrine of Immortals, he did attend the ceremonies the following year. The third annual Shrine ceremonies were held on August 17, 1962, and Foxx was present as a guest of the Maryland Professional Baseball Players Association. On this occasion Eddie Rommel and Charlie Keller were inducted into the Shrine.[27]

Foxx's economic condition, which had been precarious for years and had become worse as the result of recent illnesses, hit bottom in the fall of 1961. On November 9, 1961, newspapers in Boston, New York, Philadelphia, Miami, and elsewhere reported that Foxx had filed for bankruptcy in Cleveland, Ohio. His bankruptcy plea listed debts of $4,260.00 and assets as "clothing and household goods." His principal creditors were the Palmer House in Chicago, rent owed in Miami, the Valley National Bank in Phoenix, Arizona, hospitals in Miami and Galesburg, Illinois, and a hotel in the Cleveland area.[28] At the time Foxx filed for bankruptcy he was working for the Ohio Bureau of Unemployment Compensation. The attorney who assisted Jimmie in filing explained that the bankruptcy action "was meant to give Foxx a breather" until his economic fortunes improved; he would then satisfy his creditors. Foxx's explanation for his bankruptcy plea was that a food company he was once associated with collapsed and "all of a sudden I got a big bill that wasn't mine. I had no choice."[29]

Foxx's friends and others who were acquainted with Jimmie were not surprised by news of his bankruptcy. Foxx had a reputation, going back to his early days with the Athletics, of being overly generous or irresponsible with his money. One columnist who had known Jimmie for a number of years wrote that if Foxx was with a group at a restaurant "he couldn't stand to see others pick up the check.... [M]oney was a convenience to him, something one used to help friends." He concluded by saying, "Money went through his fingers like quicksilver." Another who knew Jimmie stated that Foxx seemed to have had a pathological dread of being thought of as "cheap."[30] Friends who knew him claimed that Jimmie would often tip a cab driver five dollars on a two dollar and thirty-five cent fare. He once tipped a Boston tailor fifty dollars for a $150.00 suit.[31] Harold Kaese, sports columnist for the *Boston Globe*, claims that Foxx was a "warm ... kind-hearted fellow who was an easy mark for well-wishers and cute promoters." He was "painfully helpless when it came to protecting himself," and "thrift was not one of his virtues." In his playing days Foxx customarily paid all room, phone, valet, and food bills charged to both him and his roommate.[32] Jimmie also financed various ventures for his brother Sammy Dell, as well as paying his debts, and for items Sammy would charge in Jimmie's name. Sammy once told a Sudlersville acquaintance that for a period of time "my brother gave me $5,000.00 a year." This was perhaps an exaggeration, but Jimmie's financial assistance to his brother was one item mentioned in Helen Foxx's petition for divorce in 1943.[33]

Foxx's reckless use of his resources was noted by Abe Goldblatt, a columnist for the *Norfolk Virginia Pilot* when Foxx was at Portsmouth in August–September, 1944. Goldblatt wrote that Foxx "dressed expensively and wore tailor-made suits." "He lived lavishly," Goldblatt wrote, and "he spent money as if there were no tomorrow." Foxx, he claimed, "never took time to send a suit to the cleaners or shirts to the laundry. He bought a suit a week and shirts by the dozen" during his stay in Portsmouth.[34] Jimmie never blamed anyone for his economic misfortune except himself. He admitted that he earned about $250,000 playing baseball and acknowledged that he "blew most of it.... It was my own fault."[35]

In the fall/winter of 1961–62, at the time Foxx filed for bankruptcy, he was removed from his job with the Ohio Office of Unemployment because civil service officials, once again, declared that he was unqualified for the position he had held for a year.[36] Jimmie then found employment with the May Company, a large department store in Cleveland. He was employed as a salesman in the sporting goods division of the company. Among the featured items that spring were bats and gloves authorized by Roger Maris. Maris was the Yankee outfielder who, in 1961, broke Ruth's record of sixty home runs for a season by hitting sixty-one round trippers.[37]

The May, 1962, issue of the magazine *Baseball Monthly* featured the last article Foxx wrote, and it summarized his attitude toward baseball and the treatment he had received from those who managed or directed the game.

The article was entitled "I'm Through with Baseball Forever." Foxx related that people often asked him, "Jimmie, how come you are not in baseball ... as a coach or manager?" His answer was that "baseball doesn't want guys like me.... Baseball has no room for fellows who built up a lot of prestige as ball players." What management wants today, he asserted, is the "young executive-type managers," people like Ralph Houk of the Yankees and Mel McGaha of the Indians. Baseball managing and coaching, he declared, has become a "young man's field" and "old-timers" might as well accept the fact. "General managers," he stated, "don't want to be bothered" by older men, regardless of their earlier contributions to the game as players.[38]

Part of Jimmie's duties with the May Company in the spring and summer of 1962 involved working with a series of baseball clinics. These clinics were arranged by local recreation departments, and the May Company helped to sponsor them. A number were held in the Cleveland area; they were for boys and were aimed at improving their skills and techniques for playing baseball. Foxx spoke to and worked with youngsters at a number of clinics in the summer of 1962.[39] On one occasion in the summer of 1962 Foxx was given leave to travel to Baltimore, where he was a guest of the Maryland Professional Baseball Players Association. He attended the ceremonies honoring those being inducted into the Maryland Shrine of Immortals. While in Baltimore he talked with personnel from Pictronics, Inc., of Wilkes-Barre, Pennsylvania, about serving as a host on a projected television series. The series, as reported, would feature stars of the "Golden Age of Sports" and would consist of thirty-nine half-hour episodes and they would be "distributed nationally." This announcement, as several similar ones in past years concerning Foxx and a sport series or biography, was never mentioned in the press again and nothing developed from this account which appeared in *The Sporting News*.[40]

Foxx continued his association with the May Company in 1963. That summer the major league All-Star game returned to Cleveland and Jimmie Foxx, the hero of the first All-Star game played in the city, was present as a guest. He was introduced to the crowd prior to the game and talked with reporters about the home run he hit in 1935. Later that year, after the close of the baseball season, the St. Louis Cardinals hosted a testimonial dinner to honor Stan Musial, who retired at the end of the 1963 season after twenty-two years with the Cardinals. Foxx was invited to attend this function as a guest of an Ohio businessman and sportsman. Raymond R. Tucker, mayor of St. Louis, proclaimed October 20, the date of the testimonial dinner, "Stan Musial Day."[41] Among those present at the dinner were Foxx, Willie Mays, Yogi Berra, Gil Hodges, Al Kaline, Warren Spahn, Bob Feller, Robin Roberts, Commissioner Ford Frick, Warren Giles (president of the National League), and Joe Cronin (president of the American League). At the dinner various guests and old-timers related their experiences with Musial. Foxx revealed that he carried with him a permanent memento from Musial. He explained that in 1945,

in a game when he was playing third base for the Phillies, Musial slid into the
bag on a close play and spiked him on the hand. The scar on one of his knuck-
les was his Musial memento.[42]

Foxx was planning to return to his home in Cleveland on October 22, his
fifty-sixth birthday. However, when he awoke that morning he experienced
dizzy spells and asked the hotel to send a physician to his room. Dr. J.W. Prob-
stein, the Chase-Park Plaza physician, sent him to Faith Hospital in St.
Louis.[43] The press reported that Foxx had suffered a heart attack. Physicians
at the hospital described his condition as "an acute heart ailment" and as "a
decompensation of the heart." Hospital spokesmen said that his condition was
serious but not critical. Foxx was released before the end of the month and
returned to his home. However, he never completely recovered from this attack,
and his attempts to work were greatly restricted.[44]

While Jimmie was home recuperating he received another honor. In the
fall of 1963 the Philadelphia Sports Writers Association, the senior organization of its kind in the country, conducted a poll to determine the All-Star baseball team for Philadelphia during the past fifty years. Players from the Athletics and Phillies were considered eligible for selection to this team. When
the All-Stars were announced, Jimmie Foxx was chosen for first base. Other
members included Frank Baker, Ty Cobb, Chuck Klein, Lefty Grove, Al Simmons, Mickey Cochrane, Tris Speaker, Napoleon Lajoie, and Dave Bancroft.[45]

A short time after he returned home the Association of Professional Baseball Players began to provide Jimmie some financial assistance. As his condition remained precarious and his physician constantly warned him about "over-
doing it," Foxx applied to the Social Security Administration for disability
benefits. After reviewing his application Social Security authorities decided
that he qualified for benefits, and he began receiving monthly checks of ninety-
eight dollars.[46]

In the spring of 1964 Foxx traveled to Portsmouth, Virginia, where he was
the guest at ceremonies honoring Frank Lawrence. Lawrence, a prominent
sportsman of the city, was owner of the Cubs when Foxx served as interim
manager of the team in 1944.[47] Also this spring Jimmie, Jr., graduated from
Lakewood High School. He was an exceptional athlete and was offered a
minor league contract by the Red Sox. Young Foxx, however, decided to forgo
professional sports and pursued a college education. He was awarded an athletic (football) scholarship by Kent State University and he enrolled at this
institution, receiving his degree in 1969.[48]

In the summer of 1964 the Foxx family moved back to the Miami area.
Jimmie's brother, Sammy Dell, was now living there and the family was familiar with the area. Upon arriving in Miami the family lived for a short while
with Jimmie's stepson, John, who was a member of the Florida State Police
force. Later Jimmie rented a house in southwestern Miami, and the family lived
there. Foxx, essentially, was retired from 1964 on. His only exercise was an

occasional swim and short walks. He worked at several part-time jobs in an effort to supplement his Social Security benefits. On one occasion he attempted to drive a coal truck and at another time he worked as a part-time filling station attendant.[49]

Foxx's stepdaughter, Nanci Canaday, states that although Jimmie never officially adopted her and her brother John, they "always went by the name Foxx." At school and elsewhere they were known as Nanci and John Foxx. She refers to Jimmie as her father and declares that he was a very loving, considerate, and caring father; that he would "do anything" for the children. However, she acknowledges that Foxx was addicted to alcohol and contributed to her mother Dorothy developing a weakness for the same.[50]

In 1962 the sports writers in Pennsylvania assumed the initiative and created the Pennsylvania Sports Hall of Fame. Each year the writers selected certain individuals for induction into the Hall. The criteria for choosing members was that one must have been born in the state or have achieved recognition in a given sport while a resident of Pennsylvania. In the fall of 1965 it was announced that the new inductees for membership in the Pennsylvania Hall of Fame were Jimmie Foxx, Lefty Grove, and Jimmy Dykes. They were invited to be the guests of the directors of the Hall of Fame and were to be honored and officially inducted in the Hall at an awards dinner on December 11. Foxx was grateful for this honor and would have attended the ceremonies, but he was prevented because he was ill with the flu.[51]

On Saturday, May 7, 1966, Jimmie's wife Dorothy was taken to the Baptist Hospital in Miami where in a short while she died. The *Miami Herald* reported that she died of a heart attack. However, her daughter claims that "mother was eating dinner and became choked on a piece of pork which lodged in her throat," that she was rushed to the hospital and expired almost immediately. Funeral services for Dorothy Foxx, age 48, were held on Tuesday, May 10, at St. Thomas Episcopal Church and interment was in Miami's Flagler Memorial Cemetery.[52] This sad event in the life of the Foxx family was also the occasion for Jimmie to renew family bonds with his youngest son from his first marriage. Kenneth Foxx was only six years old when his parents became estranged, and when the family split he remained with his mother, who shortly moved from Philadelphia and later remarried. Kenneth had little, if any, contact with his father from the 1940s on, but out of respect for his father, whom he knew was not well, he attended Dorothy's funeral. It was the first time he had seen his father in years and the first time he had ever seen Jimmie Jr., II. It was also the last time he would see his father before Jimmie's death.[53]

In the summer of 1966 baseball fans were following with interest the hitting exploits of the San Francisco Giants' outfielder, Willie Mays. In mid-August the right-handed hitting Mays eclipsed the home run total of the one whom many considered the greatest right-handed hitter of them all—Jimmie Foxx. On August 17 Mays hit home run number 535 to put him one ahead of

Foxx on the all-time home run list. Foxx, of course, was following Mays' exploits, and the day Willie surpassed his home run total Jimmie sent him a telegram of congratulations and said that he hoped Willie would hit over 600 before his career ended. Foxx told a reporter that he was happy to see "that another right-hander can prove he can hit." However, at the same time Jimmie expressed his doubts that Willie would break Ruth's total of 714.[54]

In September, 1966, Jimmie and his brother, Sammy Dell, made a return visit to their home county and Sudlersville. It was Jimmie's first appearance in the area since his father's death nine years earlier and would be his last visit to the Eastern Shore. The principal purpose of Foxx's visit was to see Gil Dunn. Charles Gilbert "Gil" Dunn owned and operated a pharmacy at Stevensville on Kent Island in Queen Anne's County. When Dunn was a youngster he became a baseball fan, and his "hero" from childhood was Jimmie Foxx. He followed Foxx's career until Jimmie retired. When Dunn opened his pharmacy in 1953, in Foxx's home county, his interest in Foxx prompted him to seek out persons who knew Jimmie and to acquire as much knowledge as possible about his favorite baseball player. He collected stories about Foxx and also began to accumulate a number of photographs. He searched local newspapers for accounts of Jimmie's early exploits. He had some of the pictures and newspaper stories pertaining to Foxx framed and hung them on the wall in a corner of his pharmacy. By the early 1960s Dunn's collection had increased as he had elicited contributions of several baseballs, bats, and other artifacts from persons in Boston, Philadelphia, and elsewhere. In 1965 Dunn's interest in Foxx had expanded to include baseball stars from Maryland who had become members of the Baseball Hall of Fame, and he envisioned establishing in a section of his pharmacy a small museum to honor Foxx and others. However, before he did this, he obtained Jimmie's Miami address from one of Foxx's Sudlersville relatives. He wrote to Jimmie, introduced himself, and explained that he was one of his lifelong fans. He asked if Jimmie would have any objections to his establishing a museum in his honor. Foxx did not reply to Dunn's letter, nor did he answer a second letter which Dunn sent him sometime later. Dunn, however, was not deterred by Jimmie's silence; instead, he took his silence for consent and proceeded to create his exhibition and museum. He called it "Jimmie Foxx: From Queen Anne's County to the Hall of Fame." One evening in January (1966) about 6:00 P.M., Dunn received a phone call from Miami. When he picked up the phone a deep voice said, "Hello, this is Jimmie Foxx." Astonished, Dunn replied,"What is this, some kind of joke?" Foxx said, "I don't know what you're talking about but this is Jimmie Foxx. What are you trying to do up there anyway?" Dunn explained to Foxx what he was doing and Jimmie agreed to bring him some items one day.[55]

There was no further communication with Foxx, but one day the following summer, Dunn relates, this big fellow with greying hair, walking with a cane and wearing a Red Sox cap came into the pharmacy and introduced himself as Jimmie Foxx. Foxx seemed favorably impressed by Dunn's exhibition and after a brief conversation told Dunn to come out to the car with him, as he had something for him. Dunn followed Foxx, who was accompanied by his brother, to the car. Jimmie opened the trunk and said, "Here is some stuff you may have. ... Nobody else wants it." The "stuff" included a couple of Jimmie's Most Valuable Player award plaques, a bat, several baseballs, gloves, mitts, and a catcher's mask. Also included were a Red Sox shirt and the uniform Foxx wore on the 1934 All-Star tour of Japan. After leaving Dunn, Jimmie and his brother spent a few days traveling around Queen Anne's County. This was the first and last time Dunn saw Foxx. Several years later Dunn placed some of his Foxx memorabilia in the Babe Ruth Museum and Maryland Baseball Hall of Fame in Baltimore.[56]

On this visit to his home area Foxx stopped by Sudlersville to renew some old acquaintances and view his boyhood surroundings. While in Sudlersville he attempted to cash a personal check for $100.00, but no one in the town would honor his check. Everywhere he tried to cash it, he was refused. A businessman in a nearby town cashed Jimmie's check and "found it was good." This episode reveals the almost total estrangement of a native son from his home community and also the low esteem in which he was held by citizens of his home town.[57]

After their visit to the Eastern Shore, Foxx and his brother returned to Miami. He made a final visit to his home state in January, 1967, when he was the honored guest at a sports banquet in Baltimore. The Maryland Professional Baseball Players Association banquet on January 13 honored two men by presenting them "the Babe Ruth Crown," signifying that they were among the "tops in sports." The honorees, Foxx and Frank Robinson of the Orioles, were both MVP recipients, triple crown winners, and the possessors of more than 500 home runs.[58]

Jimmie was scheduled to fly to Cooperstown, New York, on Sunday, July 23, to appear as a guest at the annual Hall of Fame baseball game and for the induction into the Hall of its three newest members—Branch Rickey, Red Ruffing, and Lloyd Waner.[59] However, on Friday evening, July 21, while Jimmie was visiting his brother Sammy Dell, who lived nearby in southwest Miami, he choked on a piece of steak at dinner and was unable to dislodge the meat; he lost consciousness and was rushed to the Baptist Hospital, but was pronounced dead upon arrival. Since Foxx had a serious heart condition it was first reported that he died of natural causes. However, following an autopsy, the Dade County medical examiner ruled that Foxx "died of asphyxiation after choking on a piece of meat" while eating dinner at the home of his brother."[60]

Funeral services for Foxx were conducted on Tuesday, July 25, at 11:00 A.M. at the Van Orsdale Funeral Home Chapel on Bird Road. Interment was in Flagler Memorial Cemetery, beside the grave of his wife Dorothy. The Reverend Jiles Kirkland, pastor of First Methodist Church of South Miami, officiated

and delivered a eulogy to Jimmie. Pall bearers were members of the Old Timers
Professional Baseball Association of Miami and included Max Carey, Rube
Walberg, and Bobby Hogue. Umpire Charlie Berry was present as a representative of the American league and Connie Mack, Jr., was also among the
sixty people who attended Foxx's funeral.[61] At this time Foxx's bronze plaque
in the Hall of Fame at Cooperstown was draped in black and sportswriters
and commentators throughout the nation eulogized Jimmie. One described
him as always a humble and compassionate man, a person who "made no ene-
mies" and had "an apparently genuine liking for everyone he met."[62] Joe Cronin,
a former teammate and now president of the American League, declared that
Foxx "was one of the greatest baseball players who ever lived." He was a team
player who could play any position and do everything well. Cronin said that
Foxx "hit the ball farther than any right-handed hitter," that he could "run as
fast as anybody," and was able to play "just about any position." Red Smith, in
commenting on Foxx's death, wrote that baseball was "a very big loser."[63] Jimmie's tragic death brought an end to more than twenty years of frustration and
disappointment for one who felt discarded by a profession in which he excelled
and to which he had devoted his life. His disappointment probably exacer-
bated his alcohol problem, which, in turn, adversely affected his health and
contributed to his death at the relatively young age of fifty-nine.

Notes

1. *Boston Herald,* January 12, 1959.
2. *Ibid.,* January 13, 1959; *St. Paul Dispatch,* January 13, 1959.
3. *Boston Herald,* January 12, 13, 1959.
4. *Miami News,* January 13, 1959.
5. *Cleveland Press,* September 19, 1960.
6. *Boston Herald,* April 29, 1959.
7. *Ibid.,* April 29, 1959.
8. *Philadelphia Evening Bulletin,* April 29, 1959; *Boston Herald,* May 20, 1959.
9. *Philadelphia Evening Bulletin,* May 20, 1959; *Boston Herald,* May 20, 1959.
10. *The Sporting News,* August 5, 1959.
11. *Philadelphia Evening Bulletin,* September 1, 1959; *Boston Herald,* September 2, 1959.
12. *Boston Herald,* September 2, 1959; *Philadelphia Evening Bulletin,* September 11, 1959.
13. *Boston Herald,* July 7, 8, 1960; *Philadelphia Evening Bulletin,* July 10, 1960.
14. *Cleveland Press,* September 19, 1960; *Boston Herald,* January 21, 1962.
15. *Boston Herald,* July 8, 1960.
16. *Ibid.,* August 26, 1960; *Philadelphia Evening Bulletin,* August 25, 26, 1960.
17. *Cleveland Press,* September 19, 1960.
18. *Boston Herald,* September 19, 1960, January 21, 1962.

19. Assorted clippings, Nanci Canaday item.

20. *Boston Herald*, November 9, 1961.

21. *The Sporting News*, March 16, 1961.

22. *Baltimore Sun*, August 18, 1962.

23. Program, Shrine of Immortals Day, September 2, 1960. Copy in Babe Ruth Museum, Baltimore, Maryland.

24. *Baltimore Sun*, September 3, 1960.

25. *Ibid.*, September 3, 1960.

26. *Ibid.*, August 12, 13, 1961.

27. *Ibid.*, August 18, 1962.

28. *New York Times*, November 9, 1961; *Boston Herald*, November 9, 1961; assorted clippings, November 9, 1961, in Foxx files, Baseball Library, Cooperstown; assorted clippings, November 9, 1961, Nanci Canaday item.

29. *Boston Herald*, November 9, 1961; *Philadelphia Evening Bulletin*, January 21, 1962.

30. Al Hirshberg's column, assorted clippings, in Dell Foxx scrapbook #2; *Cleveland Press*, February 28, 1956; *Boston Globe*, July 10, 1960.

31. *Boston Globe*, July 10, 1960, January 29, 1951.

32. *Ibid.*, July 23, 1967; Harold Kaese, "Foxx in Many Halls" in *Baseball Digest* (April, 1951), pp. 37-38.

33. *Easton Star-Democrat*, August 28, 1981.

34. *Norfolk Virginia Pilot*, July 25, 1967.

35. For example, see *Chicago Daily News*, December 24, 1963.

36. *Philadelphia Evening Bulletin*, January 21, 1962.

37. *Ibid.*, January 21, 1962; *New York Times*, January 21, 1962.

38. Foxx, "I'm Through with Baseball Forever" in *Baseball Monthly* (May, 1962), pp. 14-15.

39. *Ibid.*, p. 56.

40. *The Sporting News*, September 1, 1962.

41. Bob Gorman, *Double X, the Story of Jimmie Foxx—Baseball's Forgotten Slugger* (Camden, New Jersey: Holy Name Society, Diocese of Camden, New Jersey, 1990), p. 187; *The Sporting News*, September 2, 1963; *St. Louis Post Dispatch*, October 20, 1963..

42. *St. Louis Post Dispatch*, October 21, 1963.

43. *Ibid.*, October 23, 1963.

44. *Ibid.*, *Boston Herald*, October 23, 1963; *Philadelphia Evening Bulletin*, October 23, 1963; Gorman, *Double X ...*, p. 187.

45. *Philadelphia Evening Bulletin*, December 27, 1963.

46. Assorted clippings, December 24, 1963, and June, 1964, in Foxx files, Baseball Library, Cooperstown.

47. Assorted clippings, May 30, 1974, in Foxx files, Baseball Library, Cooperstown.

48. Assorted clippings, April 24, 1965, in Foxx files, Baseball Library, Cooperstown; Gorman, *Double X ...*, p. 188.

49. Assorted clippings, August 17, 1966, in Dell Foxx scrapbook #1; conversation with Nanci Canaday, February 15, 1992; Peter Golenbock, *An Unexpurgated*

History of the Boston Red Sox (New York: G.P. Putnam's Sons, 1992), p. 86; conversation with Jimmie Foxx, Jr. II, February 1, 1992.

50. Conversation with Nanci Canaday, February 15, 1992.

51. *Philadelphia Inquirer*, November 18, December 12, 1965.

52. *Miami Herald*, May 8, 1966; *Queen Anne's Record Observer*, May 12, 1966; conversation with Nanci Canaday, February 15, 1992.

53. Conversation with Kenneth Foxx, January 11, 1992; Gorman, *Double X...*, pp. 193-94.

54. *Boston Globe*, August 17, 1966; *Boston Herald*, August 18, 1966. Mays' career home run total would be 660.

55. *The Talbot Banner* (Cambridge, Maryland), July 11, 1979.

56. Conversation with Gil Dunn, July 10, 1992.

57. *Easton Star-Democrat*, August 28, 1981.

58. *Philadelphia Inquirer*, December 26, 1966; assorted clippings, Dell Foxx scrapbook #1.

59. *Miami Herald*, July 23, 1967.

60. *Ibid.*, July 22, 23, 1967; *New York Times*, July 22, 1967.

61. *Boston Herald*, July 26, 1967; *Miami Herald*, July 26, 1967.

62. *Boston Globe*, July 22, 1967.

63. Quoted in Bob Gorman, *Double X, the Story of Jimmie Foxx*, p. 195.

Epilogue

At the time of Foxx's death his home county newspaper, the *Queen Anne's Record-Observer*, published an extended account of his life and baseball achievements and included in its account several photographs loaned to the paper by Gil Dunn.[1] For the next decade it seems that the only person in Foxx's home area of Maryland who remembered or cared to remember him was Gil Dunn at his Kent Island Pharmacy. Several years later one native of the Sudlersville area declared that after Foxx's baseball career he became an embarrassment to his family and community. His divorce, talk about his drinking, his seeming inability to hold a job, his reckless use of resources—all of these contributed to his "fading from the memory" of the Sudlersville people.[2] Another local inhabitant, and one who had known Jimmie when he was a boy, asserted that Foxx was "at loose ends" after his baseball career ended. "All he knew," according to this acquaintance, "was baseball and when he could no longer play, he had nothing."[3]

It seems that in the decade following Foxx's death most of the people in his home area, with the exception of Gil Dunn, were content, if not eager, to forget Jimmie Foxx. Older people rarely mentioned his name and youngsters grew up unaware that a member of the Baseball Hall of Fame once lived in the county. However, during these same years an increasing number of persons from beyond the region were becoming interested in Foxx. Some of these were baseball buffs, but others were historians and biographers, scholars conducting research pertaining to Foxx and his environment. In the 1960s sport history became recognized by professional historians as a legitimate and acceptable area for research and publication. A landmark in the evolution of sport history as an area of investigation was Harold Seymour's 1956 doctoral dissertation at Cornell University on the early history of baseball. This manuscript was published in 1960 by the Oxford University Press.

In 1971 baseball enthusiasts, historians, and others associated with the game formed the Society for American Baseball Research (SABR). The membership of this organization quickly expanded to include thousands. The principal aim of SABR was and is to promote research and publication related to the history of baseball and those who played the game. In 1972 the North American Society for Sport History was created. A year later this Society began the publication of a quarterly scholarly journal devoted to research in sport history. Closely related to the increased scholarly interest in baseball was the growing number of university as well as commercial presses which began, in the seventies, to publish more books about baseball's history and players.

Much of the research by this first generation of sport historians was focused on baseball. By the late seventies it was not uncommon for persons engaged in research pertaining to baseball to visit Sudlersville. They would inquire of inhabitants about Foxx, wanting to know just where he had lived, where he went to school, if any of his contemporaries were still living and, if so, would it be possible to talk with them? These and similar questions were being asked more and more by outsiders who were coming to Sudlersville by 1979.[4]

Increasing interest in Foxx during the two decades following his death was also related to the passion for sport collectibles, an avocation for a growing number in American society. This interest was reflected in the monetary value associated with terms concerning Foxx. For example, a visitor to Dunn's museum sought unsuccessfully to purchase for $20,000.00 the uniform that Jimmie had worn on the 1934 tour of Japan. By the 1980s Foxx's Goudey chewing gum three-inch-square card, dating from the 1930s, was selling for up to $650.00. At the end of this decade a Jimmie Foxx 1942 jersey sold for $200,000.00, nearly as much as Foxx earned in a twenty-year major league career.[5] Interest in Foxx, exhibited by an increasing number of persons, helped to stimulate a revived interest in Jimmie in his home area. There was ample and growing awareness by a number of people in Queen Anne's County that Foxx was a significant figure. University professors, graduate students, prominent biographers, collectors, and others were inquiring about Sudlersville's forgotten native son.

Outside interest in Foxx, together with the increasing popularity of Gill Dunn's museum, prompted the citizens of Sudlersville to revive and move to preserve the memory of their best-known son. Leadership in the attempt to restore the memory of Foxx was taken by the ladies in the Sudlersville Community Betterment Club. This organization was formed in 1918 and Jimmie's mother, Mattie Smith Foxx, had been a charter member.[6] After considerable discussion, the club decided in the spring of 1981 to sponsor Sudlersville's first "annual appreciation day." At that time they would honor "native son, James Emory Foxx" by dedicating a small park in the town to his memory and by the unveiling of a "simple white sign on a corner lot at the crossroads center of the community." The sign would read "Welcome to Sudlersville, Birthplace of Jimmy Foxx."

The ceremonies for Sudlersville's first appreciation day were held on

Memorial Day, 1981, and there were festivities throughout the day. There was a parade through the town sponsored by the Sudlersville Volunteer Fire Company, and a prize was given for the most attractive float. Bands from a number of the county's schools participated in the parade, and later there was square dancing in a section of one of the streets which had been cordoned off for the occasion. The sign of welcome was unveiled by a niece of Jimmie Foxx, Mrs. Sarah Foxx Vansant.[7]

The women of the Community Betterment Club did not limit their honoring the memory of Foxx to the erection of the welcome sign and the creation of a park. During the summer they planned the observance of a "Jimmy Foxx night." As one of the club members stated, "We decided a night for Jimmy would be a good way to tell people just who Jimmy was." She noted that there were many new people in the community who did not know of him and a number of the younger people had never heard of him. The club wanted to inform people who Jimmie was and "what he did for our town."[8]

The appreciation night ceremony was held on Tuesday, September 8, 1981, in the Calvary Asbury United Methodist Church. The event had been publicized by local newspapers on the Eastern Shore, and more than 200 persons were present. Al Cartwright, sports columnist for the *Wilmington, Delaware, News-Journal* served as master of ceremonies. A number of persons who had known Foxx, including some of his high school classmates, made brief speeches recalling Jimmie or certain aspects of his career. One recalled Jimmie's "good-hearted nature" and his "generosity" toward his friends. Another long-time acquaintance said that he could not remember ever seeing Jimmie angry or mad. Another quoted Arthur Daley's comment that "Foxx had the strength of a gorilla and the disposition of a collie." The highlight of the evening was provided by Gil Dunn, who told the assembled gathering about his lifelong interest in Foxx, the establishment of his museum, and the visit from Foxx in 1966 when Jimmie gave Dunn a number of items for his museum.[9]

The sign erected by the Betterment Club in 1981 welcoming people to "Sudlersville, the Birthplace of Jimmy Foxx," was only a temporary memorial. Some of the members of the club and others in the community thought that a more permanent memorial was needed, one that was not subject to the ravages of weather and would not have to be replaced or restored every few years. After all, if you are going to memorialize the town's most famous son—one who had compiled a spectacular career in major league baseball, one who was enshrined in Baseball's Hall of Fame and in the state's "Shrine of Immortals," and one who, all agreed, "had put Sudlersville on the map"—the community should erect a more lasting memorial. After the passing of several years a movement was begun by the ladies of the Community Betterment Club to provide a permanent memorial to Jimmie Foxx in the town. Under the leadership of club president Lillian Merrick and several of her associates, including Loretta Walls, Julia Cronshaw, and Marjorie Clements, the club attempted in 1984–85 to elicit support in the community and county for a memorial to Foxx. As the discussions progressed, the concept of a memorial received a sympathetic response from the townspeople of Sudlersville, town officials, merchants, civic leaders, and members of the Queen Anne's County Historical Society. After a period of time and thought concerning the type of memorial that would be appropriate, it was decided that an engraved stone memorial or monument would be erected in the center of the town on a lot provided by the Town Council. The lot was located at the corner of Church and Main Streets, which had the town's only traffic light.[10]

The memorial, it was agreed, would be a simple three-tier structure, constructed from white granite stones that had been saved when the old Sudlersville bank building was demolished in 1984. The engraved portion of the monument would be on a marble step from the site of the old bank. Once the decision was made concerning the memorial, Ron Gatton, an engraver from Chestertown, and Irving Spy, a stone mason, were contracted to build the memorial. The engraving was to read "Sudlersville, Birthplace of James E. (Jimmy) Foxx, 1907–1967, Baseball Hall of Fame." By late spring of 1987 the memorial was complete, and it was decided to have the unveiling ceremony on or near Foxx's eightieth birthday, October 22, 1987.[11]

Throughout the spring and summer, plans were formulated for the dedication and unveiling ceremony and invitations were sent to over 300 guests and "dignitaries." Saturday, October 24, was selected as the day for the dedication, and Maryland's governor, William D. Schaefer, issued a proclamation declaring October 24 as "Jimmy Foxx Day" in the state.[12]

"Jimmy Foxx Day" was clear, sunny, and mild. It was estimated that more than 1,100 persons were in Sudlersville for the occasion. Among those present were two of Jimmie's sons—W. Kenneth of Decatur, Alabama, and Jimmie Jr., II, of Lakewood, Ohio—and three of his grandchildren. A photographer was present to record the events of the day, souvenir items prepared for the day were available in the town, and a Betterment Club member was assigned to collect and preserve items and artifacts associated with this celebration. The ceremonies began at noon with the dedication of the memorial. The master of ceremonies was William Sudler Goodhand, one of the town's Commissioners, and music was provided by the Sudlersville school band. Following the invocation by Dr. Frederick Seyfert, pastor of the Calvary Asbury United Methodist Church, the gathering was welcomed by Lillian Merrick. Prior to the introduction of special guests, Commissioner Goodhand led the gathering in the pledge of allegiance. After brief comments by several town and county officials the principal address was given by Gil Dunn. Dr. Seyfert then presided over the dedication in which the crowd participated. Programs which had been prepared for the occasion and made available to all attending the ceremonies, provided for a brief leader-audience response honoring Jimmie. The audience participation portion of the program was followed by the unveiling of the memorial by Jimmie's sons Kenneth and Jimmie Jr., II, and the placing of a wreath of flowers at the base of the memorial by his three grandchildren. After a moment of silence in memory of Foxx the school band played the Star Spangled Banner, and Dr. Seyfert pronounced the benediction.[13]

After the dedication of the memorial, more than 400 persons who had earlier purchased luncheon tickets (at $7.50 each) moved to the volunteer fire company building for a "ham and chicken salad luncheon." Special commemorative placemats were provided for the tables and a program for the ceremonies was available for all. The luncheon gathering was welcomed by Mrs. Lillian Merrick, and the invocation was given by Sudlersville's Episcopal rector, William P. Chilton. Music for the luncheon was provided by a group from Seaford, Delaware, and the master of ceremonies was Hurtt Derringer, editor and publisher of the *Kent County News* in Chestertown, Maryland. He introduced a number of guests who offered brief testimonials to Jimmie. Among those who spoke were Al Cartwright, former sports editor of the *Wilmington News Journal*; Bill Nicholson, Foxx's teammate when Jimmie was with the Cubs; William Mowbray, former editor of the *Daily Banner* in Cambridge, Maryland; Greg Schwalenberg of the Babe Ruth Museum; and Gil Dunn. Two "celebrities" who were unable to be present were Ted Williams and baseball commissioner Peter Uberroth. They, however, sent regrets and testimonials which were read at the luncheon. Williams stated that he would "never forget his old teammate" and how "nicely he had treated him" when Ted was "a brash young rookie." "I don't believe," he wrote, "that anyone ever made the impact of the ball and bat sound like it did when Foxx got hold of it." "I felt lost," he explained, "when he left the Red Sox in 1942. I loved him ... and all his friends miss him." Uberroth referred to Jimmie as "one of baseball's all-time sluggers" and complimented the people of Sudlersville for erecting a memorial to him.

The keynote speaker at the luncheon was John Steadman, sports columnist for the *Baltimore Evening Sun*. After Steadman's address two members of the Foxx family, Jimmie's son Kenneth and his nephew S. Dell Foxx, III, responded with appreciative remarks. Dell Foxx, a bank executive in Elkton, Maryland, declared with tears in his eyes, "I have always hoped that there would be a day like today." The proceedings concluded with the benediction by the Reverend Chilton.[14]

Twenty years after his death Sudlersville erected a permanent memorial to Jimmie Foxx, a monument which would preserve his memory for coming generations. The Sudlersville public library established the Foxx Memorial Collection to gather and preserve materials pertaining to Jimmie, his family, and his career. This collection of sources and photographs has become a magnet for researchers investigating the history of major league baseball and the career of Jimmie Foxx. Also in 1987 the Betterment Club, assisted by revenue from the sale of souvenirs, established the Jimmie Foxx Book Scholarship.

Memorial erected to Foxx, 1987 (photo by author).

This award is made annually to a high school graduate who attended the elementary or middle school in Sudlersville where Foxx went to school. This award was first presented in 1988 to Jill Coleman, the granddaughter of a man who once played local baseball with Jimmie.[15]

The memory of Jimmie Foxx and his baseball achievements will be preserved for posterity not only by the Hall of Fame and others who have honored him, but also by the citizens of his home town and county. The Jimmie Foxx Museum at the Kent Island Pharmacy, the Foxx Memorial Collection at the Sudlersville public library, the Foxx scholarship awarded by the Betterment Club, and the granite monument and park in the center of Sudlersville will preserve for ages the memory of one of the greatest players the game of baseball has ever known.

Notes

1. Assorted clippings, July, 1967, *Queen Anne's Record-Observer*, in Sudlersville Memorial Library.
2. Assorted clippings, March 21, 1979, Dell Foxx scrapbook #2.
3. *Queen Anne's Record-Observer*, March 21, 1979.
4. Assorted clippings, 1979, Dell Foxx scrapbook #2.
5. *Atlanta Journal and Constitution* (Atlanta, Georgia), July 12, 1992.
6. *News-Journal* (Wilmington, Delaware), August 29, 1981.
7. *Kent County News* (Chestertown, Maryland), May 27, 1981. In his home town Foxx is referred to as "Jimmy." Local inhabitants assert that when he was a school boy he spelled his name "Jimmy"; later, after going to Philadelphia, he changed the spelling of his name to "Jimmie."
8. *News-Journal*, August 29, 1981.
9. *The Star-Democrat*, August 28, 1981; *Queen Anne's Record-Observer*, September 16, 1981; *Delaware State News*, September 10, 1981; *Baltimore Evening Sun* (Baltimore, Maryland), September 16, 1981; assorted clippings, Foxx files, Sudlersville Memorial Library.
10. *News-Journal*, September 10, 1987; *Delaware State News*, October 23, 1987; *Philadelphia Inquirer*, October 26, 1987; *Washington Post*, October 24, 1987.
11. *News-Journal*, September 10, 1987; *Queen Anne's Record-Observer*, October 21, 1987.
12. Assorted clippings, unidentified item, October 26, 1987, in Sudlersville Memorial Library.
13. See program entitled "Sudlersville's Tribute to Our Native Son," copy in possession of author.
14. *Ibid.*, copies of responses from Williams and Uberroth in Sudlersville Memorial Library; *Kent County News*, October 28, 1987.
15. Assorted clippings, Sudlersville Memorial Library.

Appendix: Foxx's Lifetime Statistics

James "Jimmie" Emory Foxx. B. Oct. 22, 1907; d. July 22, 1967. Hit right, threw right. Hall of Fame, 1951

Year	Team	League	G	AB	R	H	2B	3B	HR	RBI	BB	SO	SB	E	FA	BA	SA
1924	Easton	Eastern Shore	76	260	33	77	11	2	10			1	0	0		.296	
1925	Philadelphia	American	10	9	6	6	1	0	0	0						.667	.778
1925	Providence	International	41	101	12	33	6	3	1	15	11	16	3	0	1.000	.327	
1926	Philadelphia	American	26	32	8	10	2	1	0	5	1	6	1	7	.976	.313	.438
1927	Philadelphia	American	61	130	23	42	6	5	3	20	14	11	2	17	.971	.323	.515
1928	Philadelphia	American	118	400	85	131	29	10	13	79	60	43	3	7	.995	.328	.548
1929	Philadelphia	American	149	517	123	183	23	9	33	117	103	70	10	14	.990	.354	.625
1930	Philadelphia	American	153	562	127	188	33	13	37	156	93	66	7	15	.986	.335	.637
1931	Philadelphia	American	139	515	93	150	32	10	30	120	73	84	4	11	.992	.291	.567
1932	Philadelphia	American	154	585	151	213	33	9	58	169	116	96	3	15	.990	.364	.749
1933	Philadelphia	American	149	573	125	204	37	9	48	163	96	93	2	10	.993	.356	.703
1934	Philadelphia	American	150	539	120	180	28	6	44	130	111	75	11	4	.997	.334	.653
1935	Philadelphia	American	147	535	118	185	33	7	36	115	114	99	6	13	.990	.346	.636
1936	Boston	American	155	585	130	198	32	8	41	143	105	119	13	8	.994	.338	.631
1937	Boston	American	150	569	111	162	24	6	36	127	99	96	10	19	.987	.285	.538
1938	Boston	American	149	565	139	197	33	9	50	175	119	76	5	10	.992	.349	.704
1939	Boston	American	124	467	130	168	31	10	35	105	89	72	4	10	.991	.360	.694
1940	Boston	American	144	515	106	153	30	4	36	119	101	87	4	14	.989	.297	.581
1941	Boston	American	135	487	87	146	27	8	19	105	93	103	2			.300	.505
1942	Boston	American	30	100	18	27	4	0	5	14						.270	
1942	Chicago	National	70	205	25	42	8	0	3	19	40	70	1	10	.987	.205	.344
1943	out of baseball																
1944	Chicago	National	15	20	0	1	1	0	0	2	2	5	0	0	1.000	.050	.100
1944	Portsmouth	Piedmont (mgr.)	5	2	0	0	0	0	0	0	0		0			.000	
1945	Philadelphia	National	89	224	30	60	11	1	7	38	23	39	0	8	.978	.268	.420
1946	out of baseball																
	Major League Totals		2317	8134	1751	2646	458	125	534	1921	1452	1311	88	192	.990	.325	.609

Year	Team	League		G	AB	R	H
				6	6	0	1
1947	St. Petersburg	Florida-International (mgr.)					
1948	out of baseball						
1949	Bridgeport	Colonial (interim mgr.)—month of August					
1952	Fort Wayne	All American Girls Professional Baseball League (mgr.)—won the pennant for first time, lost championship playoffs					
1956	Univ. of Miami, Fla. baseball coach						
1956	Miami	International (coach)					
1957	Univ. of Miami, Fla. baseball coach						
1958	Minneapolis	American Association (coach)					

World Series record

Year	Club	League	G	AB	R	H	2B	3B	HR	RBI	E	B.A.	F.A.
1929	Philadelphia	American	5	20	5	7	1	0	2	5	0	.350	1.000
1930	Philadelphia	American	6	21	3	7	2	1	1	3	0	.333	1.000
1931	Philadelphia	American	7	23	3	8	0	0	1	3	1	.348	.986
World Series Totals			18	64	11	22	3	1	4	11	1	.344	.994

All Star records

Year	Pos.	AB	R	H	2B	3B	HR	RBI	E	B.A.	F.A.
1934	3b	5	1	2	1	0	0	1	0	.400	1.000
1935	3b	3	1	2	0	0	1	3	0	.667	1.000
1936	3b	2	1	1	0	0	0	0	0	.500	1.000
1937	ph	1	0	0	0	0	0	0	0	.000	.000
1938	1b-3b	4	0	1	0	0	0	0	1	.250	.857
1940	1b	3	0	0	0	0	0	0	0	.000	1.000
1941	1b	1	0	0	0	0	0	0	0	.000	1.000
All-Star Totals		19	3	6	1	0	1	4	1	.316	.962

Pitching record

Year	Club	League	G	IP	W	L	Pct.	H	R	ER	SO	BB	ERA
1939	Boston	American	1	1	0	0	.000	0	0	0	0	0	0.00
1945	Philadelphia	National	9	23	1	0	1.000	13	4	4	10	14	1.57
Major League Totals			10	24	1	0	1.000	13	4	4	10	14	1.50

Bibliography

Newspapers

Baltimore Sun
Banner, Cambridge, Maryland
Boston American
Boston Herald
Centreville Observer, Centreville,
  Maryland
Chicago Tribune
Cleveland Plain Dealer
Cleveland Press
Evening-Journal, Wilmington,
  Delaware
Fort Wayne Journal-Gazette
Kent County News, Chestertown,
  Maryland
Los Angeles Times
Miami Herald
Miami News
Minneapolis Star
Minneapolis Tribune
New York Herald Tribune
New York Times
News Leader, Richmond, Virginia
Philadelphia Evening Bulletin

Philadelphia Evening Ledger
Philadelphia Inquirer
Pilot, Chestertown, Maryland
Portsmouth Star, Portsmouth, Virginia
Providence Journal, Providence,
  Rhode Island
Queen Anne's Journal, Centreville,
  Maryland
Queen Anne's Record-Observer, Cen-
  treville, Maryland
Star-Democrat, Easton, Maryland
The Sporting News
St. Louis Post-Dispatch
St. Paul Dispatch, St. Paul, Minnesota
St. Petersburg Times, St. Petersburg,
  Florida
Talbot Banner, Cambridge, Maryland
Times-Dispatch, Richmond, Virginia
Virginian-Pilot, Norfolk, Virginia
Washington Post
Winnipeg Free Press, Winnipeg, Man-
  itoba, Canada

Interviews

Ms. Nanci Canaday, Sumterville, Florida
Gilbert Dunn, Stevensville, Maryland
Jimmie Foxx Jr., II, Lakewood, Ohio
Kenneth Foxx, Decatur, Alabama
S. Dell Foxx, III, North East, Maryland

Unpublished thesis

Merrie A. Fidler. "The Development and Decline of the All-American Girls Baseball League, 1943–1954," M.S. Thesis (University of Massachusetts, 1976).

Books

Alexander, Charles C. *John McGraw* (New York: Viking, 1988).
_____. *Our Game: An American Baseball History* (New York: Henry Holt and Company, 1991).
_____. *Ty Cobb* (New York: Oxford University Press, 1984).
Allen, Ethan. *Major League Baseball: Technique and Tactics* (New York: The Macmillan Company, 1939).
Allen, Leo. *The Hot Stove League* (New York: A.S. Barnes and Company, 1955).
Allen, Lee, and Meany, Tom. *Kings of the Diamond: The Immortals in Baseball's Hall of Fame* (New York: Putnam's, 1965).
Appel, Martin, and Goldblatt, Burt. *Baseball's Best: The Hall of Fame Gallery* (New York: McGraw-Hill, 1977).
Barber, Red. *The Broadcasters* (New York: The Dial Press, 1970).
Barber, Red, and Creamer, Robert. *Rhubarb in the Catbird Seat* (Garden City: Doubleday, 1968).
Bartlett, Arthur. *Baseball and Mr. Spalding: the History and Romance of Baseball* (New York: Farrar, Strauss and Young, 1951).
Berry, Henry. *Baseball's Great Teams: Boston Red Sox* (New York: Macmillan, 1975).
Bjarkman, Peter C., editor. *Encyclopedia of Major League Baseball Team Histories: American League* (Westport, Conn.: Meckler Publishing Company, 1991).
_____, editor. *Encyclopedia of Major League Baseball Team Histories: National League* (Westport, Conn.: Meckler Publishing Company, 1991).
Blount, Roy, Jr., Boswell, Thomas, and others. *The Baseball Hall of Fame Fiftieth Anniversary Book* (New York: Prentice Hall, 1989).
Broeg, Bob. *Super Stars of Baseball* (St. Louis: The Sporting News, 1971).
Broeg, Bob, and Miller, William J., Jr. *Baseball from a Different Angle* (South Bend, Ind.: Diamond Communications, Inc., 1988).
Brown, Warren. *The Chicago Cubs* (New York: Putnam's, 1946).
Browne, Lois. *Girls of Summer: In Their Own League* (Toronto, Canada: Harper-Collins, 1992).
Carmichael, John P., editor. *My Greatest Day in Baseball* (New York: A.S. Barnes, 1945).
Chadwick, Bruce. *The Boston Red Sox: Memories and Mementoes of New England's Team* (New York: Abbeville Press, 1992).
Charlton, James, editor. *The Baseball Chronology* (New York: Macmillan, 1991).
Clark, Ellery H., Jr. *Boston Red Sox, 75th Anniversary History, 1901–1975* (Hicksville, New York: Exposition Press, 1975).
_____. *Red Sox Forever* (Hicksville, New York: Exposition Press, 1977).
Cochrane, Gordon S. *Baseball, the Fan's Game* (New York: Funk and Wagnalls Company, 1939).

Creamer, Robert W. *Babe: The Legend Comes to Life* (New York: Simon and Schuster, 1974).

Crepeau, Richard C. *Baseball, America's Diamond Mind* (Orlando: University Pressses of Florida, 1980).

Curran, William. *Big Sticks: The Batting Revolution of the Twenties* (New York: William Morrow and Company, Inc., 1990).

Daley, Arthur. *All the Home Run Kings* (New York: Putnam's, 1972).

_____. *Kings of the Home Run* (New York: Putnam's, 1962).

Danzig, Allison, and Reichler, Joe. *History of Baseball: Its Great Players, Teams and Managers* (Englewood Cliff, New Jersey: Prentice Hall, 1959).

Dickey, Glenn. *A History of the World Series Since 1903* (New York: Stein and Day, 1984).

_____. *The History of American League Baseball Since 1901* (New York: Stein and Day, 1980).

DiMaggio, Dom, and Gilbert, Bill. *Real Grass, Real Heroes: Baseball's Historic 1941 Season* (New York: Kensington Publishing Corporation, 1990).

Dykes, Jimmie, and Dexter, C.O. *You Can't Steal First Base* (Philadelphia: Lippincott, 1967).

Einstein, Charles, editor. *The Second Fireside Book of Baseball* (New York: Simon and Schuster, 1958).

Fleming, G.H. *The Dizziest Season: The Gas House Gang Chases the Pennant* (New York: William Morrow and Company, 1984).

Foxx, Jimmie. *How I Bat* (New York: Courier-Citizen Publishing Company, 1933).

Frommer, Harvey. *Baseball's Greatest Managers* (New York: Franklin Watts, 1985).

Gehrig, Eleanor, and Duros, Joseph. *My Luke and I* (New York: Thomas Y. Crowell Company, 1976).

Gilbert, Bill. *They Also Served: Baseball and the Home Front, 1941-1945* (New York: Crown Publishers, Inc., 1992).

Goldstein, Richard. *Spartan Seasons: How Baseball Survived the Second World War* (New York: Macmillan, 1980).

Golenbock, Peter. *Fenway: An Unexpurgated History of the Boston Red Sox* (New York: Putnam's, 1992)

Gorman, Bob. *Double X, The Story of Jimmie Foxx—Baseball's Forgotten Slugger* (Camden, New Jersey: Holy Name Society, Diocese of Camden, New Jersey, 1990).

Graham, Frank. *Lou Gehrig, a Quiet Hero* (New York: Putnam's, 1942).

Grayson, Harry. *They Played the Game: The Story of Baseball Greats* (Freeport, New York: Books for Libraries Press, 1944).

Green, Paul. *Forgotten Fields* (Waupava, Wisconsin: Parker Publications, 1984).

Greenberg, Hank. *The Story of My Life* (New York: Times Books, 1989).

Gregory, Robert. *Diz: Dizzy Dean and Baseball During the Great Depression* (New York: Viking, 1992).

Grobani, Anton, editor. *Guide to Baseball Literature* (Detroit: Gale Research Company, c. 1975).

Gutman, Dan. *Baseball Babylon: From the Black Sox to Pete Rose, the Real Stories Behind the Scandals That Rocked the Game* (New York: Penguin, 1992).

Guttman, Bill. *Famous Baseball Stars* (New York: Dodd, Mead, 1973).

Hirshberg, Al. *From Sandlots to League President: The Story of Joe Cronin* (New York: Julian Messner, Inc., 1962).

_____. *The Red Sox, the Bean and the Cod* (Boston: Waverly House, 1947).

Holway, John B. *Black Diamonds: Life in the Negro Leagues from the Men Who Lived It* (Westport, Conn.: Meckler Books, 1988).

Holway, John B. *Blackball Stars, Negro League Pioneers* (Westport, Conn.: Meckler Books, 1988).

Holway, John B. *The Sluggers* (Alexandria, Virginia: Redefinition, 1989).

Honig, Donald *Baseball America: The Heroes of the Game and the Times of Their Glory* (New York: Macmillan, 1985).

_____. *Baseball in the '30s* (New York: Crown Publishers, Inc., 1989).

_____. *Baseball's Ten Greatest Teams* (New York: Macmillan, 1982).

_____. *The All-Star Game: A Pictorial History, 1933 to the Present* (St. Louis: The Sporting News, 1987).

Johnston, Charles H. L. *Famous American Athletes of To-Day*, fourth series (Boston: L.C. Page and Company, 1934).

Kaufman, Louis, Fitzgerald, Barbara, and Sewell, Tom. *Moe Berg: Athlete, Scholar, Spy* (Boston: Little, 1974).

Kuenster, John, editor. *From Cobb to Catfish* (Chicago: Rand McNally, 1975).

Kuklick, Bruce. *To Every Thing a Season: Shibe Park and Urban Philadelphia, 1909–1976* (Princeton: Princeton UP, 1991).

Langford, Walter M. *Legends of Baseball: An Oral History of the Game's Golden Age* (South Bend, Ind.: Diamond Communications, Inc., 1987).

Lee, Ken, editor. *1990 University of Miami Hurricane Baseball Yearbook* (Miami: Swanson Printing, 1990).

Levine, Peter, editor. *Baseball History: An Annual of Original Baseball Research* (Westport, Conn.: Meckler Books, 1989).

Libby, Bill. *Baseball's Greatest Sluggers* (New York: Random House, 1973).

_____. *Heroes of the Hot Corner* (New York: Watts, 1972).

Lieb, Frederick G. *Connie Mack, Grand Old Man of Baseball* (New York: Putnam's, 1945).

Lowenfish, Lee, and Lupien, Tony. *The Imperfect Diamond: The Story of Baseball's Reserve System and the Men Who Fought to Change It* (New York: Stein and Day, 1980).

MacFarlane, Paul. *Hall of Fame Fact Book* (St. Louis: The Sporting News, 1983).

MacPhail, Lee. *My 9 Innings: An Autobiography of 50 Years in Baseball* (Westport, Conn.: Meckler Books, 1989).

Mack, Connie. *From Sandlot to Big Leagues: Connie Mack's Baseball Book* (New York: Knopf, 1950).

_____. *My 66 Years in the Big Leagues* (Philadelphia: John C. Winston Company, 1950).

Mead, William. *Baseball Goes to War* (Washington, D.C.: Farragut Publishing Company, 1985).

Meany, Thomas. *Baseball's Greatest Hitters* (New York: A.S. Barnes, 1950).

_____. *Baseball's Greatest Players* (New York: Grosset and Dunlap, 1933).

Michener, James A. *Sports in America* (New York: Random House, 1976).

Mowbray, William W. *The Eastern Shore Baseball League* (Centreville, Md.: Tidewater Publishers, 1989).

Murdock, Eugene. *Baseball Players and Their Times: Oral Histories of the Game, 1920–1940* (Westport, Conn.: Meckler Publishing Company, 1991).

Obojski, Robert. *Bush League: A History of Minor League Baseball* (New York: Macmillan, 1975).

_____. *The Rise of Japanese Baseball Power* (Radnor, Pa.: Chilton Book Company, c. 1975).

Okkonen, Marc. *Baseball Uniforms of the 20th Century* (New York: Sterling Publishing Company, Inc., 1991).

Oleksak, Michael M., and Oleksak, Mary A. *Beisbol: Latin Americans and the Grand Old Game* (Grand Rapids, Mich.: Masters Press, 1991).

Phillips, Paul W. *Sudlersville, Queen Anne's County on Maryland's Eastern Shore* (n.p:n.p., n.d.).

Porter, David L., editor. *Biographical Dictionary of American Sports* (Westport, Conn.: Greenwood Press, 1988).

Reibling, R.L. *Sports Lighting* (Cincinnati: Spalding Company, 1970).

Reidenbaugh, Lowell. *Cooperstown, Where Baseball's Legends Live Forever* (St. Louis: The Sporting News, 1983).

Ritter, Lawrence S. *Lost Ballparks* (New York: Viking, 1992).

Ritter, Lawrence S., and Honig, Donald. *The 100 Greatest Baseball Players of All Time*, revised (New York: Crown Publishers, 1986).

Rogosin, Donn. *Invisible Men: Life in Baseball's Negro Leagues* (New York: Atheneum, 1985, reprint of 1983 edition).

Romanowski, Jerome C. *The Mackmen* (Camden, N.J.: Graphic Press, 1979).

Ruth, George Herman. *Babe Ruth's Own Book of Baseball* (Lincoln: University of Nebraska Press, 1992, reprint of 1928 edition).

Scully, Gerald W. *The Business of Major League Baseball* (Chicago: University of Chicago Press, 1989).

Seymour, Harold. *Baseball, the Golden Age* (New York: Oxford UP, 1971).

_____. *Baseball, the People's Game* (New York: Oxford UP, 1990).

Shapiro, Milton J. *Champions of the Bat: Baseball's Greatest Sluggers* (New York: Julian Messner, 1967).

_____. *The Year They Won the Most Valuable Player Award* (New York: Julian Messner, 1966).

Shatzkin, Mark, editor. *The Ballplayers: Baseball's Ultimate Biographical Reference* (New York: William Morrow, 1990).

Smith, Carl. *Voices of the Game: The Acclaimed Chronicle of Baseball Radio and Television Broadcasting from 1921 to the Present* (New York: Simon and Schuster, 1987).

Smith, Ira L. *Baseball's First Basemen* (New York: A.S. Barnes, 1956).

Smith, Myron J., Jr., compiler. *Baseball: A Comprehensive Bibliography* (Jefferson, N.C.: McFarland, 1986).

Stang, Mark, and Harkness, Linda. *Rosters* (Smyrna, Ga.: n.p, c. 1991).

Statler, Oliver. *All-Japan: The Catalogue of Everything Japanese* (New York: Quarto Marketing Ltd., 1984).

Stotz, Carl E., and Balwin, M.W. *At Bat with the Little League* (Philadelphia: Macrea Smith Company, 1952).

Sullivan, George. *Sluggers: Twenty-Seven of Baseball's Greatest* (New York: Atheneum, 1991).

Thorn, John, and Palmer, Pete. *Total Baseball* (New York: Warner Books, 1989).

Veeck, Bill. *Veeck, As in Wreck: The Autobiography of Bill Veeck* (New York: Bantam, 1963).

Vlasich, James A. *A Legend for the Legendary: The Origin of the Baseball Hall of Fame* (Bowling Green, Ohio: Bowling Green State University Popular Press, c. 1990).

Voigt, David Quentin. *American Baseball*, 3 volumes (Norman: University of Oklahoma Press, 1966–1983).

_____. *America Through Baseball* (Chicago: Nelson-Hall, 1976).

_____. *Baseball, an Illustrated History* (University Park: Pennsylvania State UP, 1987).

Walton, Edward H. *This Date in Boston Red Sox History* (New York: Stein and Day, 1978).

Warfield, Don. *The Roaring Redhead, Larry MacPhail—Baseball's Great Innovator* (South Bend, Indiana: Diamond Communications, Inc., 1987).

Weygand, James. *Nite Time Baseball* (Fort Wayne, Ind.: Press of the Indiana Kid, 1970).

Whiting, Robert. *You Gotta Have Wa* (New York: Vintage Books, c. 1990).

Williams, Ted. *My Turn at Bat: The Story of My Life* (New York: Simon and Schuster, 1969).

Windhausen, John D. *Sports Encyclopedia, North America*, vol. 4 (Gulf Breeze, Fla.: Academic International Press, 1990).

Wolff, Rick, editorial director. *The Baseball Encyclopedia*, eighth edition (New York: Macmillan, 1990).

Zaharias, Babe Didrickson as told to Harry Paxton. *This Life I've Led: My Autobiography* (New York: A.S. Barnes and Company, 1955).

Zimbalist, Andrew. *Baseball and Billions: A Probing Look Inside the Big Business of Our National Pastime* (New York: Basic Books, 1992).

Articles

Abodaher, W. J. "Baseball via the Ether Waves," *Baseball Magazine* (November, 1929).

Bevis, Charles W. "A Home Run by Any Measure: The Baseball Players' Pension Plan," *Baseball Research Journal* (1993).

Bilstein, Roger E. "Aviation and the Changing West," *Journal of the West* (January, 1991).

Carlson, Lewis. "The Universal Athletic Sport of the World," *American History Illustrated* (April, 1984).

Clark, Dick, and Holway, John B. "1930 Negro National League," *Baseball Research Journal* (1989).

Crusinberry, James. "Women Fans and Their Effect on the Game," *Baseball Magazine* (November, 1949).

Curran, Nick. "How World Series Broadcasts Were Started in 1922," *Baseball Digest* (October, 1964).

Daniel, Daniel M. "Night Baseball Irresistible," *Baseball Magazine* (January, 1940).

Doerer, Tom. "Jimmy Foxx and His Brilliant Future," *Baseball Magazine* (October, 1928).

Driscoll, David, Jr. "Should Baseball Banish the Radio?," *Baseball Magazine* (January, 1933).

Feldman, Jay. "Glamour Ball," *Sports Heritage* (May/June, 1987).

_____. "The Real History of Night Ball at Wrigley Field," *Baseball Research Journal* (1993).

"50 Years of American Legion Baseball," *American Legion Magazine* (July, 1975).

Fincher, Jack. "The Belles of the Ball Game Were a Hit with Their Fans," *Smithsonian* (July, 1989).

Foxx, Jimmie. "Life Story of Jimmie Foxx," *Fort Wayne Journal-Gazette*, April 6, 1952.

_____. "A Master Batter Discusses His Craft," *Baseball Magazine* (December, 1929).

_____. "I'm Glad I Was a Ballplayer," *Sport* (March, 1952).

_____. "I'm Through with Baseball Forever," *Baseball Monthly* (May, 1962).

_____. "The Secret of Jimmy Foxx's Slugging Power," *Baseball Magazine* (August, 1934).

_____. "When I Was a Boy," *St. Nicholas Magazine* (November, 1935).

Glaser, Lulu. "The Lady Fan," *Baseball Magazine* (September, 1909).

Gould, James. "Is the Radio Good for Baseball?," *Baseball Magazine* (July, 1930).

Grossbandler, Stan. "40 Years Ago: First Night Game in the Majors," *Baseball Digest* (May, 1975).

Guilfoile, Bill. "Jimmie Foxx: Tape-Measure Homers Were His Trade-Mark," *Baseball Digest* (October, 1981).

Hadley, Lawrence, and Gustafson, Elizabeth. "Major League Baseball Salaries: The Impact of Arbitration and Free Agency," *Journal of Sport Management* (July, 1991).

Hadley, Lawrence, and Gustafson, Elizabeth. "Who Would Be the Highest-Paid Baseball Player?," *Baseball Research Journal* (1993).

Hartman, Harry. "In Defense of Baseball by Radio," *Baseball Magazine* (October, 1930).

Hern, Gerry. "The Unbelievable Beast," *Baseball Digest* (July, 1954).

Hilligan, Earl. "Foxx, A. L.'s Long Drive Champ," *Baseball Digest* (September, 1948).

Lane, Frank C. "A New Claimant for Babe Ruth's Slugging Crown," *Baseball Magazine* (March, 1936).

_____. "Flashing the World Series to Waiting Millions," *Baseball Magazine* (November, 1922).

_____. "The Greatest Individual Punch in the American League," *Baseball Magazine* (March, 1934).

_____. "The Greatest Player in the American League," *Baseball Magazine* (March, 1933).

_____. "The Romance of Night Baseball," *Baseball Magazine* (October, 1930).

_____. "The Strong Arm Slugger of the Fighting Athletics," *Baseball Magazine* (September, 1929).

_____. "The Sweeping Success of Night Baseball in the Minors," *Baseball Magazine* (January, 1937).

_____. "Will the Major Leagues Adopt Night Baseball?," *Baseball Magazine* (October, 1935).

MacPhail, Larry. "The Triumph of the Arc Lights," *Baseball Magazine* (September, 1936).

McEligot, J. Warren. "From Gridiron to Diamond," *Baseball Magazine* (February, 1933).

Meany, Tom. "The Beast, They Called Him," *Baseball Digest* (September, 1967).

Mercer, Sid. "Foreign Tours Date Back to '74," *Baseball Digest* (November, 1943).

Nason, Jerry. "Foxx Was King of Tape Measure Home Run Hitters," *Baseball Digest* (February, 1970).

O'Connor, Edwin. "What the Lights Have Done," *Baseball Digest* (May, 1951).

Percoco, James A. "Baseball and World War II: A Study of the Landis-Roosevelt Correspondence," *Organization of American Historians Magazine of History* (Summer, 1992).

Phelan, William A. "Inside Baseball Over the Radio," *Baseball Magazine* (June, 1922).

"Playing the Game: The Threat to Babe Ruth's Home Run Record," *The Literary Digest* (August 12, 1933).

Rainovic, Al. "Baseball's First Radio Broadcast," *Newsletter, National Baseball Hall of Fame and Museum* (July, 1984).

Robinson, Kay. "Columbia's Other Hall of Famer," *Columbia, The Magazine of Columbia University* (Spring, 1981).

Roden, Donald. "Baseball and the Quest for National Dignity in Meiji Japan," *American Historical Review* (June, 1980).

Rumill, Ed. "Looking Backward with Jimmie Foxx," *Baseball Magazine* (November, 1944).

Sanborn, Irving. "Flashing the Series to 50,000,000 People," *Baseball Magazine* (November, 1920).

Sawyer, C. Ford. "The Lowdown on Night Ball Play in the Major Leagues," *Baseball Magazine* (June, 1946).

Stann, Francis. "The Day Foxx Tried to Hang a Curtain," *Baseball Digest* (November, 1961).

Steadman, John F. "Foxx's Unbelievable Power," *Baseball Digest* (December, 1962).

Tarvin, A.H. "The Origin of 'Ladies Day'," *Baseball Magazine* (July, 1934).

"The Threat to Babe Ruth's Home Run Record," *The Literary Digest* (August 12, 1933).

Tiemann, Robert. "Join the Majors, See the World," *The National Pastime, A Review of Baseball History* (1990).

Time Magazine (July 29, 1929).

Voigt, David Quentin, review of "Gerald W. Scully, The Business of Major League Baseball," *Journal of Sport History* (Spring, 1990).

_____. "Sex in Baseball: Reflections on Changing Taboos," *Journal of Popular Culture* (Winter, 1978).

Whiting, Robert. "Zen and the Art of Baseball," *New York Times* (March 25, 1990).

Winerip, Harold. "Opinions on Ladies Day," *Baseball Magazine* (July, 1939).

Young, David. "Seasons in the Sun," *Women's Sports* (October, 1982).

Index